Georgia

John T. Edge
Photography by Robb Helfrick

COMPASS AMERICAN GUIDES
An Imprint of Fodor's Travel Publications, Inc.

Georgia
First Edition

Copyright © 2000 Fodor's Travel Publications, Inc.
Maps Copyright © 2000 Fodor's Travel Publications, Inc.
Compass American Guides and colophon are trademarks of Random House, Inc.
Fodor's is a registered trademark of Random House, Inc.

Compass American Guides, Inc., 5332 College Ave., Suite 201, Oakland, CA 94618, USA
ISBN: 0-679-00245-6

Editors: Kit Duane, Lesley Bonnet   Designers: Christopher Burt, Julia Dillon
Managing Editor: Kit Duane   Production Editor: Julia Dillon
Creative Director: Christopher Burt   Map Design: Mark Stroud, Moon Cartography
                                           Cover design: Siobhan O'Hare
10 9 8 7 6 5 4 3 2 1
Production House: Twin Age Ltd., Hong Kong; Manufactured in China

PUBLISHER'S ACKNOWLEDGMENTS
Abby Aldrich Rockefeller Folk Art Center p. 19; Atlanta History Center pp. 37, 125; Augusta-Richmond County Museum p. 168; Bettman Photo Archives, Corbis p. 40; The Columbus Museum pp. 23, 197; Kelly Duane pp. 119, 164, 180; Dr. John Duncan, photo by Richard Sommers p. 16; Georgia Dept. of Archives & History pp. 17, 20, 44, 46, 83, 112, 141, 169, 216; Georgia Dept. of Natural Resources p. 54; Georgia Museum of Art, Univ. of Georgia, gift of Mrs. Will Moss p. 95; Mr. & Mrs. Harvey Granger Jr. p. 285; Greenville County Museum of Art p. 18; The Henry Francis du Pont Winterthur Museum p. 259; Herndon House p. 130; Muriel Gassett James files, Sacramento, California p. 139; Library of Congress pp. 21, 24, 25, 28, 32, 34, 35, 38, 39, 41, 45, 47, 60, 111, 113, 244, 260, 262, 288; Mariner's Museum p. 263; Metropolitan Museum of Art, New York, New York, Gift of Edgar William and Berenice Chrysler Garbisch, 1963 (63.201.3), photograph © 1984 The Metropolitan Museum of Art p. 29; The Morris Museum p. 165; National Park Service p. 15; New Britain Museum of American Art, © T.H. Benton and R.P. Benton Testamentary Trusts/Licensed by VAGA, New York, New York p. 50; New York Historical Society p. 276; Kenneth Rogers p. 45; Richard Sommers p. 275; Mr. & Mrs. Richard and Kay Tarr p. 267; Underwood Archives, San Francisco pp. 146, 196; Univ. of Georgia Press p. 229.
     Thanks also to Ellen Klages for proofreading and to Lesley Bonnet for indexing, and thanks to Michael Brubaker of the Atlanta History Center and to Nelson Ross for their expert reading.

Photographer Robb Helfrick would like to dedicate his work in this book to his parents, Bill and Peg.

For Blair, on the road and off.

AUTHOR'S ACKNOWLEDGMENTS

The author would like to thank the faculty and staff of the Center for the Study of Southern Culture at the University of Mississippi, the staff of the Washington Memorial Library in Macon, the good folks at the University of Georgia Library in Athens, and the Georgia Department of Archives in Atlanta.

Individuals who gave advice, provided shelter, and shared their tales of Georgia past and present include: Nelson Ross of Atlanta, Bert Way of Hawkinsville, John and Mary Anne Edge of Macon, Charlie and Laura Hammond of Savannah, Greg Coleson of Atlanta, Richard Fausset at Flagpole in Athens, Christianne Lauterbach at Knife and Fork in Atlanta, Judy Long and the folks at Hill Street Press in Athens, Kevin Gantz of Ball Ground, and Spyros Dermatas at Nu Way in Macon. Thanks to sometime Georgian Jay Hale for pointing the way to the Power Line, to David Nelson of Living Blues for telling me about Andrew's Oyster Bar, and to the Yacht Club for the beers. The offices of tourism in the towns of Athens, Atlanta, Macon, Columbus, Augusta, and Americus were especially helpful.

Without the determined efforts of Kit Duane, my editor at Compass, this book would be but a shell. She is a marvel of patience and editorial talent. Thanks to Lesley Bonnet, copy and map editor extraordinaire, who did yeoman's duty. To Chris Burt of Compass, thanks for the wonderful design. And for Blair Hobbs, my bride, thanks for the support and for all the welcomes home.

CONTENTS

Literary Extracts and Topical Essays

Maps

O V E R V I E W

GEORGIA

With the Appalacian Mountains in the north, a fertile agricultural plain across its center, and lush sea islands hugging the coast, Georgia's landscape is diverse and inviting. In addition to two great cities—bustling, modern Atlanta and sedate, charming Savannah—Georgia also has regal plantation homes, meandering back roads, small cities with historic downtowns, and the magical Okefenokee Swamp.

NORTHWEST GEORGIA

Beautiful and remote, the mountains of the northwest contain many interesting pockets of culture. Come here to visit New Echota, last home of the Cherokee people before they were expelled to Oklahoma, and Chickamauga National Battlefield, where the Confederacy held off the Federals in a bloody battle. Visit Paradise Gardens, home of famed visionary artist Howard Finster.

NORTHEAST GEORGIA

Known for Blue Ridge Mountain scenery and Appalachian culture, this is an area with many small resorts. Come for a country music and crafts festival, or to rent a cabin and hike through the woods. Rent a canoe or try your hand at cane-pole fishing. Rushing rivers and towering trees provide a soothing backdrop to all adventures.

ATLANTA

Founded in 1835 and staked as a railway terminus in 1837, Atlanta was of great importance to the Confederate war effort and became the target of the Union's General Sherman, who burned the city on his march to Savannah. Today it is a sprawling metropolis with huge hotels, a dynamic nightlife and music scene, and sophisticated restaurants. Although the city can be difficult for the outsider to navigate, those with a car and good directions can visit lovely intown neighborhoods such as Virginia-Highland and Inman Park.

MIDDLE GEORGIA

Athens, home to the beautiful University of Georgia campus, has a charming downtown, a vital music scene, and innovative restaurants. Augusta, Macon, and Milledgeville are all easily accessible and exude charm. This is a beautiful region of small historic cities, undulating farmland, and a gracious way of life. Come here to eat barbecue at roadside cafes, to browse in antique stores, and to soak up the comfortable ambiance of a courthouse square on a warm winter afternoon.

SOUTH GEORGIA

From the piney woods near Augusta, to wet, mysterious Okefenokee Swamp with its canoe trails and alligators, southern Georgia is a delight. Pecan and peach orchards line the roadways, and traffic goes slow. Take in Plains, hometown of former President Jimmy Carter and capital of the peanut-growing region. If you're lucky, he'll be teaching Sunday school at the local church. Visit country resorts, float down a lazy river, and drink in the sunshine.

SAVANNAH

Founded in 1733 as a British colony that would offer a new start to England's economic unfortunates, Savannah retains the city plan designed by James Oglethorpe, the city's idealistic founder. Twenty-one lovely green spaces—or squares—each with benches, walkways, and abundant greenery, are surrounded by fine old homes, many dating from the early 1800s. Savannah is one of America's most beautiful and cities.

THE GEORGIA COAST

Long ago the province of Muscogee Indians, and later unsuccessfully colonized by Spanish missionaries, the Sea Islands were planted with rice, sugar, and long-staple cotton on vast plantations owned by an aristocratic planter society. So many slaves were imported into this region that by the time of the Civil War the area was 80 percent African, and the people of some of the more remote islands developed a unique culture still in evidence today. This is a lush region, with tropical vegetation, white sand beaches, and luxurious resorts.

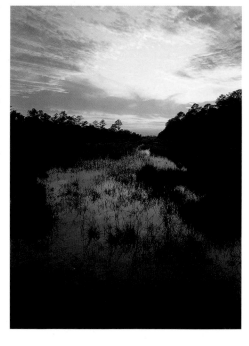

INTRODUCTION

I SPENT THE BETTER PART OF MY YOUTH on a five-speed Schwinn bicycle, burning up the blacktop road that ran between my home, a modest Federal-style farmhouse built in 1814, and Old Clinton Barbecue, a wonderful roadhouse shrouded in what seemed a perpetual wreath of sweet smoke. Behind the counter stood Mrs. Coulter, mother of the proprietor, keeper of the flame. Always kind, and nearly as sweet as the tea she mixed up by the gallon, she dished out barbecue, coleslaw, and Brunswick stew to the boys of Jones County, dispensing a good measure of motherly love at no charge. I can still taste the smoked pork napped with pepper-laced vinegar; I can still hear shoes shuffling on the sawdust-covered floor.

The community I grew up in was called Clinton, Georgia, and by the time I remember noticing, it appeared a humble collection of regal older homes, a few new redbrick faux colonials, and more than a few tumbledown tarpaper shacks. There was a time, my parents always told me, when Clinton was the third largest town in Georgia. But when the railway diverted to Gray, three miles up the road, Clinton receded from view. By the time I came into the world, the past had a stranglehold on Clinton that the present couldn't loosen.

I spent early fall mornings traipsing through the woods, sometimes with my father, other times with friends. We were digging for Confederate relics. They must be buried close by, I reasoned, for my house had once been the home of Confederate brigadier general Alfred Iverson Jr. Surely there were bayonets and muskets, minié-balls and buttons to be exhumed from the red clay. Instead we found treasures of another sort—rusted tin cans, busted bottles, and shattered plates—the detritus of the more recent past.

I was born in 1962. I was old enough to watch and listen as the Civil Rights Movement swirled around me. I recall sitting in a federal courtroom, rapt, watching my father work to put away white men accused of murdering a black Georgian. I came of age in Clinton. The Civil War and the Civil Rights Movement held equal sway. In my pantheon Alfred Iverson Jr. and Martin Luther King Jr. were compatriots, not combatants.

Though I would leave for college in Athens, later moving to Atlanta and beyond, it was in Clinton that I learned the lessons that would define my life. And though I don't make it back to Old Clinton Barbecue as often as I once did, I can't think of another place I would rather be come dinnertime.

HISTORY & CULTURE

GEORGIA WAS CONCEIVED AS A SOCIAL EXPERIMENT to lessen crowding in England's debtor prisons, realized as a military buffer between colonial Spain and England, tortured like much of the American South by more than two centuries of slavery, and finally heralded as the jewel in the crown of the Sunbelt economy. Thus Georgia's history is not easily encapsulated. Nor is the physical landscape of this, the largest state east of the Mississippi River. Whether your destination be the Blue Ridge Mountains of norther Georgia, the stooped irregularity of the red clay Piedmont, the piney woods of the sandy lowlands, or the wetlands and inlets of the seashore, Georgia's landscape is as diverse as its people.

■ IN THE BEGINNING

The first inhabitants of Georgia, nomadic tribes of big game hunters, made their way to the southeast of present-day America some 12,000 years ago. Save a scattering of spearheads and the skeletal remains of a few of these Paleo-Indian peoples, there is little that remains of their presence.

About 3,000 years ago, a new Native American culture emerged. Its people built hundreds of earthen mounds over the next several thousand years, some as burial mounds, others as ceremonial stages of a sort. Kolomoki Mounds is one of the more famous examples still existent in Georgia. It was also during this era that the bow and arrow came into use, farming became commonplace, and the use of pottery became widespread.

As agriculture became more important, the settlements in which people

This Mississippian-era figurine, once a bottle top, was found at an Indian burial site at Ocmulgee. (National Park Service)

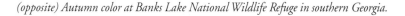

(opposite) Autumn color at Banks Lake National Wildlife Refuge in southern Georgia.

This 1837 engraving, Village Indien, *was done after an illustration by Theodore de Bry in the 1590s. (courtesy Dr. John and V. Duncan)*

lived grew increasingly large and complex. Soon, moats and wooden palisades protected villages. Not long thereafter, most people were living in wood-framed, thatched houses. In time, chiefdoms were established whereby a single powerful ruler might govern a network of many villages.

Since most of these tribal groups lived in the bottomlands along the Mississippi River, this period—from around a thousand years ago until the arrival of Europeans—has come to be known as the Mississippian era. It was during this era that Native American culture in the region reached its zenith.

In 1540, when Spanish explorer Hernando de Soto arrived in Georgia, he found large permanent farming villages built around enormous earthen temple mounds. De Soto's expedition and the European settlement that followed destroyed much of the original population of Georgia. Skirmishes fought between these two groups killed people on both sides, but it was European diseases—in particular measles and smallpox—that wiped out the majority of the native people. Remnants of native tribes eventually drew together in the hinterlands, and from these survivors came the formidable Creek and Cherokee nations, the histories of which are intertwined with that of the colony and state of Georgia.

HISTORY &
CULTURE

■ UTOPIAN EXPERIMENT

Created by royal decree in 1732 and entrusted to the care of British parliamentarian James Edward Oglethorpe, the colony of Georgia was, at its outset, an experiment in utopian idealism. The poor and downtrodden (including those so down on their luck that they were indeed in debtors' prison) were recruited. And in the interest of avoiding temptation, all manner of suspicious persons were prohibited, including attorneys and Catholics. Because Georgia's founders were idealists, slavery was forbidden; because they were entrepreneurial, they embarked on silk production, decreeing that two mulberry trees per acre must be planted on all land grants, as food for silkworms.

Touted by Oglethorpe and the 20 other trustees as a "lush Edenic paradise," Georgia attracted the interest of more than the poor and bankrupt it was originally intended for. Among the 114 colonists on the first ship to sail for Georgia were two merchants, five carpenters, two wig makers, five farmers, a gardener, an upholsterer, a vintner, a baker, a miller, a surgeon, a writer, and not a single convict. Perhaps it was the unflagging boosterism (a recurrent theme in Georgia history) that compelled Britain's yeoman farmers and skilled laborers to come running. But come they did, enticed by a slew of perquisites including free passage and 50 acres of land as well as a year's worth of support. One historian has gone so far as to posit that "the first Georgians were perhaps the most selectively chosen group of colonists to come to British North America." Yet the grand colonial experiment was not to last long as it was first conceived. Attempts made to raise silkworms sputtered. Ditto

Parliamentarian James Edward Oglethorpe is credited with the founding of Georgia. (Georgia Department of Archives & History)

This painting, circa 1810, shows Benjamin Hawkins at a trading post with members of the Creek nation. (Greenville County Museum of Art, Greenville, SC)

for European varietal grapes, oranges, and olives. Indeed, for its first 50 years, Georgia, the last of the 13 British colonies, floundered. In 1740, just seven years after Oglethorpe established the city of Savannah on the Yamacraw Bluff overlooking the Savannah River, traveler Henry Garret was so disturbed by what he saw of colonial Georgia that he observed: "I got into a very bad corner of the world, where poverty and oppression abound to such a degree that it has become proverbial this way to say as poor as a Georgian."

■ SLAVERY AND PROSPERITY

Just up the coast in South Carolina, planters prospered growing indigo and rice—with slave labor, of course. While Georgia farmers struggled, South Carolina planters lived a life of comparative ease, a distinction that did not escape the notice of some of the colony's more prominent business people. "The poor people of Georgia may well as think of becoming Negroes themselves—as of hoping to be ever able to live without them," argued colonist Thomas Stephens. Slavery, land-holding Georgians of wealth and influence argued, was the answer to these economic ills. By 1750, pro-slavery advocates had won out. And by 1760, thousands of Africans had been brought into Georgia. By 1773, the state could claim 15,000 slaves and 18,000 whites. Sea Island cotton flourished along the coast, and rice plantations spread up the Savannah River and down the coast. By the eve of the Revolutionary War, Georgia looked less and less like a radical utopian experiment than its antithesis, an agrarian outpost reliant upon slave labor.

Most slaves sold into Georgia bondage were of West African origin. Among them the Wolof and Mandinka peoples were prominent, though a wide variety of regions and peoples were represented, for the native region of Georgia slaves described a wide arc along the African coast, stretching from present-day Senegal through Ghana and on into Nigeria. Slaves from the Sierra Leone area were especially valuable to low-country planters, who valued their knowledge of rice cultivation.

The instruments shown in this painting—The Old Plantation, artist unknown, circa 1800—
are similar to those used by the Yoruba in West Africa.
(Abby Aldrich Rockefeller Folk Art Center, Williamsburg, VA)

This French map from 1767 shows Georgia extending west from the Atlantic coast between the Savannah River to the north and the Altamaha River to the south. (Margaret Davis Cate Collection, Fort Frederica National Monument, Georgia Department of Archives & History)

■ SHRINKING GEORGIA

As conceived, the colony of Georgia was bounded by the Altamaha River on the north and the Savannah River on the south. At the headwaters of each river a line was drawn westward to the Pacific. Had these borders been maintained, the largest city in Georgia today would be not Atlanta but Los Angeles.

Instead, in accordance with the Treaty of Paris, signed in 1763 at the conclusion of the French and Indian War, Britain gave up all claims to lands west of the Mississippi River, while in 1802, modern-day Alabama and Mississippi were ceded to the U.S. government. By the close of the 18th century, Georgia's borders were fixed much as they remain today.

■ REVOLUTIONARY WAR

Despite what the Daughters of the American Revolution may tell you, Georgia remained at the periphery of the fighting for most of the Revolutionary War, if for no other reason than that Georgia was a geographically peripheral colony, at the tail end of a region close to revolt, distanced by time and territory from the patriotic fervor of the New England colonies. Closer to home, in the Carolinas, after 100-plus years of limited self rule, some citizens may well have been chafing under the yoke of British tariffs and taxation, yet most Georgians remained content.

Exports were booming. Georgia's rich farmlands were yielding bumper crops. In short, after years of privation, many Georgians were too busy making a living (or, in some cases, making a fortune) to pay heed to the protests coming from colonies to the north. Georgia was the sole colony to comply with the Stamp Act, and when it came time to send delegates to the first Continental Congress, Georgia mustered no official delegation. Indeed, on the eve of hostilities, both Tory and Whig factions claimed the loyalty of equal numbers of Georgians.

Still, Georgia joined the other 12 colonies in declaring independence from Britain in 1776. Just two years later the British attacked and gained control of Savannah, and by the close of 1779 much of colonial Georgia was under British control. Fighting, mostly restricted to small skirmishes and guerrilla warfare, was relegated to the backwoods, far from towns of import like Savannah. Nevertheless, according to historian E. Merton Coulter in his *Georgia, A Short History:*

The war had been unusually destructive in Georgia as it developed through the bitterest partisan struggle into a war of extermination of life and property. Half the property in the state had been destroyed, the institution of slavery was upset, and the people were torn asunder through hatreds and suspicions....Robbers and murderers after the close of the war continued to infest the highways to such an extent as to endanger the life of the government....

General Casimir Pulaski died in the attempt to recapture Savannah.
(Library of Congress)

SHE'S A TOUGH GAL, NANCY HART

Cross-eyed, pockmarked, and masculine in bearing, Nancy Morgan Hart was no storybook heroine, yet to this day she remains the most lionized and mythologized of Georgia Patriots. Though the tale of her exploits may well be apocryphal, that possibility has done nothing to dampen the fervor with which her story is told.

Legend has it that Nancy's cabin in the north Georgia woods near what is now Elberton, was a refuge for Georgia Patriots intent upon escaping British troops. One afternoon, six redcoats, aware of her reputation, decided to pay her a little visit. Seeing no Patriots about, they demanded supper. Obligingly, Hart prepared a feast of venison, turkey, and hoecake, and she provided a jug of whiskey. Soon the Tories were in their cups, unaware that Hart was slipping their rifles out the cabin through a chink in the wall. When they finally realized what she was doing, she hefted a rifle and demanded that they "surrender their Tory asses to a Whig woman." Owing to Nancy's crossed eyes, the Tories were at a loss as to where her gaze fell, and when one Tory made a grab for his rifle, he guessed wrong and paid for the mistake with his life. A second guessed wrong; a second fell. By the time her husband Benjamin Hart arrived home, Nancy had the remaining four at bay and was making plans to hang them. And hang them she did.

In 1912, the veracity of this legend was strengthened when a gang of railroad workers unearthed six skeletons less than a mile from the site of the Hart cabin.

This 1855 etching shows Nancy Hart attacking the Tories.

■ EXPANSION INTO INDIAN LANDS

During the late 18th and early 19th centuries, the population of Georgia swelled, moving northward and westward as Revolutionary War veterans bought up acreage in exchange for service, and land lottery winners laid claim to nearly three-quarters of present-day Georgia at a rate of around seven cents an acre.

Much of this newly settled land had previously been part of the Cherokee and Creek nations. By hook, crook, and "treaty," Georgia wrested lands away from these indigenous peoples. Land speculation was pursued at a feverish pace until the Yazoo Land Fraud—an aborted at-

This hand-tinted lithograph was made after Henry Inman's oil portrait of Creek chief William McIntosh. (The Columbus Museum, Columbus)

tempt by four land companies to bribe Georgia legislators to sanction the sale of 35 million acres of land for the paltry sum of $500,000—was exposed in 1795.

As Georgia farmers moved west, the tribal lands of the Creeks and Cherokees were encroached on again and again. Andrew Jackson's defeat of the Creeks in the War of 1812, coupled with the discovery of gold near the Cherokee capital of New Echota in 1829, signaled the beginning of the end.

In 1827, hard on the heels of a fraudulent treaty signed by Chief McIntosh, most of the Creeks were removed to Oklahoma. The Cherokee followed, though their removal was not completed until 1838, when U.S. general Winfield Scott and his men rounded up the last 15,000 Cherokee and marched them west to Oklahoma, on a journey now remembered as the Trail of Tears. Forced to travel on foot more than 1,000 miles in the dead of winter, nearly one in three Cherokee died on the five-month march, now considered one of the more shameful acts in American history. Missionary Daniel Buttrick, a firsthand observer of the removal, wrote in 1838 that, "from their first arrest, the Cherokees were obliged to live very much like brute animals, like hogs. Driving them is only a most expensive and painful way of putting the poor people to death." One Georgia soldier in Scott's company was so disturbed by what he witnessed that, writing many years later, he observed: "I fought through the Civil War, and have seen men shot to pieces and slaughtered by the thousands, but the Cherokee removal was the cruelest work I have ever seen."

Though Georgians of the day rationalized the removal of the Cherokee as being in the best interest of a savage people, the Cherokee culture, even when measured by European standards, was far from uncivilized. Aware that their homeland was under siege, the Cherokee adopted Western modes of government and conduct. Under the leadership of Sequoya, the Cherokee devised a constitution modeled in part after that of the United States, and they set fixed borders for what was to be a sovereign country. With New Echota, Georgia, as the capital, the Cherokee nation stretched across four states.

Concurrently, the Cherokee developed what was called a syllabry, a set of written symbols, each representing a different syllable in the Cherokee language. Today, the press used in printing the bilingual *Cherokee Phoenix* newspaper offers visitors to New Echota a glimpse of the accomplishments of these native Georgians.

Sequoya—Cherokee warrior, silversmith, and painter—invented the Cherokee syllabry in 1821. He created a system of 86 symbols, adapting letters from English, Hebrew, and Greek. (Library of Congress)

Because it increased the speed with which cotton fibers could be separated from the seeds, the cotton gin made short-fiber cotton commercially viable. (Library of Congress)

■ KING COTTON

The years between Independence and the Civil War were ones of progress and prosperity for Georgia. Cotton may well have emerged as king, but its ascendance was the result of neither rich soil nor agricultural acumen. Instead, the introduction of two "engines" would transform Georgia from an isolated state at the new nation's periphery into the South's leading economic force.

In the fall of 1792, fresh from Yale College, Eli Whitney, a New Englander by birth, accepted a job as the tutor at Catherine Greene's Mulberry Plantation just outside Savannah. Whitney may have earned his keep as a tutor, but it was his tinkering with a mechanical means of separating cotton lint from seeds that was to win him fame.

Intrigued by neighboring planters' tales of the difficulty and expense involved in combing the precious white cotton fibers from the seeds, Whitney set about finding a solution. By the spring of 1793, he had completed a model for what he called a cotton engine or "gin," as we now know it. It was a simple affair consisting of a cylinder studded with wire teeth; when turned by hand, it pulled the fiber

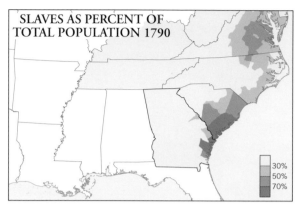

SLAVES AS PERCENT OF
TOTAL POPULATION 1790

*Increased cotton production
between the Revolutionary
and Civil Wars was directly
related to the growth of
slavery during that period.*

from the seed. At the suggestion of Mrs. Greene he further refined the gin when he added a row of brushes that rotated in the opposite direction, pulling the cotton from the teeth. The gin, even in its most rudimentary form, could do the work of ten men.

Whitney's invention revolutionized cotton production in the South. Previously, most cotton farming had been restricted to the coastal areas where the long-staple Sea Island cotton flourished. The short-fiber variety of cotton, though it grew well in the interior and produced more cotton per acre, had been little cultivated because it was difficult to seed. With Whitney's invention, the short-staple cotton became commercially viable, thousands of acres of land were planted with it, and planters sought many more slaves to work the newly planted acres.

Georgia came late to the institution of slavery. At the time of the American Revolution, New York had five times as many slaves as Georgia. And yet Georgia wasted little time in catching up and finally surpassing almost everyone else. By 1790, the slave population was almost 60,000, by 1840 more than 280,000, and by the eve of the Civil War, Georgia was second only to Virginia in number of bondsmen, and 40 percent of its population was enslaved.

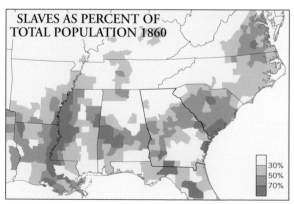

SLAVES AS PERCENT OF
TOTAL POPULATION 1860

In 1790 only 1,000 bales of cotton were grown in Georgia, but by 1840 the figure was

Between 1820 and 1860 farmland in western Georgia, Alabama, Mississippi, and Louisiana, was increasingly planted in cotton.

COTTON PRODUCTION 1820

Each dot represents 2,000 bales

400,000 bales, and by 1860 it exceeded 700,000. And as cotton acreage skyrocketed, so did the dependence on slave labor. The cotton gin may well have been a labor-saving device, but it did nothing but fuel the seemingly insatiable desire for enslaved black laborers. It should come as no surprise to learn that, though in the days just before the cotton gin, the price for a good field hand had hovered around $300, by 1850 the price was over $1,000, and by 1860 the average was nearly $1,800. In 1844, a Scottish visitor to Georgia observed, "Nothing was attended to but the rearing of cotton and slaves. The more cotton the more slaves and the more slaves the more cotton!"

■ COTTON AND THE RAILROAD

The second engine of import employed in Georgia pulled railroad cars rather than cotton fibers. In December of 1833 the Georgia legislature chartered two railroads to connect the cotton market towns of the day, one from Augusta to Athens and another from Savannah to Macon. Rail lines proved to be a highly efficient means of transporting cotton, and Georgians set about building them at a remarkable rate. By 1836, the legislature had passed a law calling for a state-owned railroad

COTTON PRODUCTION 1860

Each dot represents 2,000 bales

connecting Georgia's existing rail lines and thus affording Georgia farmers better access to U.S. markets, as well as to ports serving trade with England and its textile mills. The new railroad, the Western and Atlantic, would run from the Chattahoochee River in Dekalb County north to the Tennessee border. Surveyors drove a stake in the ground at the southernmost point of the new line and named this spot Terminus. Soon, with construction in high gear, Terminus was booming. By the 1850s, sporting the more cosmopolitan moniker of Atlanta, the city was one of the South's most important rail centers. And the cotton kept coming.

■ PLANTERS AND FARMERS

Thanks to novels like *Gone With the Wind*, antebellum Georgia is often perceived as being a genteel land of moonlight, magnolias, and mint juleps. In this world white Georgians raised cotton on plantations run by devoted, amusing slaves. Flirtatious girls in gorgeous pastel gowns went to balls on neighboring estates, young men galloped about on fine horses, and chivalry was in the air.

In reality, by 1860 less than one percent of Georgians belonged to the planter class (roughly defined as men owning more than 20 slaves). Though grand plantations worked by hundreds of slaves furnished a very small oligarchy with a sumptuous lifestyle, reality was more picaresque than picturesque. Often times, slave and master worked the fields side by side, up one row and down another, from

Rail lines facilitated the export of cotton to markets around the world. (Library of Congress)

An idealized version of a plantation, done by an unknown artist in 1825. (Metropolitan Museum of Art, Gift of Edgar William and Bernice Chrysler Garbisch, 1963; photograph © The Metropolitan Museum of Art)

first light to first dark.

If most white Georgians were small farmers, owning few or no slaves, they considered themselves respectable family people, churchgoing frontiersmen. The lowest class of whites—called by blacks and whites alike white trash—lived on the fringes of society.

■ THE "LATE UNPLEASANTNESS"

Ask a native why Georgia seceded from the Union and you are not likely to get a straight answer. For years, Georgia schoolchildren were taught that the primary issue was that of states' rights. Few Georgians, black or white, replied with the single word answer uppermost in most outlanders' minds: slavery.

Today, most Georgians will concede that the South seceded from the Union in order to protect the institution of slavery from a rising tide of abolitionist sentiment in the North. And leading historians concur that much of the impetus

HISTORIC GEORGIA

| 0 | 25 | 50 Miles |
| 0 | 25 | 50 | 75 Kilometers |

Map shows current shoreline, drainage, and boundaries

☐ *Major Archeological Site*
▭ *De Soto 1535-1542*
⊡ *Fort*
✸ *Atlanta Campaign Battles*
✷ *Wilson's Battles*
✳ *Other Battles*

Chattanooga
Chickamauga
Dalton
Resaca
Fort Mountain
Nacoochee
New Echota Cherokee Capitol
Estatoe
Chauga
Tugalo
Gregg Shoals
Wilbanks
Clyde Gulley
Van Creek
Etowah
Picketts Mill
Ruckers Bottom
Kennesaw
Fort Yargo
Tate
Beaverdam Creek Mound
New Hope Church
Peachtree Creek
Dallas
Atlanta
Utoy Creek
Ezra Church
Jonesborough
Dyar
Scull Shoals
Stallings Island
Silver Bluff
Hollywood
SHERMANS MARCH
Shoulderbone
Sunshine Church
West Point
Shinholser
SRP
Griswoldville
Lawton
Macon Plateau
Ocmulgee
Lamar
Columbus
De Soto 1535-42
Roads Landing
Haver Home
Irene
Savannah founded 1733
Fort Pulaski
Fort Mc Allister
Fort Mc Allister
Fort Pulask
Cemochechobee
Kolomoki
Fort King George
Fort Frederica

Elevation
in feet
4,784
2,600
2,200
1,800
1,400
1,000
Sea Level

N
W — E
S

NATIVE GROUPS

Iroquoian
☐ Cherokee

Gulf
☐ Kasihta
☐ Hitchiti
☐ Muskogee

Other
☐ Guale

IMPERIAL ZONES 1780

☐ Great Britain
☐ France
☐ Spain

for Georgia's exit was the need to defend the state's greatest repository of economic capital and its primary means of agricultural production—in short, slave labor.

Georgia seceded from the Union on January 21, 1861, the fifth state to do so. Contrary to popular belief, Georgia did not secede and then immediately join the Confederate States of America. Instead, for two months Georgia considered itself a sovereign nation, even going so far as to name ambassadors to Britain, France, and Belgium.

But when the other Southern states convened in Montgomery, Alabama, for the purpose of forming a new nation, the Confederate States of America, delegates from Georgia were in attendance. Alexander Stephens was elected vice president, while another Georgian, Thomas Cobb of Athens, crafted the new nation's constitution. The constitution, modeled in part on that of the United States, assuaged the fears of slaveholding Southerners by expressly prohibiting the Confederate Congress from passing any law to abolish slavery.

The first few years of the war were relatively quiet ones in Georgia. Though tens of thousands of Georgians volunteered and served in the Confederate Army, little fighting took place this far south. Meanwhile, Georgians were at work in munitions plants and textile mills churning out firearms, clothing, and other essentials for the boys in gray. Soon the cities of Macon, Augusta, Columbus, and Savannah were among the Confederacy's primary manufacturing centers. And thanks to its location at the center of Georgia's umbilical network of rail lines, Atlanta was the most important transportation center in the Confederacy.

By early 1864, Atlanta had become the prime target in General Grant's plan to divide and thus decimate the Confederate States of America. With Atlanta in Union hands, Confederate supply lines would be severed. Backed by 99,000 men and charged with orders from Grant to "get into the interior of the enemy's country as far as you can, inflicting all the damage that you can against their war resources," Gen. William Sherman marched southward from Chattanooga, Tennessee. Just 30 or so miles south, Gen. Joseph Johnston and his 62,000 Confederate soldiers dug into defensive trenches.

All spring long, the armies of Sherman and Johnston did battle. At Dalton, Resaca, and New Hope Church, Johnston's men fought and lost, retreating again and again, only to dig a new set of trenches and fight another day. When on June 27, Sherman attacked Johnston's troops head-on at Kennesaw Mountain, the Confederates dealt Sherman a nasty blow, killing more than 3,000 of his troops. But the victory was short lived. Soon the Confederates were retreating and digging in yet again, this time to defend Atlanta.

In an attempt to turn the tide, Confederate president Jefferson Davis replaced General Johnston with General John Hood—to no avail. Sherman pressed on, and for 40 days his artillery bombarded the city of Atlanta. "War, fearful and bloody, was each hour coming nearer," wrote one Atlantan. "Terrific cannonading on every side, continual firing of muskets, men screaming to each other, wagons rumbling by or pouring into the yard." By September 1, most Atlantans had evacuated; the next day, Mayor James M. Calhoun surrendered a largely abandoned city. In less than two weeks, Sherman gave orders that Atlanta be burned.

A Union soldier wrote of what he witnessed:

> On the night of November 15th, the torch was applied to the railroad shops, foundries, and every one of the many buildings that has been used in fitting out the armies of the enemy in this vast "workshop of the Confederacy," as Atlanta was called. The flames spread rapidly and, when morning came, it is doubtful whether there were a score of buildings remaining in the city, except on the very outskirts.

This photograph of Sherman (in foreground, leaning on breach of cannon) was taken in Atlanta in the fall of 1864. (Library of Congress)

The next day, Sherman began his "March to the Sea." Southward and eastward out of Atlanta, through Macon, Madison, and Milledgeville and on into Savannah, Sherman cut a swath of destruction unprecedented in the annals of American warfare, leaving wreck and ruin in his wake. For years thereafter the landscape was cluttered with his handiwork: "Sherman's sentinels" (blackened, lone chimneys) and "Sherman's neckties" (rails twisted around trees).

When Sherman's men entered Savannah on December 21, 1864, the general telegraphed President Lincoln with the good news:

General Johnston is the subject of this stained glass window in Rhodes Hall, Atlanta.

> *I* beg to present to you as a Christmas gift, the city of Savannah, with 150 guns and plenty of ammunition, also about 25,000 bales of cotton.

By the spring of 1865, the Southern armies were hapless, the Southern fight for independence hopeless. Of the 120,000 Georgians who had marched off to war, more than one in five did not return. On April 26, 1865, General Johnston formally surrendered the state of Georgia to Sherman, and soon thereafter, on May 10, Union forces captured a fleeing President Jefferson Davis near Irwinville in South Georgia.

■ RECONSTRUCTION AND REDEMPTION

With the defeat of the Confederacy and effective release of all slaves from captivity, $400 million vanished overnight from the coffers of white Georgia. This loss of slave capital, coupled with the physical destruction of nearly all important rail lines and manufacturing facilities, left Georgia in a postbellum economic lurch.

Many black Georgians, emboldened and empowered by their newfound freedom, left the old plantations, striking out for points north. Others remained, forging an uneasy alliance with their former masters, working the same fields, tending the same cash crop.

Meanwhile, Northern profiteers, intent upon taking advantage of the economic and social turmoil of the day, descended upon Georgia. Derided as carpetbaggers by white Southerners because they often carried baggage made from old carpets, these men were, in effect, land speculators who sought to buy up Georgia's decimated acreage at a pittance and resell at a monstrous profit.

While economic change came swiftly, it would be two years before real governmental change came, and only then at the threat of force. When Georgia and nine other former Confederate states refused to ratify the Fourteenth Amendment guaranteeing all citizens "equal protection of the laws," Congress acted. Early in 1867, the 10 states were placed under military stewardship. Georgia was governed by a U.S. Army general, and his decisions were enforced by federal troops. Soon the occupying troops set about registering black voters and making plans for the adoption of a new state constitution.

Concurrently, the federally mandated Freedmen's Bureau was at work in the state, providing support and education to struggling black Georgians. Among the bureau's most important tasks was helping freed slaves negotiate labor contracts with white landowners, a development that eventually gave rise to the

President Ulysses S. Grant is here depicted as a wealthy tyrant atop the huge carpetbag crushing the "Solid South." (Library of Congress)

sharecropping system.

From 1867 through 1870, Georgia flirted with a true overhaul of its governmental system. In 1868, 32 black Republicans were elected to Georgia's General Assembly, but 28 of the 32 were soon expelled on the grounds that the state constitution did not grant blacks the right to hold office. The four who remained were judged to be mulattos and thus worthy of service.

By the time the federal troops finally withdrew in 1870, a new force in Georgia politics was ascendant: the Ku Klux Klan, a fraternal order of sorts dedicated to the preservation of Protestant, Anglo-Saxon rule. For the next century, these white-hooded hooligans would exercise extralegal control over the affairs of Georgians both black and white.

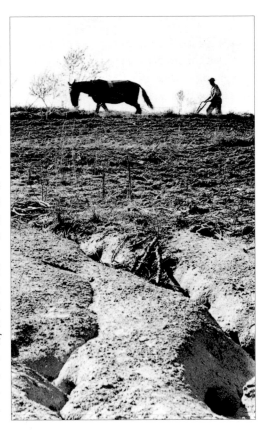

A farmer plows a deeply eroded field in Heard County. (photo by Jack Delano, Library of Congress)

■ BLEAKEST OF YEARS

As the century came to a close, the entire nation sank into an economic depression, with the South suffering the worst fate. Interest rates skyrocketed. Cotton prices plummeted. Once-fertile land, spent from years of one-crop farming, washed away in ruddy torrents, leaving deep red gorges cut into the landscape, a testament to years of abuse and neglect.

While planters scrambled to reassemble their fiefdoms, Georgia's smaller farmers eked out the barest of livings, raising cotton for cash and corn for feed. Black Georgians, rather than work for their former masters in a gang-style arrangement as they had done in the days of slavery, took to sharecropping. Their white neighbors worked beside them, subsisting on the same meager and monotonous diet of cornbread, molasses, and fatback.

With cash in short supply, Georgians depended on the sharecropping system as their de facto banking system. It worked this way: Farmers secured loans from planters and other large landholders under the guise of a crop lien, leveraging not the value of the land they were to be working but the crop they would bring in come fall. Planters provided what was called "the furnish"—seeds, tools, and other essentials necessary for survival. At "settlement time," the planter would weigh and price the cropper's harvest, deduct his half for the lease of the land, and then deduct an amount of his own divination for the furnish. All too often, no matter how large the crop, no matter how high the going price of cotton, the cropper came up short.

Frustration with the inequities of the sharecropping system gave birth to a short-lived biracial alliance of farmers, who, at the turn of the century, joined forces with Populist Party advocates, seeking governmental assistance in bringing an end to the usurious system. Among the more vociferous advocates of such agricultural reform was Georgian Tom Watson. When opponents attempted to wreck the movement by pitting the races against one another, Watson intoned that, "the accident of color can make no difference in the interest of farmers, croppers, and laborers." No matter, the effort failed, and a defeated and dejected Watson was soon spouting the same racist rhetoric he had once decried.

■ NEW SOUTH, NEW DEAL

It would take more than 60 years and the accumulated effects of large infusions of Northern fiscal investment and federal legislative intrusion to transform the Georgia economy and by extension the lives of the Georgia people.

During the 1870s and 1880s, *Atlanta Constitution* editor Henry Grady sold Southerners and Northerners alike on the idea that a "New South" was emergent. The *New York Times* called him "the great interpreter of a new spirit which was awakening in the South, exhorting the people to concern themselves no longer about what they had lost, but to busy themselves with what they might find to do:

to put the whole strength of their minds and bodies into the building up of a New South."

Grady charmed the industrialists with his mellifluous speech and promises of eager, cheap labor, even while he chided General Sherman for being "kind of a careless man about fire." Under Grady's leadership, and with Atlanta at its center, a new South did begin to take shape. Between 1870 and 1910, almost $200 million was invested in Georgia manufacturing concerns. Yet Grady never lived to see his dream come to fruition. He died in 1889 at the age of 39.

Henry W. Grady, seen here in bathing costume with Mrs. Bessie Johnson (left) daughter-in-law of President Andrew Johnson, in 1884. (Atlanta Historical Society)

The late 19th and early 20th centuries saw Georgia prosper only modestly. Atlanta boomed with industry, but the rest of the state plodded along, suffering through boll weevil infestations that ruined cotton crops, and droughts that left farmlands parched and puckered.

In response, Georgians of all hues and hometowns lit out for the North, intent on securing manufacturing jobs in New York, Detroit, and Chicago. Between 1920 and 1925 alone, Georgia's farm population decreased by 375,000.

By the 1930s, Georgia, like the rest of the nation, was in the grip of the Great Depression. At a time when President Roosevelt was pledging to provide all possible aid to a South that he considered, "the nation's number one economic problem," Gov. Eugene Talmadge, Georgia's firebrand champion of the common man, was making every effort to resist Roosevelt's roster of relief and assistance programs on the grounds that they threatened "Georgia's way of life." For the first four years

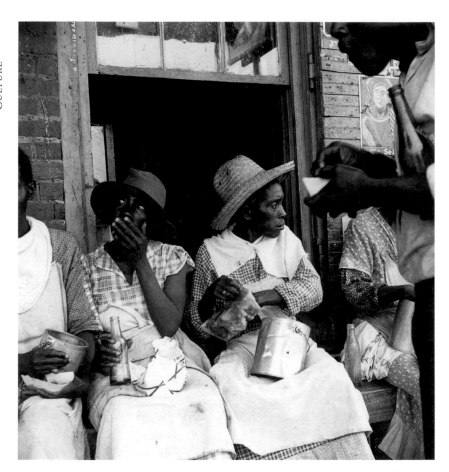

Farm Security Administration photographer Dorothea Lange took this picture of peach pickers during their lunch break in Muscella, Georgia, in 1936. (Library of Congress)

of Roosevelt's administration, Talmadge successfully forestalled Roosevelt's agenda, but in 1936, Eurith D. "Ed" Rivers was elected governor, and Georgia fully embraced the New Deal.

Though the New Deal brought immediate relief to many Georgians, it was not until the outbreak of World War II that Georgia fully recovered from the ravages of the previous years. War brought true prosperity to Georgia as military bases opened across the state and manufacturing concerns geared up to produce airplanes, ships, and weapons. By the fall of 1943, 20,000 civilians were working at one new facility alone, the Bell Aircraft Corporation in Marietta. At the close of the war, the annual income of the average Georgian was twice what it had been when the Japanese bombed Pearl Harbor.

■ CIVIL RIGHTS MOVEMENT

For almost a century after the demise of slavery, African-American Georgians chafed under the yoke of a white majority intent on denying them the most basic of civil rights. A de facto system of segregation known as Jim Crow specified where blacks were allowed to study, eat, and work. In addition, steps were taken to ensure that black Georgians would be excluded from the electoral process, culminating in 1908 with the passage of a constitutional amendment that disenfranchised potential black voters by requiring proof of Confederate lineage and property ownership. But in 1946, the U.S. Supreme Court declared the "white only" primary illegal, paving the way for black inclusion in the electoral process. In 1954 the Supreme Court declared that separate but equal schools were inherently discriminatory.

The effects were not immediate, but by 1960, Atlanta—under the leadership of its remarkably progressive mayor, Ivan Allen—was admitting black students to previously all-white high schools. In 1961, against the strong protests of racist demagogues like Herman

In 1964, Danny Lyon, staff photographer for the Student Nonviolent Coordinating Committee, took this photo of 17-year-old activist Taylor Washington being arrested at Lebs Delicatessen during a demonstration in Atlanta. (Library of Congress)

Talmadge (Eugene's son) and Lester Maddox, the University of Georgia admitted its first two African-American students, Charlayne Hunter and Hamilton Holmes.

Meanwhile, in the southwest Georgia town of Albany, Student Nonviolent Coordinating Committee (SNCC) members organized a massive, grassroots voter-registration drive. In November of 1961, Martin Luther King Jr. came to their aid, but the local movement was ultimately frustrated by the efforts of police chief Laurie Pritchett. Though the Albany Movement did not achieve its goals, it did represent a turning point in the struggle of black Georgians to achieve equal rights under the law, as seasoned activists joined with students and members of the black middle class in a systemic effort of organized resistance that would set the precedent for similar efforts in Birmingham, Alabama, and elsewhere.

Across the state, the Civil Rights Movement spread. Leaders like Andrew Young, Julian Bond, and John Lewis led sit-ins and launched protests. Compared to states like Alabama and Mississippi, the Civil Rights Movement in Georgia was relatively peaceful. Cities like Atlanta and Augusta, faced with well-organized sit-in campaigns targeted at local restaurants and other public accommodations, negotiated compromises and quickly got back to work. Thanks to its comparatively tolerant racial policies and its reputation for business savvy, Atlanta was soon

known as "the city too busy to hate."

Though the state would come close to riot at the news of the murder of favorite son Martin Luther King Jr.—and would flirt with racial demagoguery once again under the governorship of Lester Maddox—the 1970s held great promise for all Georgians.

Before he became the governor of Georgia, Lester Maddox refused to serve two African-American divinity students in his cafeteria the day after Johnson signed the Civil Rights Act of 1964. Here he models a pair of water buffalo horns sent to him by a Georgia soldier serving in Vietnam. (UPI/Bettmann)

Like Lester Maddox, Jimmy Carter was a self-made man from rural Georgia who became governor—but their opinions on segregation could not have been more different.

■ JIMMY CARTER AND MODERN TIMES

By the early 1970s, Henry Grady's vision of the New South was fast becoming a reality. In a fit of bravado worthy of the great Grady himself, newly elected Georgia governor Jimmy Carter declared in 1971 that, at the end of his term, "We shall be able to stand up anywhere in the world—in New York, California, or Florida— and say 'I'm a Georgian' and be proud of it." And much to the chagrin of some of the more conservative members of his own Democratic party, this onetime peanut farmer from Plains announced, "I say to you frankly that the time for racial discrimination is over."

With Carter at the helm, Georgia businesses boomed, Georgia schools received dramatic funding increases, and Georgia prisons were remodeled and reformed. By 1974, Carter was plotting a leap from the Georgia governor's mansion to the White House. In 1977 he took the oath of office as President of the United States.

While Carter was in the White House, change was afoot in Georgia. In search

*With its ever-increasing numbers of skyscrapers and highways, Atlanta is today the
largest city in the South.*

of manufacturing and service-industry employment, Georgians left farms in droves, moving to the urban center of the state—metropolitan Atlanta—in a trend that continues to this day. By 1990, metropolitan Atlanta accounted for more than 40 percent of the state's population.

Today, Atlanta is recognized as one of the world's premier corporate centers. Among the companies that call Atlanta home are such international powerhouses as Coca-Cola, CNN, UPS, and Delta Airlines.

Other regions of Georgia have also been affected by the booming economy. Change, in the form of urban sprawl, has come even to the hinterlands. Of modern north Georgia, Mary Hood writes: "Toward the interstate, pastures have been carved into streets. Oaks and horse barns have been shouldered out by apartments.

It is only a matter of time before there will be a car wash, cleaners, convenience store, tanning salon, racquetball center, roller rink, and video rental club."

So is this progress? Are Georgians of today better off than they were a hundred years ago, a generation ago? Well, as a precocious child might say, that depends.

There is little debate as to whether Georgians are a different people than they were even a generation ago. No longer are we a segregated land of black and white, almost all of whom vote the Democratic ticket and live within a couple hours' drive of where we were raised.

No, we are all grown up now—so grown up that in 1996 we hosted the Summer Olympic Games. But that doesn't mean Georgia has lost its quirks. That doesn't mean our last shred of Southern distinctiveness has been mortgaged to build yet another strip mall. Should you doubt me, just point your car toward the little hamlet of Box Springs in western central Georgia. West of town, you'll spot the Giggle Box Cafe. Pull over, order yourself a mess of fried okra, and then tell me what you think.

In 1996, Atlanta hosted the Summer Olympic Games. American track star Michael Johnson ran in the 200-meter heat shown here.

SOUTHERN WRITERS ON SOUTHERN CULTURE

Visitors to Georgia encounter a variety of cultures. Life in Appalachian Georgia is a far cry from life in the university town of Athens, and Atlanta's old-money black elite has little in common with peanut or sugar-cane farmers in the south part of the state. And yet the idea that there exists such a thing as "Southern culture" has enormous staying power. Southerners themselves have no doubt made the largest contribution to the literature on the subject. The following excerpts offer glimpses of how Southerners see or have seen themselves.

◆ SOUTHERN GENTLEMEN

*B*eside being of faultless pedigree, the Southern Gentleman is usually possessed of an equally faultless physical development. His average height is about six feet, yet he is rarely gawky in his movements, or in the least clumsily put together; and his entire *physique* conveys to the mind an impression of firmness united to flexibility.... the Northern people have been told so incessantly of the lazy habits of Southerners, that they honestly believe them to be delicate good-for-nothings, like their own brainless fops and nincompoops.... The gentlemen of the South owe their physical perfectness in part, doubtless, to those mailed ancestors who followed Godfrey and bold Coeur de Lion to the rescue of the Holy Sepulchre....

Much more reasonably, however, we think we may attribute the good size and graceful carriage of the Southern Gentleman, to his out-of-doors and a-horseback mode of living. For we might as well here inform our readers, the genuine Southern Gentleman almost invariably lives in the country. But let them not conclude from

from this circumstance that he is nothing more than the simple-hearted, swearing, hearty, and hospitable old English or Virginia Country Gentleman, of whom we have all heard so repeatedly.

—Daniel R. Hundley, *Social Relations in Our Southern States*, 1860

George Washington Lay (left) and his cousin, James Berry Lay, a couple of Southern gentlemen, photographed in 1855. (Georgia Department of Archives and History)

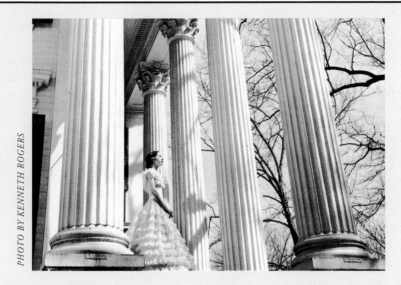

PHOTO BY KENNETH ROGERS

◆ SOUTHERN LADIES

In her 1975 collection of essays, titled Southern Ladies and Gentlemen, *author Florence King explains the thrall in which Southern women hold many of us, writers included:*

Novelists prefer complex women for their protagonists, which is why the Southern woman has been the heroine of so many more novels than her Northern sister. The cult of Southern womanhood endowed her with at least five totally different images and asked her to be good enough to adopt all of them. She is required to be frigid, compassionate, sweet, bitchy, and scatterbrained—all at the same time. Her problems spring from the fact that she succeeds.

Antebellum Southern civilization was built upon the white woman's untouchable image. In order to keep her footing on the pedestal men had erected for her, she had to be aloof, aristocratic, and haughty. These qualities have always been required of women in societies based upon vast, entailed estates, but they were especially necessary in the South. They enabled the white woman to maintain her sanity when she saw light-skinned slave children, who were the very spirit of Old Massa, running around the plantation. By being sufficiently frosty and above it all, she was able to ignore and endure the evidence of intercaste sexuality that surrounded her.

—Florence King, *Southern Ladies and Gentlemen*, 1975

◆ SOUTHERN HOSPITALITY

Integral to the Southern mystique is the reputation Southerners enjoy for gracious accommodation. A distant relative, a neighbor, a statesman, or otherwise distinguished man, a stranger who came with letters of introduction from friends: all could be assured of a warm welcome. In his informal history, *Eating and Drinking in the South*, published in 1982, historian Joe Gray Taylor observes:

> *Of* the hospitality of the planters and well-to-do townsmen of the Old South there can be no doubt; the witnesses are too abundant. The story of the lonesome lord of many acres who at rifle point forced passersby to partake of his hospitality, is probably apocryphal, but it does make the point that life on the plantation could be isolated and lonely; the visit of a well-informed traveler could be a much welcomed break in the routine of the seasons."

Naturalist William Bartram was quite impressed by the cordial reception he received in Georgia in the 1770s. He noted that on one rice plantation he was entertained "in every respect as a worthy gentleman—A stranger spent the evening very agreeably and the day following (for I was not permitted to depart sooner)."

Bartram's observations were confirmed by another traveler of that era, Sir Charles Lyell, who noted that "they alone who have traveled in the southern states can appreciate the ease and politeness with which a stranger is received."

A Southern-style family reunion circa 1900. (Georgia Department of Archives and History)

Baptism at Triplett Creek in 1940. (Library of Congress)

◆ SOUTHERN RELIGION

Author Flannery O'Connor wrote that Georgia is "Christ-haunted." If a Georgian asks you what church you belong to, he's probably assumed you're either Baptist or Methodist. Here is O'Connor's evocation of a preacher:

"*I* seen you cure a woman oncet!" a sudden high voice shouted from the hump of people. "Seen that woman git up and walk out straight where she had limped in!"

The preacher lifted one foot and then the other. He seemed almost but not quite to smile. "You might as well go home if that's what you come for," he said.

Then he lifted his head and arms and shouted, "Listen to what I got to say, you people! There ain't but one river and that's the River of Life, made out of Jesus' Blood. That's the river you have to lay your pain in, in the River of Faith, in the River of Life, in the River of Love, in the rich red river of Jesus' Blood, you people!"

His voice grew soft and musical. "All the rivers come from that one River and go back to it like it was the ocean sea and if you believe, you can lay your pain in that River and get rid of it because that's the River that was made to carry sin. It's a River full of pain itself, pain itself, moving toward the Kingdom of Christ, to be washed away, slow, you people, slow as this here old red water river round my feet."

—Flannery O'Connor, "The River," from *A Good Man is Hard to Find, and Other Stories*, 1955

N O R T H W E S T

■ HIGHLIGHTS

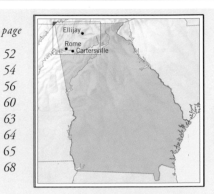

■ TRAVEL BASICS

Remote and relatively undeveloped, northwest Georgia is a delight. Natural beauty abounds, from Cloudland Canyon with its breathtaking views and waterfalls, to the rugged Cohutta Mountains and the rolling hills of the Civil War battlefield at Chickamauga. Vestiges of Native American life are well preserved at New Echota, the last eastern capital of the Cherokee nation, and at the Etowah Indian Mounds near Cartersville. For a glimpse at what man has wrought, make your way to visionary folk artist Howard Finster's Paradise Gardens, or to Fort Mountain, where an unexplained rock wall more than 800 feet long winds its way through the wilderness.

Getting Around: To appreciate the natural beauty of the region, head east or west from the I-75 corridor and wander the mountain roads. And by all means, get out of the car and take a hike. Rome, the largest town in north Georgia, can be toured on foot.

Climate: Cool and wet winters with temperatures ranging from the low 20s F to the mid-50s. Occasional snowfall possible. Summers are warm and humid with frequent thunderstorms; temperatures in the 80s. Fall is usually dry and pleasant. Spring peaks in April.

Food & Lodging: Good restaurants and inns are few and far between in this corner of Georgia. But there are a few surprises tucked away, including a suite for let in Pennsville that's situated in the gardens of a renowned visionary folk artist, and a tidy little diner in Rossville that serves near perfect cheeseburgers. Cabins are available at many state parks, including Cloudland Canyon and Fort Mountain. For food and lodging listings, see pages 70 to 73.

■ OVERVIEW

Viewed in late fall, the mountains of northwest Georgia resemble a rumpled shag carpet of kaleidoscopic color, each tuft a different mix of russet and gold, purple and chocolate, dusky green and bleached black.

Here at the tail end of the Appalachian Mountains, the Cherokee nation once flourished. The settlement at New Echota—now a state historic site—is a testament to a valiant and ill-fated attempt to assimilate and survive in the face of European encroachment. Those first Europeans were for the most part Scotch-Irish settlers. Their descendants, living in the comparative isolation of these mountains, remain a people apart, friendly and welcoming, but not as likely to invite a stranger in as their low-country neighbors. Welcoming they are; gullible they are not.

Though the region remains remote, development is spreading north from Atlanta along the interstate highway system. From Calhoun to Dalton, north to Chattanooga, Tennessee, the I-75 corridor cuts a swath of development and industry that stands in stark contrast to the remote and comparatively unspoiled lands that lie to its east and west. Unlike the mountains of northeast Georgia, which were long ago claimed as vacation getaways by Atlantans, the Cohutta Mountains and the remote canyons and cave-riddled ridges farther west are remarkably devoid of ticky-tacky tourist development. Here the land is unspoiled, the people unassuming and welcoming.

Thomas Hart Benton's Arts of the South, *1932. (New Britain Museum of Art, New Britain, CT; © T. H. Benton and R. P. Benton Testamentary Trusts/Licensed by* VAGA, *New York, NY) (opposite) Cloudland Canyon State Park.*

■ ROME *map page 49, B-4*

On the southern fringe of the region is Rome—a population of 30,000 makes it the largest city in the state north of Atlanta. Once known as "the stove center of the South," modern-day Rome is still a manufacturing center, albeit one overshadowed by the behemoth that is Atlanta, located just an hour south. In 1863 the town was ably defended against Union forces by Confederate colonel Abel D. Streight, but the following year it was occupied by the Federals, and in November of 1864 its factories were destroyed.

Today, the graceful Victorian downtown district and natural splendor of the Berry College campus are the primary attractions.

Romulus and Remus

Perhaps because the founders realized they'd sited the city on seven rolling hills, they named their town for that other city on seven hills. Rome, Georgia, even claims a sculpture of Romulus and Remus and their lupine mother. In Rome, Italy, the original Etruscan sculpture sits atop Capitoline Hill; in Rome, Georgia, a replica guards the entrance to City Hall: a ferocious, almost fiendish she-wolf, fangs bared, protects the mythical boy twins, founders of the city. The inscription below is a bit unnerving: "From Ancient Rome to New Rome during the consulship of Benito Mussolini in the year 1928." *At the corner of Broad Street and Sixth Avenue.*

Rome Area History Museum

Three blocks away from the City Hall is the Rome Area History Museum, a great-aunt's attic of a display space, stuffed to the gills with ephemera and homespun exhibits detailing local history in a provincial yet charming fashion. *305 Broad Street; 706-235-8051.*

Clock Tower Museum

Up the hill at Fourth Avenue and Third Street is the Clock Tower Museum, a brick water tower 100 feet tall and topped with an 1871 clock. Inside, a spiral staircase leads to the top, where visitors may take in a sweeping view of the city's seven hills. *706-236-4430.*

Myrtle Hill Cemetery

An equally lofty perspective on the city is offered at Myrtle Hill Cemetery, located on Rome's southwestern edge at the confluence of the Etowah and Oostanaula Rivers. Named for the hundreds of crepe myrtle bushes that grace the grounds and explode with purple each spring, the cemetery rises six terraced levels high and is the last resting place of Rome native Ellen Axson Wilson, first wife of President Woodrow Wilson.

Also of interest, if for nothing more than the florid prose, is the cemetery's **Women of the Confederacy Monument,** which pays homage to the women of Rome, "whose purity, whose fidelity, whose courage, whose genius in love and in counsel kept the home secure, the family a school of virtue, the state a court of honor, who made of war a season of heroism and of peace a time of healing, the guardians of tranquility and our strength." *South Broad and Myrtle Streets.*

Chieftains Museum

Heritage of another sort is on display at the Chieftains Museum, once home to Major Ridge, one of the leaders of the Cherokee nation. Ridge signed the U.S. removal act on behalf of the Cherokee people and followed them to Oklahoma. He was eventually executed by his tribe for having sold their tribal lands.

The clapboard home houses an odd juxtaposition of Native American exhibits and gilded Victorian furniture, intended to convey the Cherokee people's attempts at assimilation. *A few miles north of town on Riverside Parkway; 706-291-9494.*

Berry College

On the northern outskirts of Rome is the beautiful campus of Berry College, founded in 1902 by Martha Berry. Near the entrance to the 28,000-acre campus (the world's largest in geographical size) is the cabin where Berry, daughter of a wealthy

The Old Mill Wheel at Berry College.

planter, first began teaching the sons and daughters of those less fortunate. From here, the campus sprawls along Highway 27. Roadways are lined with towering oaks, and the pasture-like expanse of campus green space is dotted with Gothic stone halls and simple cabins. At the northern extreme, some three miles from the main campus, the Berry College Mountain Campus sits atop Lavender Mountain. Here the Old Mill Wheel still turns; the 1930 water wheel is one of the largest overshot wheels in the world. *Campus information: 706-232-5374.*

Today, 2,000 students call the campus home. And thanks to Martha Berry's commitment to the interdependence of work and study, most students earn their keep by working at the college's farms and research facilities. Also on campus is the Berry family home, known as **Oak Hill,** a magnificent Georgian mansion filled with family mementos and ringed by boxwood gardens. And on this site is the newly renovated **Martha Berry Museum,** a tribute to Berry's life and legacy; *706-291-1883.*

■ CARTERSVILLE AREA *map page 49, D-4*

Thirty miles east of Rome (and 45 miles northwest of Atlanta via I-75) is Cartersville, a tidy town that boasts two quaint cafes and a bucolic business district. On the east wall of Main Street's Young Brothers Pharmacy, you can take a gander at the first outdoor sign painted to advertise Coca-Cola. These signs, once a ubiquitous a part of the Southern landscape, are now, in the words of a local, "scarce as chicken teeth."

Nearby are the **Etowah Indian Mounds**, a series of three large temple mounds and four smaller ones, constructed on the north bank of the Etowah River between A.D. 1250 and 1550. Constructed basket by dirt-filled basket, the largest of these flat-topped earthen knolls is more than six stories high, with a base covering three acres. Also of note are the restored fish traps built of stone and woven wood. When the river is low, these can be viewed from the riverbank. *Located a few miles southwest of town, down Highway 113, past the Bow and Arrow Mobile Home Park; 770-387-3747.*

These Etowah Indian human figures date from the Mississippian era, circa A.D. 1200–1400. (Georgia Department of Natural Resources)

The Etowah Mounds State Historic Site, south of Cartersville.

■ NORTH OF CARTERSVILLE

North of Cartersville along Highway 293 is the little village of **Kingston,** where in 1864 Union general William T. Sherman received permission from Ulysses S. Grant, commander of the Union Army, to begin his infamous March to the Sea.

Today, the village is but a ghost of its former self. In days past, the downtown business district teemed with shoppers on Saturday afternoons. Perhaps the sole diversion on a Saturday now is the **Church of the Lord Jesus Christ,** one of the few snake-handling churches in Georgia, which by evening comes alive with worshippers.

Dennis Covington, in his book *Salvation on Sand Mountain,* describes a service in this way:

> *It's* not true that you become used to the noise and confusion of a snake-handling Holiness service. On the contrary, you become enmeshed into it. It is theatre at its most intricate—improvisational, spiritual jazz. The younger the worshipper, the easier it seems to be for the Holy Ghost to descend and speak—lips loosened, tongue flapping, eyes rolling backward in the head....

At a typical service, three or four guitarists join a bassist and maybe a couple of drummers behind the altar. As they crank out a raucous back beat, the preacher begins his sermon, alternately chanting, shouting, praying, and singing as church members rise from their seats, some merely raising their hands in the air, others off on a jig of their own divination, while still others make their way to the pulpit, intent upon drinking "the deadly thing" (strychnine) or handling rattlesnakes, as prescribed in Mark 16:18: "They shall take up serpents."

Services can last upwards of three hours, and visitors should bear in mind that they are attending a religious ceremony. Potential guests are advised to write to the church in advance at General Delivery, Kingston, Georgia 30145.

■ BARNSLEY GARDENS *map page 49, C-4*

A world away from the raw-boned life of Appalachia is Barnsley Gardens, once described by Union general James McPherson as being "one of the most beautiful spots on earth." The gardens were the site of a grand antebellum mansion built by British-born cotton exporter Godfrey Barnsley.

Today the house is but a shell, though the gardens, designed by pioneering landscape architect Andrew Jackson Downing, are a marvel of boxwood mazes and ancient gnarled rosebushes. The gardens and grounds have been reborn as a resort and golf course. *Located equidistant between Kingston and Adairsville, 10 minutes off I-75; 770-773-9495.*

■ NEW ECHOTA *map page 49, C-3*

Fifteen miles north of Barnsley Gardens, off Highway 225, is New Echota, the last eastern capital of the Cherokee nation, established on November 12, 1825. New Echota was a planned community, laid out by Cherokee surveyors and intended from its inception to serve as the seat of government. In the face of continuing pressure from the United States, the Cherokee adopted a system of government based on the U.S. model, dividing the nation into eight districts represented by a bicameral legislature.

It was here that a Cherokee named Sequoyah first devised a written language for his people—a syllabry of 86 characters, put to practical use in 1828 with the publication of a bilingual newspaper, the *Cherokee Phoenix.*

Despite such efforts to assimilate, the Cherokee nation came to an end when,

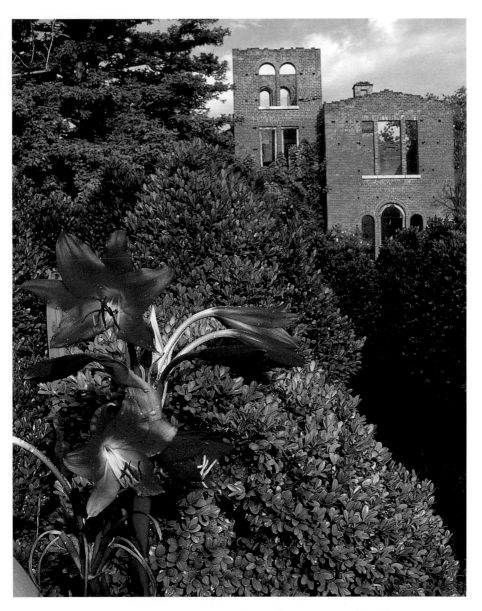

Early light on the ruins of the Barnsley Gardens estate, near Adairsville.

on December 29, 1835, the Treaty of New Echota was signed, ceding all Cherokee lands east of the Mississippi River to the United States. In exchange, the Cherokee received $5,300,000 and a large parcel of Oklahoma land. In May 1836, over the objections of the many Cherokee who considered the treaty unjust, President Andrew Jackson signed the treaty into law, thus beginning the two-year-long removal along a route that came to be known as the Trail of Tears. Over the course of the 1,000-mile journey, more than 4,000 Cherokee lost their lives.

Faced with the prospect of removal, Elias Boudinot, first editor of the *Cherokee Phoenix,* composed this remarkably prescient statement in November of 1836:

> The time will come when the few remnants of our once happy and improving nation will be viewed by posterity with curious and gazing interest as relics of a brave and noble race...perhaps only here and there a solitary being, walking as a ghost over the ashes of his fathers to remind a stranger that such a race once existed.

Soon after the Cherokee were installed in Oklahoma, the three principal signers of the treaty, the editor Elias Boudinot, Major Ridge, and his son John Ridge, were assassinated by their fellow tribesmen for selling tribal lands.

Today, New Echota is the living embodiment of Boudinot's words. Walking along the dusty lanes that crisscross the settlement, past the reconstructed print shop, courthouse, council house, and tavern, it seems the dwelling place of ghosts.

A Cherokee farmstead in spring at New Echota State Historic Site. A planned community, New Echota was the last eastern capital of the Cherokee nation.

Here and there you come upon another visitor, but for the most part, the buildings are empty, their displays dust-covered. Eight major buildings are on view, and all save the Worchester house, home of a missionary who remained even after the removal, were the dwelling and meeting places of the Cherokee.

After a tour of the grounds, stop at the museum to see exhibits on Cherokee building techniques and language. Those interested in the Cherokee syllabry may listen to recordings of the language and gaze at an original copy of the Cherokee nation's newspaper.

Chief Vann House, built in 1804.

◆ CHIEF VANN HOUSE

The opulent Chief Vann House, known as the "showplace of the Cherokee nation," was built by Chief James Vann in 1804. A two-story brick home, it stands in tribute to the great wealth the Vann family amassed farming cotton. At one point, Vann's 110 slaves worked 4,000 acres of land. The home sits on a grassy knoll, surrounded by a clump of trees with a log cabin behind. Inside, the mantelpieces are hand-carved, the staircase cantilevered, and the whole of the house painted a vibrant palate of iron-hued red, baby blue, earthy brown, and green.

Forced to leave their home in 1835 after the Treaty of New Echota was signed, Vann's descendants traveled in style, with a stint on a luxurious steamboat, on their way to the Cherokee reservation in Oklahoma. James Vann's son, Joseph, built a replica of his Georgia home in Weber Falls, Oklahoma.

Since 1958, the original Vann home has been managed by the state of Georgia as a historic site. *Eighteen miles north of New Echota along Highway 225 in Spring Place; 706-695-2598.*

■ PIEDMONT HILLS AND CHICKAMAUGA

To the north, rolling hills give way to the stooped irregularity of the Piedmont-Plateau, and soon you are approaching Dalton, Georgia, the self-proclaimed "carpet capital of the world." Though there is little of interest in this city, its industrial might is changing the cultural face of northwest Georgia. Mexican immigrants are moving to the area in search of work in the plants, and in small towns like Dalton and Chatsworth, taquerias are now as common as cafes.

Close to the Tennessee border, the Piedmont erupts with geological complexity. Here, high plateaus long ago eroded into mountains, and gulleys deepened into gorges. On this rough, unforgiving terrain was fought the bloodiest two-day battle of the Civil War: Chickamauga.

On September 19 and 20 of 1863, 124,000 soldiers fought and 34,000 fell. Lt. Col. James Abernathy of Kansas remembered the battle this way:

> We advanced under a perfect shower of bullets, sometimes driving the enemy and in turn being driven by them, until we had fought over the ground over and over again, and almost half our number lay dead and wounded.

The Battle of Chickamauga was one of the costliest Civil War battles for both sides.

CHICKAMAUGA VICTORY

January and February of 1864 passed, full of cold rains and wild winds, clouded by pervasive gloom and depression. In addition to the defeats at Gettysburg and Vicksburg, the center of the Southern line had caved. After hard fighting, nearly all of Tennessee was now held by the Union troops. But even with this loss on the top of the others, the South's spirit was not broken. True, grim determination had taken the place of high-hearted hopes, but people could still find a silver lining in the cloud. For one thing, the Yankees had been stoutly repulsed in September when they had tried to follow up their victories in Tennessee by an advance into Georgia.

Here in the northwesternmost corner of the state at Chickamauga, serious fighting had occurred on Georgia soil for the first time since the war began. The Yankees had taken Chattanooga and then had marched through the mountain passes into Georgia, but they had been driven back with heavy losses.

Atlanta and its railroads had played a big part in making Chickamauga a great victory for the South. Over the railroads that led down from Virginia to Atlanta and then northward toward Tennessee, General Longstreet's corps had been rushed to the scene of the battle. Along the entire route of several hundred miles, the tracks had been cleared and all the available rolling stock in the Southeast had been assembled for the movement.

Atlanta had watched while train after train rolled through the town, hour after hour, passenger coaches, box cars, flat cars, filled with shouting men. They had come without food or sleep, without their horses, ambulances or supply trains and, without waiting for the rest, they had leaped from the trains and into the battle. And the Yankees had been driven out of Georgia, back into Tennessee.

It was the greatest feat of the war, and Atlanta took pride and personal satisfaction in the thought that its railroads had made the victory possible.

—Margaret Mitchell, *Gone With the Wind,* 1936

The battle, though a victory for Confederate forces, was quickly followed by a Union victory at the Battle of Lookout Mountain outside Chattanooga, Tennessee. That winter Union general Sherman plotted an attack on Atlanta from his Chattanooga lair.

Soon after the end of the Civil War, Chickamauga was established as a national military park, the first in the country. Today, more than 600 stone and brass monuments (most erected by Chickamauga veterans) stand in tribute to the battlefield losses of blue- and gray-clad boys and men.

Florida Monument at Chickamauga and Chattanooga National Military Park.

A series of plaques—blue for Union, gray for Confederate—mark troop movements, while pyramids of cannonballs stand where brigade commanders were killed and headquarters established.

Deer now graze amid Chickamauga's monuments and children play games of tag, but reminders of the carnage of war are never far away. Though the setting is pleasing, the grounds of the park look like a vast graveyard filled with mausoleums and obelisks. Along Battle Line Road, the marble monuments face one another: the 90th Ohio Infantry squaring off against a Confederate unit from Alabama.

Among the most striking monuments is an imposing pedestal crowned with a statute of four soldiers and dedicated to Confederate soldiers from Georgia, "those who gave much and those who gave all."

Thanks to the miles of footpaths and roadways that wend their way through the park following old battle lines, this huge greensward can be explored at a leisurely pace. Spend an hour or so driving through, or an afternoon on foot, exploring some of the more remote sites.

◆ Visitor Center

A 30-minute introductory film offered at the graceful, flagstone visitor center, as well as an audiocassette-narrated tour of the park, put the battle in historical perspective and explain the major engagements. Also in the visitor center is the Fuller Gun Collection, a stockpile of rifles old and new, some of which feature fencing bayonets made from whalebone. *The military park is nine miles south of Chattanooga on US 27; 706-866-9241.*

❖

Others may want to journey north to Chattanooga and the Point Park and Lookout Mountain battlefields. Unfortunately, the drive there is through a rather ugly commercial stretch.

■ Cloudland Canyon State Park *map page 49, A-1*

West of Chickamauga, almost at the Alabama border, is Cloudland Canyon State Park, perhaps the most remote spot in northern Georgia. Located on the western edge of Lookout Mountain, the park straddles a deep gorge cut in the mountain by Sitton Gulch Creek. Reached by way of an ear-popping climb on Highway 136, Cloudland Canyon offers sightseers unparalleled vistas from the parking lot, while hikers in search of more may take to two canyon-rim trails. A variety of overnight accommodations are offered, from primitive campsites to two- to-three-bedroom cabins. *Highway 136, southwest of Trenton; 706-657-4050.*

A trail through Cloudland Canyon State Park.

■ PENNVILLE AND PARADISE GARDENS *map page 49, B-3*

Down the mountain by way of Highway 27 is the little burg of Pennville, home to **Howard Finster's Paradise Gardens**. Situated on what was a patch of swampland, in the midst of a lower middle class neighborhood, this three-acre compound is a treasure trove of idiosyncratic architecture, religious iconography, and plain old funk. *706-857-2926.*

Until 1976, the Rev. Howard Finster made his living as a Baptist preacher and bicycle repairman. But one spring day he had the first of several visions that changed his life forever. On that day, while fixing a bicycle, he glanced at his thumb, covered at the time with enamel paint, and saw a small, animate human face. The face spoke to him, saying, "Paint sacred art." Howard replied, "I can't!" The little face boomed back: "How do you know? How do you know? How do you know?!"

In desperation, Finster, using a one-dollar bill as a model, painted his first work, a portrait of George Washington. Soon after, Finster began to work nonstop. He painted on cars and cast-off tin, Nyquil bottles and paint lids, Coca-Cola bottles and coffin lids. Over time he began constructing a garden of sorts in his backyard, a jumble of towers made from bicycle parts and a four-story chapel made of scrap lumber. Concrete walkways embedded with shards of brightly colored glass criss-crossed the grounds. All, says Howard, was done for the greater glory of God.

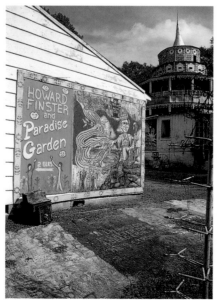

Soon the press came calling. The Sunday *New York Times Magazine* called it "a garden of art that beats anything this side of Eden." Pop artist Keith Haring called it "a Disneyland of Art."

By the 1980s Finster was painting album covers for rock groups like the Talking Heads and REM, and advertisements for Absolut vodka. Asked why he would paint an album cover for a rock band, Finster replied, "I had 26 million verses go out and reach the world. That's more than I ever reached in the 45 years I was pastoring. The rock 'n' rollers are my missionaries."

Paradise Gardens.

Howard Finster preaches/performs at Paradise Gardens on Sunday afternoons.

Today, the septuagenarian still receives guests at Paradise Gardens on Sundays from 2 to 5 P.M., when he holds a ceremony that is equal parts religious service, art show, and gospel sing-along. The gardens, however, have seen better days. In 1996, many of Finster's better outdoor pieces were moved to the High Museum in Atlanta. Yet an hour-long stroll about the gardens still offers many an unexpected delight, like a six-foot-long high-top sneaker made of concrete and emblazoned with the words "Blessed are the feet of those who spread the gospel of peace," or a mirror-covered tree house perched in the pines.

At the entrance to the gardens, Finster's daughter Beverly now operates a gallery, selling art made by Howard and his many relatives as well as CDs of Howard preaching and singing. The ultimate experience is reserved for those who book a night's stay at the Paradise Suite, located in a cabin on the property. *(See page 72 for details.)*

■ COHUTTA MOUNTAINS

An alternate approach to the mountains of northwest Georgia can be made by way of I-575; at the terminus of this interstate spur, just 45 miles north of Atlanta, urban sprawl gives way to quaint, quiet small-town life, marble quarry country, and, finally, the mountains of Appalachia. Less traveled than mountainous regions to the east, the surrounding countryside as viewed from Highway 5 rewards travelers with glimpses of towering forests and numerous geological curiosities. The Cohuttas belong to the Great Smoky Mountains, and are drier and more open than the Blue Ridge Mountains to the east. Hikers in the **Cohutta Wilderness Area** will find over 90 miles of trails, traversing both forest and wide-open vistas. At lovely Lake Conasauga, with its backdrop of Grassy Mountain, there is much wildlife to be seen. The 1.7-mile Songbird Trail crosses an area set aside to preserve habitat. Come here to see scarlet tanagers, red crossbills, and sandhill cranes, all visible at times from an observation platform.

Though Tate and Jasper are better known for their marble quarries, the little village of **Ball Ground,** located just an hour or so north of Atlanta, is a worthy detour for any rock hound: arrayed along the main drag, Gilmer Ferry Road, are eight brick storefronts, once home to hardware stores, grocery stores, and the like, and now given over to the display of rocks and minerals.

From the street, the **Rock Shop,** as the complex is called, doesn't look like much: some of the front windows are cracked, the sidewalk is a jumble of marble shards and boulders, and the whole of the block seems shrouded in a thick blanket of dust. But upon closer inspection, you come to see that the dirty display windows frame a collection of geodes, crystals, fossils, and assorted geologic whatnot worthy of a museum. Never mind that the displays are dotted with vaguely Chinese statuary and gaudy necklaces that hang from the ceiling like stalactites. If you can catch the proprietor on premises, step inside; if no one is home, window shopping will have to do.

■ TATE *map page 49, E-3*

Just north of Jasper is Tate, the undisputed epicenter of the state's marble industry and home to the Georgia Marble Company. The company's founder, Col. Sam Tate, was an inveterate promoter of all things marble, working to ensure that Georgia marble was used in the building of the Lincoln Memorial in Washington, D.C., as well as in more plebeian projects like the local elementary school, a white marble wonder on Highway 53 just a half-mile or so outside the town of Tate. On the same road is the pink marble palace Tate built in 1923, now doing business as a bed-and-breakfast inn *(see page 73).*

Just down the hill from the mansion, the smokestacks of the Georgia Marble Company loom, spewing marble dust high in the air.

Dogwood blooms in spring in Georgia's forests.

■ COOSAWATTEE RIVER AREA *map page 49, E-2*

North of Tate is **Ellijay,** located in Gilmer County, the "Apple Capital" of Georgia. The nearby (and now dammed) Coosawattee River was the setting of James Dickey's horrifying novel *Deliverance.* Dickey took whitewater canoeing trips along the river in the early '70s while he was working for the Army Corps of Engineers. Though much of the novel (and the popular film that followed) dwells upon what befalls a group of suburbanites in the wilds of Appalachia, Dickey communicates a real love for the natural splendor of this corner of the state, as evidenced by this passage from early in the novel:

> *T*here was another bend up ahead, and the river seemed to strain to get there, and we with it. Around the turn it came into view, and broadened in the white. Everywhere we were going was filled with spring bubblings, with lively rufflings, not dangerous-looking but sprightly and vivid. There was not the sensation of the water's raging, but rather that of its alertness and resourcefulness as it split apart at rocks, frothed lightly, corkscrewed, fluted, fell, recovered, jostled into helmet-shapes over smothered stones, and ran out of sight down long garden-staircase steps around another turn.

❖

Today, the biggest attraction around these parts is a roadside barbecue joint called **Colonel Poole's Bar-B-Q**, locally referred to as the "Taj Ma Hog." From humble origins, this little stand has grown to be one of the most visited 'cue spots in the state. And though the barbecue and Brunswick stew are indeed quite good, Poole's popularity is best attributed to the Colonel's flair for showmanship. Rising high on a raw red-clay hill behind the restaurant is the "Pig Hill of Fame," covered with thousands of plywood pigs, emblazoned with the names of patrons who paid $5 for the privilege to be so honored. Out front sits the Colonel's Pigmobile, a retro-fitted station wagon festooned with bright-red pig ears. It's a good laugh and—according to the Colonel—good business. Look for Colonel Poole's just south of Ellijay on Highway 515—as if you could miss it *(see page 71).*

■ FORT MOUNTAIN STATE PARK *map page 49, D-2*

West of Ellijay by way of Highway 52—perhaps the most beautiful stretch of highway in northwestern Georgia—is Fort Mountain State Park, a 3,200-acre wilderness refuge named for an 855-foot-long rock wall believed to have been

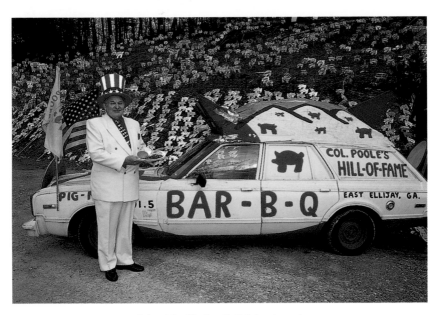

Colonel Poole's Bar-B-Q is hard to miss.

built perhaps 4,000 years ago. Explanations for the wall's existence vary: some people believe it was used as a defensive barrier by Native Americans, while others opt for a more fantastic explanation, asserting that the wall was constructed by a Welsh prince whose travels predated those of Hernando de Soto. Either way, the wall is a marvel, zigzagging across the face of Fort Mountain. A stone observation tower affords a fine view of this edifice. *Information: 706-695-2621.*

■ BLUE RIDGE

Northeast of Ellijay by way of Highway 515 is the little hamlet of Blue Ridge, a great jumping-off point for a tour of the Blue Ridge Mountains to the east or the Cohutta Mountains to the west. On the weekends, the **Blue Ridge Scenic Railway** makes a 26-mile round trip along the Toccoa River to McCaysville and back. *Information: 706-632-9833.*

With the exception of the rail depot, the town's commercial activity seems to focus on the sale of knickknacks and antiques.

To continue east along Highway 76, see "NORTHEAST GEORGIA," page 86.

Northwest Georgia Food & Lodging

✕ **Restaurant Prices:** $ = under $10; $$ = $10–20; $$$ = over $20
Restaurant price designations indicate the approximate cost of an entrée and an appetizer or desert, exclusive of drinks, tax, and tip.

▦ **Lodging Rates:** $ = under $75; $$ = $75–150; $$$ = over $150
Lodging rate designations indicate the approximate cost of a double occupancy room for one night, exclusive of surcharges and taxes.

A statewide food and lodging **reference map** can be found on page 306, and an **index of towns** with food and lodging listings in this book follows on pages 307–308. Toll-free numbers for **chain hotels and motels** can be found on page 308.

Ball Ground *map p. 49, E-4*

✕ **Two Brothers' Barbecue**
770-735-2900; 1695 Old Canton Rd.
Open since 1974, this roadside white frame restaurant has a couple of benches out front for those who like to lounge a bit after stuffing themselves with great smoked pork and stew. The interior is festooned with old farm equipment. Lunch and dinner. $

Cartersville Area
map p. 49, D-4

✕ **4-Way Lunch**
no phone; West Main and Gilmer Streets
Housed in a squat red frame building on the edge of downtown. Twelve chrome stools face the grill where an aged cook dishes out monstrous biscuits doused with cream gravy at breakfast, and beef stew for lunch. A great slice of Southern Americana. Breakfast and lunch. $

✕ **Ross's Diner**
706-382-9159; 17 Wall St.
Few towns this size can claim two venerable diners. Open since 1945, the diner is housed in a redbrick building and features a U-shaped counter at the center of the dining room. The biscuits and gravy, burgers, and chili are equally good. Breakfast and lunch. $

▦ **Barnsley Gardens Inn and Golf Resort**
770-773-7480; 597 Barnsley Gardens Rd., Adairsville
Renovations are underway to turn this estate into a full service resort, with a couple of upscale restaurants and a collection of suites for rent, each with views of the ruins and gardens. Call for details.

Chickamauga *map p. 49, B-1*

▦ **Gordon Lee Mansion**
706-375-4728; 217 Cove Rd.
Four elegant rooms are available in the 1847 manor house, while two rooms are

for let in the former slave quarters. During the Battle of Chickamauga this red-brick mansion served as headquarters for Union general Rosencrans, and there's a Civil War museum upstairs. $-$$

Ellijay *map p. 49, E-2*

✕ **Colonel Poole's Bar-B-Q**
706-635-4100; Hwy. 515
Thick, ruddy Brunswick stew and finely chopped slaw complement the smoky if a tad greasy pork at this shrine to Republican politics and entrepreneurial acumen operated by Oscar Poole, a retired minister. Lunch and dinner. $

COLONEL POOLE'S BAR-B-Q

✕ **The Pink Pig**
706-276-3311; Cherry Log
The Democratic flip-side to nearby Poole's, this joint turns out better 'cue and, thanks to its more remote location—a few miles north in Cherry Log— it isn't swamped by tourists. That said, the feel of the place is a bit drab compared to the circus atmosphere at Poole's. Lunch and early dinner. $

Fort Mountain *map p. 49, D-2*

⊡ **Cohutta Lodge**
706-695-9601; 500 Cochise Trail
Perched atop a hill with a commanding view of the surrounding countryside, this '70s–era lodge is clean and comfortable if a bit institutional in feel. There's a heated pool as well as tennis courts and a mini-golf course. $-$$

COHUTTA LODGE

⊡ **Fort Mountain State Park Cottages**
706-695-2621; Hwy. 52; for reservations call 800-864-7275.
Fifteen simple cottages ring the park. And pioneer trails lead off from the back door into the woods, through thickets of blueberries and along meandering streams. $-$$

Jasper *map p. 49, E-3*

✕ **The Woodbridge Inn**
706-692-6072; 44 Chambers St.
Might be the only restaurant in town that doesn't offer fried okra. Instead, mountain trout and meatballs with

horseradish sauce are favorites at this frumpy but charming restaurant. Lunch and dinner. $$

⊞ The Woodbridge Lodge
706-692-6072; 44 Chambers St.

From its inception in the middle years of the 19th century through the early years of the 20th century, the lodge was a railroad hotel. Now the original hotel is a restaurant. There's a lodge out back with 12 modern rooms, including the Eagle's Nest, with a second-story loft accessible by a spiral staircase. $-$$

Pennville *map p. 49, B-1*

⊞ Paradise Gardens Suite
706-857-2926; Rena St., Pennville

The floor is linoleum. And the furniture is faux maple. But for those who are fans of folk artist Howard Finster, this is the best room to rent in the region. Decorated with the work of Finster and his friends, admirers, and relatives, the suite is comfortable if not tasteful. If camp is your thing, this is your place. $

PARADISE GARDENS SUITE

Rome *map p. 49, B-4*

✕ Bubba's Barbecue
706-291-0618; One Broad St.

Serves a hot sauce the proprietor claims is "neither fittin' for man nor beast." Located at the base of the Broad Street bridge, this smokeshack does a mostly takeout business, though a few picnic tables are set up. Lunch and early dinner. $

✕ J & J Barbecue
706-234-7895; 1517 Dean St.

The better, though less conveniently located, of Rome's two barbecue joints. In addition to great ribs and Brunswick stew, try the smoked catfish on Thursday and Friday. There are fresh vegetables daily. And biscuits stuffed with streak-o-lean for breakfast. Breakfast, lunch, and early dinner. $

✕ LaScala Restaurant
706-238-9000; 513 Broad St.

An Italian-inspired cafe where salmon is served on a bed of spinach and topped with a caper sauce. Numerous pasta dishes are served as well. Lunch and dinner. $-$$

✕ The Partridge Restaurant
706-291-4048; 330 Broad St.

Set in what was once the lobby of a downtown theater, this place exudes a '60s chic. Plate lunches are the draw, with offerings ranging from grilled chicken livers over rice and stewed tomatoes to chicken-and-dumplings and baked squash. Lunch and early dinner. $

X **Schroeder's Deli**
706-234-4613; 406 Broad St.
A college hangout where the walls are lined with old quilts and sandwich offerings include a vegetarian specialty, the Salvador Deli, served hot and smothered with cheddar, mushrooms, onions, tomatoes, and olives. Pizzas and calzones are also available. Lunch and dinner. $

⊞ **Claremont House**
706-291-0900; 906 East Second Ave.
This Victorian Gothic mansion, built in 1882 and renovated in 1993, offers complimentary champagne in the evening and a full breakfast every morning. But the real draw is the unique architecture of the house itself. Soaring 14-foot ceilings and period antiques lend a graceful air to the interior. $$

⊞ **Holiday Inn Skytop**
706-295-1100; 20 U.S. 411
Probably the best chain motel in the downtown area; a sprawling complex of low-slung buildings with an indoor-outdoor pool and a hot tub. $

Rossville *map p. 49, B-1*

X **Roy's Grill**
706-866-0290; 116 Chickamauga Ave.
A blast from the past. Opened in 1934, this cleaner-than-clean diner serves hand-patted hamburgers on toasted buns and gutbomb chili to a loyal cadre of locals. Breakfast, lunch and dinner. $

⊞ **Cloudland Canyon State Park Cabins**
706-657-4050; on top of Lookout Mountain, off Hwy. 136 West; for reservations call 800-864-7275

High above the world at an ear-popping altitude, these spacious, functional cottages are perched at the canyon rim. The best cabins are numbers 6 through 16, each with a screened porch and rocking chairs. There is also a lodge on-site that sleeps up to 40, perfect for family reunions and the like. $-$$

Summerville *map p. 49, A-3*

X **Armstrong's Barbecue**
706-857-9900; 216 North Commerce St.
Open since 1965, this white-tile building proffers a fine sliced barbecue sandwich as well as chili and burgers made from fresh ground chuck. And the prices couldn't be more reasonable. Lunch and dinner. $

Tate *map p. 49, E-3*

⊞ **Tate House**
770-735-3122; Hwy. 53
Built in 1925 of locally quarried pink marble, this mansion has five suites within the main building and a clutch of log cabins out back, each equipped with a fireplace and hot tub. $$

TATE HOUSE

N O R T H E A S T

■ HIGHLIGHTS

■ TRAVEL BASICS

The Blue Ridge Mountains themselves are the main attraction here in Appalachian Georgia. Rivers and waterfalls abound—some of the best whitewater rapids in the country are here—and the Chattahoochee National Forest covers most of the region. Former mill towns dot the mountains, and visitors can still pan for gold at Dahlonega. Numerous festivals highlight mountain music and crafts, yet except at these fairs, distinctive Appalachian folk culture can be hard for the outsider to come by.

Getting Around: Give yourself time to wander the back roads and soak up the quiet; inhale the scent of oak trees and sweet mountain laurel; listen to water running in the creeks. Opportunities abound for river trips and hiking; Springer Mountain has the southern trailhead of the Appalachian Trail, which winds its way through the region.

Climate: Cool and wet winters with snow above 3,000 feet in the mountains. Temperatures usually range from 20 degrees F to the mid-40s. Spring peaks in late April. Mild summers with highs in the mid-80s and frequent thunderstorms. Heavy rain falls year-round in the far northeast corner of the region. Fall colors peak in October.

Food & Lodging: Northeast Georgia is well equipped for tourists. Inns and clusters of cabins dot the mountains, and a passel of barbecue joints line the roads. Lodging is available at many state parks. To avoid country-cute tourist haunts, look for a mixture of pickup trucks and late-model sedans in restaurant parking lots, and steer clear of inns that spell country with a "K." For food and lodging listings, see pages 99 to 105.

NORTHEAST GEORGIA

Elevation
in feet

4,784
2,600
2,200
1,800
1,400
1,000
Sea Level

0   5   10 Miles
0   5   10   15 Kilometers

N
W   E
S

SOUTH CAROLINA

Anderson

Iva

Clemson

Seneca

Walhalla

Mountain Rest

Westminster

Satolah
Sky Valley
Pine Mountain
Estatoah Falls
Mountain City
Dillard
Sky Valley
Black Rock Mountain State Park
Clayton
Tallulah Falls
Lake Burton
Seed Lake
Lake Rabun
Lake Kanee

Hiawassee
Young Harris
Blairsville
Brasstown Bald
4,784
(Highest point in Georgia)
Dicks Creek Gap
3,365
Unicoi Gap
2,963
Neel's Gap
Woody Gap
3,300
Vogel State Park
Helen
Unicoi State Park
Moccasin Creek State Park

Morganton
Mineral Bluff
Margret
Suches
Carters Lake
Nottely Lake
Chatuge Lake

Springer Mtn
3,702
Amicalola Falls State Park
Dahlonega
Auraria

Turnerville
Hollywood
Clarkesville
Leaf
Demorest
Cleveland
Tallulah Gorge/Terrora State Park
Travelers Rest State Historic Park
Toccoa Falls
Toccoa
Spring Branch State Park
Poplar Springs State Park
Tugaloo State Park
Hart State Park
Hartwell

Richard B Russell State Park
Nuberg
Hartwell Lake

Lavonia
Bowersville
Canon
Royston
Vanna
Bowman
Dewy Rose
Elberton
Middleton
Corner
Neese
Danielsville
Pocataligo
Ila
Nicholson
Center

Carnesville
V Bryant State Park
Martin
Avalon
Fort Lamar
Maysville
Homer
Commerce
Apple Valley
Jefferson
Arcade
Hoschton
Pendergrass
Talmo
Belmont
Gillsville
Lula
Clermo
Baldwin
Cornelia
Boydville
Alto
Hollingsworth

Murrayville
Price
Dawsonville
Silver City
Coal Mountain
Free Home
Cumming
Birmingham
Alpharetta
Ocee
Sugar Hill
Buford
Rest Haven
Flowery Branch
Chicopee
Gainesville
Lake Sidney Lanier
Elachee Nature Center

Chattahoochee River
Oconee River
Broad River
Hudson River
Middle Oconee River
Etowah River
Chestatee River
Chattooga River

Nottely Lake

SOUTH CAROLINA

■ TOPOGRAPHY AND LANDSCAPE

The mountains of northeast Georgia are the tail end of the Blue Ridge Range, which extends north to Pennsylvania and is part of the Appalachian Mountains. Though the exurbs of Atlanta loom but an hour south, northeast Georgia feels far removed from city life. Instead, there are the broad valleys and timber-lined ridges of the foothills, followed by the increasingly knobby, increasingly high peaks (almost 5,000 feet) of Appalachia, where the roads wend their circuitous way along wooded slopes, bordered in the spring by a profusion of dove-white laurel blossoms, and in the fall by a blanket of leaves and a kaleidoscope of colors.

Northeast Georgia's Springer Mountain marks the southern end of the Appalachian Trail, a 2,100-mile hiker's path that extends through 14 states and seven national parks, ending at Mount Katahdin in Maine. Writing of the allure of the "AT," the initials by which hikers know the trail, Bill Bryson, author of *A Walk in the Woods,* describes it as wandering "through plump, comely hills whose very names—Blue Ridge, Smokies, Cumberlands, Green Mountains, White Mountains—seem an invitation to amble." Who could but pronounce the words, Bryson asks, "and not feel an urge, as the naturalist John Muir once put it, to 'throw a loaf of bread and a pound of tea in an old sack and jump over the back fence'?"

■ BACKWOODS HISTORY

In this comparatively remote corner of the state, economic and social isolation are less a choice than a physical reality. A writer at the turn of the 19th century referred to the people of Appalachia as "our contemporary ancestors." Perhaps he was on to something. Following old-time ways, in their sparsely populated hills and hollers, the hardy Scotch-Irish who came here in the early 19th century were rugged and unyielding.

When the Civil War erupted, pitting those who worked their land with slaves against the North, many of the inhabitants of Appalachia turned their back on both sides. It was not a war in which they had a stake. Instead, as the saying goes, they took to the hills, retreating farther into the mountains and contining to live as subsistence farmers, planting corn and beans for their families' larders. Some of that corn was converted into liquid, in the form of moonshine, while the majority was served up as hoecakes and hominy, corn pudding, and succotash. They lived in chinked log cabins, later improved with tin roofs; and well into the 20th century, they made their own clothes, musical instruments, and furniture (as reflected in the well-known *Foxfire* books).

It was not until the early years of the 20th century that the region began to feel the influence of the Industrial Revolution, as mills harnessed mountain streams and rural electrification programs pushed their way through the hills. Today, much of Appalachian Georgia teeters on the brink of modernity. Clapboard and brick homes now outnumber rough-hewn log cabins, and dirt roads are being paved. And yet the mountains still act as a buffer—separating hill folk from flatlanders, old-time ways from the insistent invasions of modernity. Things are slowly changing. A local man now wears the same mesh gimme cap as his cousin in Atlanta, and his wife shops at Wal-Mart. People watch television at night rather than sitting outside on their porches playing banjos, and most work days in small local industries rather than hoeing hilly cornfields. Yet a distinctive dialect, a culture of self-reliance, and a healthy suspicion of outsiders remain.

North of Atlanta, the roadways narrow and the sky opens up—loosed from the skyscrapers that boxed it in and the almost omnipresent shroud of Atlanta smog. Soon the artifacts of a unique culture begin to appear along the road. Near the spot where Interstate 985 intersects with the Old Cornelia Highway there stands a monstrous concrete bunny emblazoned with the slogan, "**Rabbittown**—A Hoppin' Little Place."

A hundred yards east, in the crook of an especially crooked turn of that old crooked road sits the home of R. A. Miller: "the fella down the road what makes them whirligigs," as the locals say. Nowadays, he's also known as an artist, and his works fetch hefty prices in galleries across the nation. From the road you can see the "whirligigs" high on a bluff, glinting in the afternoon sun. His creations spin: vibrant red and blue scraps of tin tacked to old bicycle wheels and perched atop spindly sticks; five-foot tin cutouts of blood-red devils, pitchforks in hand; three-foot renderings of Elvis, a guitar at his side.

This odd menagerie—standing just five miles down the road from Gainesville, the largest city in the region—is a testament to the ingenuity and idiosyncrasy that defines the people of northeast Georgia.

(following pages) Spring in the Appalachians, as seen from the
Richard Russell Scenic Highway.

NORTHEAST

■ GAINESVILLE   *map page 75, B-3*

Gainesville, on the southern fringe of Appalachian Georgia, was once a mill town. Here hosiery and denim were pieced and fitted, wood for furniture cut and lathed. For the people of the mountains, Gainesville also served as a market town, a center of commerce where eggs and corn, beans and buttermilk, might be bartered for flour and sugar or bolts of cloth. Today, the city remains a center of commerce, though the mills have been replaced by a new industry: poultry processing. Low-slung and bunker-like in appearance, poultry coops are everywhere, and the trucks that transport the chickens clog the roadways, trailing a cloud of downy feathers. Thousands of workers have made their way up from Mexico in search of jobs, transforming many of the local cafes from the sorts of joints where you get a platter of grits and eggs, to taco stands where lengua and horchata are lunchtime offerings.

Yet Gainesville retains much of the feel of a county seat of yesteryear, with its redbrick business district and its tree-lined avenues bordered by columned homes.

On the city's northeastern edge, wedged between Brenau Avenue and Green Street, is the campus of **Brenau College**. Founded in 1879 as the Georgia Baptist Seminary, this liberal arts college for women boasts a museum that has featured shows by Gainesville's favorite son, Pop artist Jasper Johns.

Nearby is the **Georgia Mountains History Museum**, a "grandma's attic" sort of space where an eclectic collection of local ephemera includes a pie safe from which Union general Sherman presumably ate pies when he was billeted on a nearby farm. No record remains of the flavor, though apple is a good bet, owing to the prevalence of apple trees in these parts. *311 Green Street; 770-536-0889.*

■ LAKE SIDNEY LANIER

Sprawling west and south of Gainesville is Lake Sidney Lanier, a man-made, 38,000-acre recreational lake created in the 1950s when the Chattahoochee River was damned for hydroelectric power. Today, the lake is favored by landlocked Atlantans who treat it like a third coast, flocking north on weekends to waterski and fish, or maybe just to tool around the lake on a party barge, dipping a fishing pole in the waters once in a while but for the most part just soaking up the sunshine. With more than 15 million annual visitors, Lake Lanier is the most visited Corps of Engineers lake in the country. Accordingly, during the prime spring and summer months, the waters can be choked with boaters. But even the roar of an outboard motor can't spoil the view afforded to canoeists and kayakers who paddle to

Dockery Lake, just north of Dahlonega, lies near the southern end of the Appalachian Trail.

the more isolated coves in search of a tranquil vantage point from which to take in the mountains rising just to the north.

■ DAHLONEGA   *map page 75, B-2*

Travel 20 miles northwest of Gainesville by way of Highway 60 and you are in Dahlonega, epicenter of America's first gold rush. According to local folklore, Benjamin Parks first discovered a chunk of gold, similar to "the yellow of an egg," while hunting deer in 1828. When word of his discovery began to circulate, he recounted that it "seemed within a few days, as if the whole world must have heard it; for men came from every state I ever heard of. They came afoot, on horseback, and in wagons, acting more like crazy men than anything else."

Soon the little town of Auraria, six miles south of present-day Dahlonega, was overrun with prospectors. By 1836 Dahlonega had won out over Auraria as the county seat, and a fine brick courthouse stood at the center of town.

Today the former courthouse houses the **Dahlonega Gold Museum.** On display are pans used to sift for gold dust and coins from the days when Dahlonega was the site of one of the nation's first branch mints. By the time the mint closed in 1861, more than $6 million in gold coins had been minted in Dahlonega. *Old Courthouse, center of the town square; 706-864-2257.*

Today, weekenders rather than prospectors throng the sidewalks during the fall and spring, shopping for antiques and visiting two of the old mine sites on the outskirts of town. (You can pan for gold at either location. Pie-tin–shaped plates are provided; you do the stooping and scooping from the river bed.)

Crisson Gold Mine is an early strip mine with a still-functioning stamp mill that crushes quartz into sand so that trace elements of gold can be spotted more easily. *Highway 19 at Cavender Creek Road; 706-864-6363.*

Consolidated Gold Mine is an underground mine. *Northeast of town on highway 19 near Gold Mine Shopping Center; 706-864-8473.*

River trips are popular in this area along the Chestatee. Try Appalachian Outfitters in Dahlonega; *706-864-7117.*

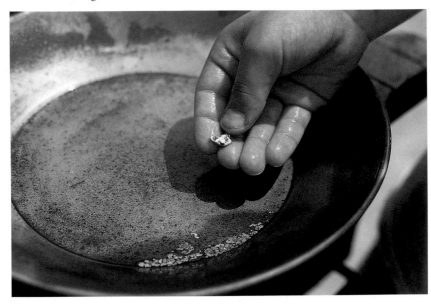

(above) A gold nugget panned near Dahlonega, epicenter of America's first gold rush.
(opposite) Gold-mining scenes at Dahlonega from a Harper's Weekly *issue, circa 1870.*
(Georgia Department of Archives & History)

PANNING

STORE HOUSE

THE CUT

STAMP MILL SHOWING WHERE GOLD PASSES OVER COPPER PLATES

■ AMICALOLA FALLS STATE PARK *map page 75, A-2*

Twenty miles west of Dahlonega is Amicalola Falls State Park, a pristine 1,200-acre park highlighted by a dramatic 729-foot waterfall, four times as tall as famed Niagara Falls. The forest is hardwood and wildflowers are abundant in spring. Beautiful, three-quarter-mile **Amicalola Falls Trail**, which begins at the parking lot at the end of the park road, climbs past cascading waterfalls to an observation deck. *Park information: 706-265-2885; lodge 706-265-8888.*

For those intrepid few considering a journey up the **Appalachian Trail** (AT), this is the trailhead for the eight-plus-mile AT approach trail. A day's hike north is Springer Mountain, point of departure for the 2,100-mile trek to Maine.

■ BLOOD MOUNTAIN AREA *map page 75, B-2*

Those who prefer burning fossil fuel to burning glucose should head north of Dahlonega on Highway 19, a serpentine two-lane switchback that leads up and around Blood Mountain—home in Cherokee mythology of the Nunnehi, spirit people known to look after wayward hunters and wanderers. At **Neel's Gap** is the Walasi-Yi Center, a Civilian Conservation Corps–era building of flagstone, now given over to hiker support and sale of camping gear. One-quarter of a mile north along the highway is a spur trail named in honor of Byron Herbert "Hub" Reece, Georgia's late lamented bard of the mountains.

■ VOGEL STATE PARK *map page 75, B-1*

Farther north still on Highway 19, you come upon Vogel State Park. Nestled in a valley with Lake Trahlyta at its center, this is one of Georgia's most scenic—and by extension most visited—state parks. In summer the place can be overrun with campers and their vehicles, but the park is nevertheless a great base from which to explore any number of hiking trails. In addition to the nearly 20 miles of trails within the park (including an easy, mile-long trail that loops the lake before leading off to a waterfall), there are a number of more strenuous hikes, including a nearly four-mile loop known as the Bear Hair Trail, that winds its way through thick, wet forest. Each August, the park hosts **Old Timers Day**, a festival of mountain music and handicrafts; *706-745-2628.*

Trahlyta Falls in Vogel State Park.

■ BLAIRSVILLE   *map page 75, B-1*

As Highway 19 winds through the Chattahoochee National Forest and heads (more or less) north toward the North Carolina border, the road is lined with signs advertising sorghum—a grassy crop that yields a sticky fluid similar to molasses. Soon you are in the hamlet of Blairsville, home each October to a **Sorghum Festival** that pits brother against brother, neighbor against neighbor, in biscuit-eating and syrup-sopping contests. *Festival information: 706-745-4745.*

■ BRASSTOWN BALD AREA RAMBLES   *map page 75, B-1*

Across the top of the state, Highway 76 cuts a four-lane swath eastward through beautiful rolling countryside framed by mountain peaks. Along the way it passes the bucolic little burg of **Young Harris,** hometown of former Georgia governor Zell Miller. Each summer the town hosts *The Reach of Song*—a folk play that evokes old ways of life in Georgia through storytelling and song. Onward, the highway cuts across **Chatuge Lake,** a mountain-swaddled body of water that seems permanently shrouded in mist. Along the road, whitewashed gourds, now serving as birdhouses for tiny purple martins, stand like ghostly specters in the backyards of modest mountain homes, while billboards beckon the newly arrived—and the newly wealthy—to build luxurious log cabins in the subdivisions that are being carved deep into the woods.

◆ HIAWASSEE AND
   THE GEORGIA MOUNTAIN FAIR

Perched on the shore of Chatuge Lake is the crossroads town of Hiawassee, a popular stop with through travelers. For most of the year it is quiet enough to warrant the description sleepy. But each August the hills come alive when the **Georgia Mountain Fair** opens, a celebration of mountain music and traditional mountain crafts like split-oak basket weaving and pottery making. Though there is a good bit of hokum to be had, and the crowds can be daunting, a day's amble about the fairgrounds is, in effect, a crash course in mountain culture. *Fair information: 706-896-4191.*

MOUNTAIN MUSIC

Contrary to what some may contend, the music of Appalachia is not solely a vestige of Elizabethan-era ballads, transported to these shores by Scotch-Irish settlers and performed in much the same style as was done in the motherland. Instead, much of what we know as mountain music owes its origins to a myriad of influences, ranging from the introduction of an African instrument, the banjo, to the innovations of a singularly talented individual, the late Bill Monroe, inventor of bluegrass music. That said, many of the ballads still plucked by mountain folks have at least a tenuous connection to Great Britain, especially graphically recounted murder ballads like "Knoxville Girl."

Aside from festival events, it can be difficult to find a place to hear mountain music in a setting that comes close to seeming authentic. There are a number of Georgia performers whose work is worth listening to on a record or CD. Among the early Hillbilly bands to make their mark were the Georgia Wildcats, Lowe Stoke's Georgia Potlikkers, and Gid Tanner and the Skillet Lickers. Of these, the most famous group was the latter. In 1924 the Skillet Lickers became the first Hillbilly band to cut an album for Columbia Records. Songs like "Boil the Cabbage Down," still ring out loud, true, and honest.

Mountain musicians in Dillard, Georgia, playing banjo and guitar.

◆ BRASSTOWN BALD

One might expect Georgia's highest peak (at 4,784 feet) to be a treacherous, craggy mountain inhospitable to climbers, much less picnickers. Yet Brasstown Bald (properly called Mount Enotah), like many other so-called peaks in Georgia, is, in essence, a pasture perched atop a mountain. The Blue Ridge Range has many such "balds," and botanists have numerous theories but no definitive explanation for what has caused them.

Brasstown Bald rewards hikers who have traversed the steep half-mile trail from the parking lot with a sweeping view of four states, though the real treat may well be the mountain flora along the trail, including lush, pink rhododendron bushes that sometimes bloom late into the summer. Atop the mountain, a visitors center offers interpretive programs and operates a shuttle service that will cart you up and down the slope. *Located 10 miles southwest of Hiawassee by way of a spur road that cuts off Highway 180; 706-896-2556.*

(above) Snow-covered mountains viewed from Brasstown Bald.

(opposite) Queen Anne's lace fills a meadow in Sky Valley.

■ LAKES BURTON AND RABUN *map page 75, C-1 and D-1*

East of Hiawassee on Highway 76 lap the waters of Lake Burton, one of many lakes created in the early years of the 20th century by the Georgia Power Company. In a program that would later serve as a model for the Tennessee Valley Authority's rural electrification efforts, the company dammed the Tallulah River in stair-step fashion, creating a string of lakes including Burton and nearby Lake Rabun. Today, the lakes look as though they have been a part of the landscape for eons.

Both lakes are popular with Atlantans, who treat them as weekend getaways. Rabun is the tonier of the two, a Catskill-like enclave of cathedral-ceilinged lodges and sleek boats; Burton, to the northeast, is more the fisherman's favorite. Both are home to unique mountain inns, where accommodations harken back to simpler days and the food (cornmeal-crusted catfish and bacon-wrapped trout are favorites) is never frou-frou.

❖

East and north of the lakes is a wedge of Appalachian Georgia sandwiched between the Chattooga River and the North Carolina border. For **river trips, try calling Chattooga River Adventures** in Clayton; *800-846-7238.* In the far northeast

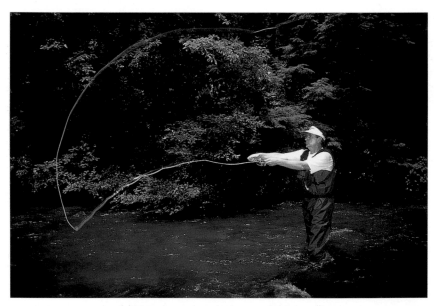

Fly-fishing on Cooper Creek in northeast Georgia.

JAMES DICKEY'S *DELIVERANCE*

"*D*o you know where you're going?" she said.

"Not exactly. Lewis does. Somewhere up in the northeast part of the state, where he's been fishing. If everything goes off OK, we ought to be back late Sunday."

"Why wouldn't it go off OK?"

"It will, but you can't predict. Listen, if I thought there was anything dangerous about it, I wouldn't go...."

Thus begins Deliverance, *James Dickey's 1970 horror novel about Georgian Appalachia, in which the darkest of the stereotypes foisted upon the people of Appalachia fuel the plot:*

*A*n old man with a straw hat and work shirt appeared at Lewis' [car] window, talking in. He looked like a hillbilly in some badly cast movie, a character actor too much in character to be believed. I wondered where the excitement was that intrigued Lewis so much; everything in Oree was sleepy and hookwormy and ugly, and most of all, inconsequential. Nobody worth a damn could ever come from such a place.

As it unfolds, Dickey's drama documents what befalls four suburban Atlantans on a white-water canoe trip down a river that everyone in these parts recognized as the Chattooga, but that Dickey called the Cahulawasee. Over the course of a weekend, the Atlantans are beset by a cast of depraved Appalachian characters, defined by their physical deformities and violence:

*E*very family I've ever met up here has at least one relative in the penitentiary. Some of them are in for making liquor or running it, but most of them are in for murder. They don't think a whole lot about killing people up here.

After Dickey's novel became a bestseller and was made into an equally horrific movie, it seemed the whole of the United States became aware of Appalachian Georgia and believed it was peopled by maniacs. Folks in northern Georgia, where Dickey once worked for the Army Corps of Engineers, still haven't forgiven him.

corner, you will find **Sky Valley,** Georgia's only ski resort, where many Georgians try their luck at skiing. The slopes are often ice-slicked rather than powder-packed, and not a few first-timers can be seen making their way down the mountain on their backsides rather than on their skis; *706-746-5302.*

■ DILLARD   *map page 75, D-1*

Seven miles north of the intersection of Highways 76 and 441 is the burg of **Dillard,** founded in 1794 by Revolutionary War veteran John Dillard and now home to a resort and restaurant run by his descendants *(see page 101).* Across the valley from this flagstone-and-glass temple of country cooking, and perched on a grassy hill, are the redbrick Colonial-style buildings that are home to the **Rabun Gap–Nacoochee School.** Founded in 1900 as the Rabun Gap Industrial School by Andrew Jackson Ritchie (a Harvard alumnus and one of the area's first college graduates) the private academy was the first to introduce the Farm Family Plan of education, whereby entire families worked their way through a course of industrial and agricultural instruction. The school continues to serve mountain families.

Nearby, on Betty's Creek Road in Dillard, is the **Hambidge Center**, an artists' retreat in operation since 1934. In addition to regular art shows and occasional concerts, the center hosts guided nature walks throughout the fall and spring; *706-746-5718.*

■ FOXFIRE   *map page 75, D-1*

Perhaps the most influential educational institution in the mountains of northeast Georgia is headquartered in the shadow of Black Rock Mountain, along busy Highway 441 in Mountain City. Foxfire—established as a literary magazine of the same name in the early 1970s by local teacher Eliot Wigginton and his students— has become an educational phenomenon of sorts, spurring a series of best-selling books, a television movie, and a new wave of interest in the ways and means of Appalachia.

Originally conceived by Wigginton as a device to motivate his high school students, the Foxfire project encouraged schoolchildren to interview their elders about such crafts as log-home construction, hominy making, and the weaving of white-oak chair bottoms. Under Wigginton's direction, the interviews were transcribed and the results published for an increasingly attentive audience. Soon,

Foxfire became an educational institution of its own, sponsoring seminars throughout the country where students and elders worked together, sharing Appalachian knowledge and lore with outlanders.

Today, the headquarters is site of a museum *(706-746-5828)*, a reconstructed Appalachian village, and a bookstore and gift shop. By special arrangement, you can arrange a tour of the entire facility.

Among the Foxfire Center's recent publications is the *Foxfire Book of Appalachian Cookery*, wherein aged local "Granny" Gibson recounts the process by which hard

PUTTING UP TOMATOES FOR WINTER

Hillard Green was almost 80 when the first Foxfire *book was published, in 1969. He lived by himself in the mountains near the North Carolina border, in a one-room cabin with a wood stove. He still grew his own food and got his water from a spring next to the cabin. The students who compiled the book were so moved by the time they spent interviewing and photographing him that they chose to close the book with his words. On the students' last visit, Hillard Green was canning tomatoes:*

*P*eople'll look at those pictures and say, "What is that crazy old man a'doin'?" You tell'em I'm puttin' up 'maters for th'winter, that's what. People might laugh at such stuff as this, but I'll tell y', I'm not about t'let'em rot. And when you've got old, you're not a'goin't'lay down and die just because you're old. Feller's got t'have somethin' t'do. Well, this is one of th' things I do, and I'm proud I can. Let 'em laugh. I'll be eatin' good this winter and laughin' back.

Everyone ought t'learn how to do such as this. One a'these days, times might get back hard again, and then what will they do? Nobody not knowin' how t'do nothin'. Might have t'live off th' land again, one day. We never had nothin' fer th' winter only what we put up. What we put up was what we had. Goin't'be a lot of hungry people someday.

Lotsa people don't even know how t'cook any more. They just go t'th' store and get it fixed already. These girls nowadays go off t'school and learn about everything but what's really important. Get home and still can't even cook a meal. If your woman can't cook whenever you get married, let me know and I'll come cook fer y'!

About his life in the mountains, Hillard Green had this to say:

[There's] nobody t'ask you where you're goin', when you'll be back, or where you've been. I do just as I please. Tomorrow? Who knows? I might put up 'maters again.

—Hillard Green, from *Foxfire*, 1969

kernels of dried corn are made into hominy, the big brother to fine-ground grits:

> People used to tie the ashes and corn in a sack and boil them a pretty long time in an old iron pot. The water going through the ashes makes lye. That's what makes the outer part of the corn scale off, and what you have left is hominy. You just wash it and wash it to get the lye out, and then you put it back in the pot with just pure water and cook it until it gets tender. Keep adding water to it because it just keeps swelling. Then you take it out, put some grease in it and fry it. It takes all day to make, but it was good.

❖

To the south, Highway 441 passes through Clayton, seat of government for Rabun County and the largest commercial center in the area, and dips down through Tallulah Falls, connecting to a number of smaller roads that lead westward to Clarkesville, Cleveland, and Helen.

■ TALLULAH FALLS AREA *map page 75, D-2*

Once the summer playground of Athens and Atlanta residents who took trains north in search of a respite from the heat, Tallulah Falls was, until the damming of the Tallulah River in 1913, site of one of the highest and most spectacular waterfalls in North America. And Tallulah Gorge, spanning more than three miles in length and plunging more than 600 feet, has long been a gawker's delight and a thrill seeker's challenge. (In 1970, tightrope artist Karl Wallenda crossed the gorge balanced on a thin wire cable, without the security of a net stretched beneath.) Today, few buildings remain from the turn of the 19th century, save the old rail station, now operated as an artists' cooperative and stocked with local honey, hand-carved toys, and the like. Most visitors are white-water enthusiasts who have come to run the recently reopened river gorge.

◆ CLARKESVILLE *map page 75, C-2*

Clarkesville, southwest of Tallulah Falls along Highway 15, was also once a summer resort destination. Today air conditioners stay the sultry heat of an August afternoon, but city folks still take to the hills around Clarkesville in search of clean mountain air and a heaping helping of solitude; the town itself beckons with country-cute shops and antique stores.

George Cooke's painting Tallulah Falls, *circa 1840, depicts a view that no longer exists. (Georgia Museum of Art, University of Georgia, gift of Mrs. Will Moss)*

◆ CORNELIA AND "ELVISIANA"

Just south of Clarkesville is the little village of Cornelia, site of an attraction that's as unlikely as any you'll find in Georgia. On a quiet side street the graceful white clapboard **Loudermilk Boardinghouse and Museum** houses one of the world's foremost collections of Elvisian memorabilia and art. In other words, this is the

NORTHEAST

best spot east of Graceland for Presley pilgrims. The displays are unconventional, to say the least. Come here to gaze upon a wart removed from Elvis, or a toenail fished from the shag carpet in Graceland's Jungle Room. Or just come here on the off chance that you will catch the proprietor, Joni Mabe, in residence. Joni is a font of Elvis lore, not to mention a talented artist in her own right, whose collages and paintings fill her home. (Her work can be found in the permanent collection of the Museum of Modern Art in New York and in the private collection of the late Andy Warhol.) Also on site is what Joni terms a bed-and-Elvis, a comfortable suite in the downstairs of the home, available to let for a reasonable price. *271 Foreacre Street; 706-778-2001.*

◆ CLEVELAND AND HANDICRAFTS   *map page 75, B-2*

The town of Cleveland is ancestral home to the Meaders clan, Georgia's most celebrated family of potters. At a little settlement just south of town called Mossy Creek, the Meaders family has been "turning and burning" pottery, fashioning functional butter churns and fanciful face jugs (influenced by West African memory vessels and English Toby jugs) since the 1890s. Though the family's patriarch and most accomplished potter, Lanier Meaders, passed away in late 1998, a new generation of Meaders has taken to the wheel and are now selling their hand-glazed, wood-fired wares throughout the South.

Down the road in Gillsville, the Hewell family still turns and burns too, making utilitarian ware like strawberry pots and, thanks to the increasingly high prices that face jugs command, oddities such as a two-faced jugs with a candelabra sprouting from the top.

Locally, **Rosehips Gallery** sells the work of the Meaders family as well as that of many other area potters; on *Highway 129; 706-865-6345.*

Handicrafts of another sort are on display at Babyland General Hospital, an "adoption center" where the folks who brought you that late-'70s fad, the Cabbage Patch Kid, fight valiantly to rescue their product from anonymity in the face of subsequent fads, such as the Beanie Baby onslaught. *Located at 73 West Underwood Street; 706-865-2171.*

(left) A Meaders face jug. (opposite) Edwin Meaders cradles an unglazed ceramic rooster with a rattlesnake on its back.

NORTHEAST

■ HELEN *map page 75, C-2*

The faux-Alpine village of Helen owes its origins to a bit of hucksterism. Faced, in the late 1960s, with a faltering lumber industry and a moribund economy, town fathers hit upon a scheme to breathe life into their town: paint building broadsides in the business district with murals of the snow-capped peaks of Germany, and tack gingerbread trim to the eaves of every house in town. In short order, a tourist attraction was born.

Today Helen, 10 miles north of Cleveland on Highway 75, sells as much baloney as bratwurst. But no one seems to mind; it's all in good fun, and it's all good for business. The primary draws in Helen are shopping, eating, drinking beer, and clogging to the incessant sound of oompah bands. Here even the local purveyor of grease, the Huddle House, is gussied up in Bavarian trim. Despite the decorations, the main strip of shops feels more like the midway at a Midwestern state fair than an Alpine village.

Truth be told, it's such a spectacle that you almost fail to notice the shallow **Chattahoochee River** rippling through the middle of town.

North of Helen, the Chattahoochee is the spectacular, fresh-running stream it's supposed to be. At **Anna Ruby Falls Scenic Area** double waterfalls crash over rocky cliffs, and a pleasant walking trail (that leads from the parking lot), will take you past mountain laurel and rhododendron. Possibly one the wild turkeys, deer, or squirrels who live in this area will step out of the woods. *Turn off Highway 75 one mile north of Helen onto Highway 356 and follow signs.*

Three miles downstream on Highway 17 is the **Norah Mill Granary**, where grits are ground from corn on the same stones that were in place when the mill opened in 1876. Here you will receive an informal education in Southern grains, learning the difference between whole-grain grits like these and the version made from ground, dried hominy; *706-878-2375.*

Just across the street at the white clapboard house that is home to the **Habersham Winery**, a tasting bar is set up, pouring samples of the dry whites and reds the company now bottles. Of special note is their port-like Chambourcin variety, a surprisingly supple and tasty dessert wine with a spicy nose; *call 770-983-1973.*

For **river trips on the Chattahoochee River** try Wildewood Outfitters in Helen; *706-878-1700.*

Northeast Georgia Food & Lodging

✗ **Restaurant Prices:** $ = under $10; $$ = $10–20; $$$ = over $20
Restaurant price designations indicate the approximate cost of an entrée and an appetizer or desert, exclusive of drinks, tax, and tip.

⊞ **Lodging Rates:** $ = under $75; $$ = $75–150; $$$ = over $150
Lodging rate designations indicate the approximate cost of a double occupancy room for one night, exclusive of surcharges and taxes.

A statewide food and lodging **reference map** can be found on page 306, and an **index of towns** with food and lodging listings in this book follows on pages 307–308. Toll-free numbers for **chain hotels and motels** can be found on page 308.

Amicalola Falls St. Park
map p. 75, A-2

✗ **Amicalola Falls Lodge Restaurant**
706-265-8888; Hwy. 52
Bountiful buffets are served in a glass-walled dining room looking out over the trees atop the mountains. Look for Southern staples like grits and eggs at breakfast, and fried chicken and yams for lunch and dinner. Breakfast, lunch, and dinner. $

AMICALOLA FALLS LODGE

⊞ **Amicalola Falls Lodge**
706-265-8888; Hwy. 52

The modern, airy lodge has more than 50 rooms. There are also 14 cabins, some hidden away in the woods, others set at the base of the falls. $-$$

Blairsville Area
map p. 75, B-1

⊞ **Blood Mountain Cabins**
706-745-9454; Hwy. 19, 14 miles south of Blairsville
Hard by the roadside but somehow still remote in feel, this collection of seven cabins is perched on the side of the mountain. Simple and functional, the cabin interiors are accented by hand-hewn timbers and outfitted with TVs and VCRs, but no telephones. $$

⊞ **Souther Country Inn**
706-379-1603; 2592 Collins Lane
This English-style country inn has 16 rooms and offers unparalleled views of the surrounding mountains. Trails lead from the inn's back door into the surrounding countryside. Rates include an evening dessert as well as breakfast. $$

Clarkesville *map p. 75, C-2*

✕ **Glen-Ella Springs Dining Room**
706-754-7295; 1789 Bear Gap Rd.
Perhaps the best white-tablecloth restaurant in the mountains. Recent offerings included smoked pork tenderloin with Vidalia onion chutney, and low-country shrimp and gravy over fried grits cakes. The restaurant's cuisine has been featured at New York's prestigious James Beard House. Dinner. $$-$$$

✕ **The Trolley**
706-754-5566; 146 Washington St.
A casual restaurant on the square, with an adventurous menu. Jerk-glazed pork chops and sautéed shrimp with white beans and basil over polenta are but two of the recent dinner specials. Lunch and dinner. $$-$$$

GLEN-ELLA SPRINGS INN

▥ **Glen-Ella Springs Inn**
706-754-7295; 1789 Bear Gap Rd.
Overlooking a peaceful meadow, the century-old inn has 16 rooms facing on the meadow, and a large pool for summertime frolics. Beyond the meadow, Panther Creek trickles by. The complimentary breakfast befits an inn with such a fine dining room. $$

Clayton *map p. 75, D-1*

✕ **Green Shutters**
706-782-3342; Old Hwy. 441
Situated hard by the highway, and serving the pinnacle of mountain cookery. Try the fried chicken and mashed potatoes at lunch and the perfect, crisp little biscuits for breakfast. All meals are served family style. The peach cobbler is splendid. Breakfast, lunch, and dinner. Seasonal hours. $-$$

Cornelia *map p. 75, C-2*

▥ **Loudermilk Boarding House**
706-778-2001; 271 Foreacre St.
Proprietor Joni Mabe calls this a bed-and-Elvis instead of a bed-and-breakfast. It's actually a comfortable suite downstairs in her family's recently refurbished house. Factor in the unique displays of Elvisian artifacts, and you've got an experience unequaled in the region. *See page 95 for details on the upstairs museum.* $

Dahlonega Area
map p. 75, B-2

✕ **Dogwood Cafe**
706-864-9169; on the square
A little cubbyhole of a restaurant with great egg salad sandwiches, burgers, and salads. During the summer, the line for ice cream often stretches out the door. Lunch and early dinner. $

✗ **Rick's Caricature Cafe**
706-219-2862; 868 South Main St.,
Cleveland
A two-story, tin-roofed Victorian house
packed to the gills with folk art, Rick's is
a visual treat. The food ain't bad either.
Offerings range from the time-honored
(hot wings) to the innovative (a smoked
chicken glazed with a delicious house
Worchestershire sauce). A Dahlonega-
area favorite. Lunch and dinner. $-$$

✗ **The Smith House**
706-867-7000; 84 South Chestatee St.
The Smith House has been open as a
boarding house since 1922, and the
basement dining room still serves fried
chicken, country ham, pole beans, fried
okra, sweet potatoes, and the like from
family-style platters passed from patron
to patron. Lunch and dinner. $$

BLUEBERRY INN AND GARDENS

▦ **Blueberry Inn and Gardens**
706-219-4024; 400 Blueberry Hill
Ten minutes north of town, this 1920s-
style farmhouse offers a wonderful perch
from which to survey the surrounding
mountains. There are 12 rooms, each
with private bath. And, yes, blueberries

grow wild on the property and are yours
for the picking. $-$$

▦ **The Smith House**
706-867-7000; 84 South Chestatee St.
This Victorian farmhouse with a shady
front porch has been a mountain favorite for more than 75 years. The pro-
prietors like to boast that it sits atop a
rich vein of gold. Rooms upstairs are
comfortable if not opulent. Conveniently located just off the town square. $-$$

WORLEY HOMESTEAD INN

▦ **Worley Homestead Inn**
706-864-7002; 168 Main St. West
This 1845 farmhouse with a two-story
front porch was renovated in 1984 by a
descendant of the original owner, Capt.
William Worley of the Confederate
Army. Eight rooms, three of which have
fireplaces, are offered. And on weekends,
a big country breakfast is served. $$

Dillard *map p. 75, D-1*

✗ **The Dillard House**
706-746-5348; Old Dillard Rd., off
Hwy. 441
An odd mixture of country farmhouse
and glassed-roof solarium, where meals

are served family style. In their rush to clear tables the servers raise a clatter—so much so that the din in the dining room can reach deafening levels —but the food satisfies. Among the best of the meats and vegetables to be piled on each table are rosy-hued country ham, gooey sweet-potato soufflé, fat green beans, and some of the tenderest, smokiest barbecue chicken you will ever taste. Tea, served in ersatz Mason jar mugs, is so sweet it'll cave your teeth. Breakfast, lunch, and dinner. $$

⌂ The Dillard House
706-746-5348; Old Dillard Rd., off Hwy. 441
Also on the grounds are a cluster of cabins and a lodge, where the rooms are plain but clean, plus a nice pool and tennis courts. From almost any vantage point, nearby Black Rock Mountain looms magisterial. $-$$

Gainesville *map p. 75, B-3*

✗ Collegiate Grill
770-532-1114; 220 Main St.
This sparkling, royal-blue and white diner first opened its doors in 1947. Menu categories have cutesy, college themes: Dorm food, Electives, Extra Credit—the latter being fries and onion rings. Breakfast and lunch. $

✗ Lantern Inn
770-887-3080; Brown Bridge Rd., Cumming
The home of Mike Jones, a fry cook who does decent work with catfish. But his real claim to fame—and the real reason to seek out this restaurant—is that, between batches of fish, he drops his apron, dons a cape, and slips on a pair of gaudy sunglasses, reappearing in full Elvisian garb. Between Mike's sets of "Hound Dog" and "Teddy Bear," his sister does her own Patsy Cline act. Come for the laughs, not the food. Dinner. $$

✗ Luna's
770-531-0848; 200 Main St.
Dominican Republic native Juan Luna is the capable chef at the helm of this restaurant smack dab in the middle of downtown. The look is subdued and tasteful, almost hip. Try the paella or an innovative dish like a macadamia nut–crusted snapper. Best wine list in town. Dinner. $$-$$$

✗ Rudolph's on Green Street
770-534-2226; 700 Green St.
The finest dining room in these parts. Set in a handsome Tudor home, this continental restaurant features scallops en papillote and beef filet in a béarnaise sauce, among other entrees. Children swoon over the deep-fried ice cream for dessert. Dinner, Sunday brunch. $$-$$$

✗ Taqueria Los Rayos
770-297-0905; 323 Washington St.
A branch of the Atlanta location, the tacos *al pastor* are as tasty as ever. Wash your meal down with a glass of horchata, a sweet rice-water drink. Lunch, dinner. $

✗ 2 Dog Cafe
770-287-8384; 109 Bradford St.
Exposed brick walls and colorful local art give this cafe a cheery atmosphere. Try the chicken and portabello mush-

room quesadilla or the mojo-marinated pork sandwich. Good, economical wine selection. Lunch and dinner. $$-$$$

⊞ **General lodging information**
A number of chain motels line Jesse Jewell Parkway on Gainesville's southern fringe, including a **Hampton Inn** *(770-503-0300; 450 Jesse Jewell Pkwy.)* and a **Holiday Inn** *(770-536-4451; 726 Jesse Jewel Pkwy.)*. But the best place to stay in Gainesville is at the Dunlap House.

⊞ **Dunlap House**
770-536-0200; 635 Green St.
Built in 1910, this 10-room B&B has a large, welcoming front porch shaded by a tasteful green-and-white awning. Renovated in 1985, the inn has all the modern conveniences and serves a full breakfast every morning. $$

Helen *map p. 75, C-2*

Despite what you may see advertised, Helen is not a great town in which to sample German food. Most of the restaurants serve Americanized dishes, and the selection of German beers proffered is no better than you will find in a good Atlanta pub.

✕ **The Hofbrauhaus Inn**
706-878-2248; One Main St.
For those intent on eating German, the inn slings schnitzel and spaetzel, and has a pleasant outdoor beer garden. $

⊞ **Chattahoochee Riverfront Motel**
706-878-2184; 8849 North Main St.
Just up the road from downtown, this low-slung motel is perched on the banks of the shallow Chattahoochee. Alpine Helen is but a short walk away, but this place is a far remove from the hubbub. $

CHATTAHOOCHEE RIVERFRONT MOTEL

Hiawassee *map p. 75, C-1*

✕ **The Pitz**
706-896-6232; 1088 Bell Creek Rd. (Hwy. 75)
Run by the Dorta family, formerly of Ybor City, Florida. At this family restaurant, Cuban sandwiches, juicy with mojo sauce, and thick Brunswick stew are equally good. Or maybe you'd prefer a slab of ribs and a side of black beans and rice. You won't find better Cuban food in the state. And the barbecue is the best to be had north of Danielsville. Lunch and early dinner. $

⊞ **Fieldstone Inn**
706-896-2262; 3499 U.S. 76, just west of the bridge
On the shores of ChatugeLake, this modern resort features more than 65 rooms, many of which boast private balconies overlooking the lake. Also on-site is a large swimming pool and a full service marina where jet skis and powerboats are for rent. $$

▣ **Town Creek Cabins**
706-745-8891; 4863 Seabolt Rd.
Perched on a hillside overlooking a
stream, these new cabins feature porches
with a view of the mountain scenery.
Flagstone fireplaces, eat-in kitchens,
and outdoor grills. $$

Lake Burton *map p. 75, C-1*

✕ **LaPrade's**
706-947-3312; Hwy. 197, 18 miles
north of Clarkesville
Set right on the lake, this first-class
country-cooking restaurant is famed for
its fried chicken and country ham with
red-eye gravy. The sprawling green tim-
ber building was built in 1916 to house
workers who were in the area building
hydroelectric dams. Breakfast, lunch,
and dinner. $$-$$$

▣ **Burton Woods Cabins**
706-754-7442; 155 Fox Valley Rd.
Just a half-mile from the lake, these new
cabins feature stone fireplaces and full
kitchens. Tucked away in a remote,
heavily wooded area, they seem a far
remove from civilization. Cabins, which
ring the main building, are rustic to say
the least. But in a day of chain hotels,
their quaint charm is refreshing, and
screened porches front many. Rates in-
clude three meals per day. Open from
April 1 to December 1. $-$$

▣ **LaPrade's Cabins**
706-947-3312; Hwy. 197, 18 miles
north of Clarkesville

The fish camp of your dreams. Surrounding the lodge *(see left)* are 20 rustic
fisherman's cabins (all with bathroom)
and 3 cottages with full amenities. Rates
for the cabins include three meals a day.
$-$$

Lake Rabun *map p. 75, D-1*

LAKE RABUN HOTEL

▣ **Lake Rabun Hotel**
706-782-4946; Lake Rabun Rd.
Built in 1922, this inn looks like it
belongs in the Catskill Mountains of
New York rather than on the edge of a
Georgia lake. In the lobby, a massive
stone fireplace gives a cozy glow to the
surroundings, and the 16 rooms are
decorated with locally made twig furniture. In the morning, treat yourself to
fresh-baked muffins and coffeecake. $

Mountain City
map p. 75, D-1

▣ **Mountain State Park Cottages**
706-746-2141; Hwy. 441; for reservations call 800-864-7275

At the highest state park in Georgia, 10 simple cottages are available to let. Make your reservations early; these are among the most sought-after cabins in the mountains. $

⊞ The York House
706-746-2068; York House Road off Hwy. 441

In business since 1896, this charming inn is ringed by a wonderful veranda dotted with rocking chairs, and features 13 antique-appointed rooms. Begun as a two-room cabin, this is the oldest inn in the state in continuous operation. $-$$

THE YORK HOUSE

Vogel State Park

⊞ Vogel State Park Cottages
706-745-2628; Hwy. 19, south of Blairsville; for reservations call 800-864-7275

There are nearly 40 cottages for rent, ranging from compact, one-bedroom affairs to large three-bedroom cabins. The nicest are the lakeside flagstone and timber ones constructed by the Works Progress Administration in the '30s. $-$$

Young Harris

✗ Enrico's Restaurant and Pizzeria
706-379-1950; 687 Main St.

Pizzas and steaks share menu space, but the locals know to leave the beef alone and plunge into a plate of pasta or a slab of pie. Dinner. $-$$

✗ Mary Ann's Country Kitchen
706-379-2136; US 76, east of town

Renowned for breakfasts of hand-patted sausage, thick creamy grits, and ethereally light biscuits. Plate lunch specials are offered at noontime. The setting is pure '50s. Breakfast, lunch, and dinner. $

BRASSTOWN VALLEY RESORT

⊞ Brasstown Valley Resort
706-379-9900; 6321 US 76

Set amid a 500-acre forest, this new resort features a beautiful lodge with a soaring central hall lit by antler chandeliers. Rooms and separate cottages are filled with "nouveau mountain" furnishings and folk art. $$-$$$

A T L A N T A

■ TRAVEL BASICS

Atlanta is the citadel of both the mythical and the modern South. It's a place where old and new Georgia manage to coexist socially, but where older, graceful buildings are being overwhelmed by massive highrises encircled by freeways, at the expense of a comfortable civic life. Often, visitors who come to stay at big downtown hotels feel Atlanta is uninteresting, as street life, local restaurants, and stores aren't much in evidence. Even Midtown can be daunting, although the blocks of huge buildings do rise alongside older, walkable streets where charming façades and cafes still exist. To enjoy Atlanta, you must get in a car and drive out to the older neighborhoods, where you'll find lovely old homes, vital commercial districts with funky stores, and restaurants serving good Southern cooking.

Getting Around: Atlanta is not easily explored on foot—you'll be best off in a car. Central Atlanta is known to locals as I.P. (inside the perimeter highway), new suburban Atlanta as O.P. (or outside the perimeter freeway).

Climate: Cool and wet winters with temperatures ranging from the low 20s F to the mid-50s. Occasional snowfall possible. Summers are warm and humid with frequent thunderstorms; temperatures in the upper 80s. Fall is usually dry and pleasant. Spring peaks in April.

Food & Lodging: Atlanta offers an array of world-class restaurants and hotels, palaces of haute cuisine like Seeger's, and temples of luxury like the flagship Ritz-Carlton Hotel Buckhead. But there are bargains to be had as well, in unassuming neighborhood haunts where the fried chicken is crunchy and the tea (in the Southern tradition) is tooth-achingly sweet. For food and lodging listings, see pages 148 to 161.

(above) Gridlock, suburban Atlanta, 1998.
(below) Gridlock, suburban Atlanta, 1908.
(below photo, Georgia Department of Archives & History)

■ OVERVIEW

Natives of genteel Savannah like to dismiss the bustle and boosterism of Atlanta, citing an oft-repeated bit of doggerel: "If Atlanta could suck as hard as it can blow, it would be a seaport." True, such sentiment seems mean-spirited, but compared to historic, refined Savannah, Atlanta is indeed an upstart, a city built on salesmanship and speculation rather than tradition.

According to the prevailing wisdom, Atlanta is the quintessential modern American city, sprawling outward from a threatened inner core. Its roadways are choked with commuters, its borders ringed by a barrier of glass and steel skyscrapers, its population mostly newly arrived, its identity in question. In a recent *New York Times* story, Atlanta was deemed (and damned) the "new Los Angeles." Though the *Times* article referred to Atlanta's burgeoning traffic problems, the observation might well be applied to many aspects of life in what critics are now labeling a loosely connected series of exurbs and suburbs rather than a cohesive collection of neighborhoods.

And yet, there exists another Atlanta, far removed from suburban blight. This Atlanta remains approachable, enjoyable, swaddled in green spaces, and shaded by

Downtown skyline at night: Atlanta has grown into a sprawling city that many have compared to Los Angeles.

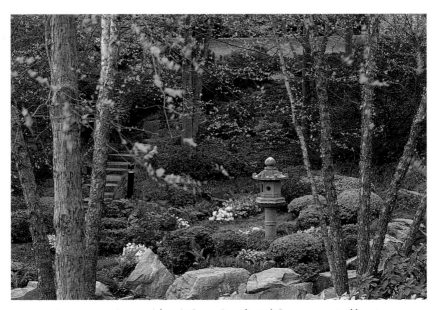

Springtime visitors to Atlanta's Carter Presidential Center can enjoy blooming cherry trees and azaleas as well as historic exhibits.

the boughs of towering oak and pine trees. In the springtime, when dogwood trees and azaleas burst forth from their dull winter slumber, Atlanta is a magical place, awash in pastel-hued splendor. In the fall, a patchwork of orange and russet blankets the hills.

■ HISTORY

Located atop the Piedmont Plateau, 50 miles or so south of the Appalachian Mountains, this city of three million is an anomaly among Georgia cities. Most Georgia cities of import grew up along navigable waterways or natural harbors. Not so Atlanta, a latter-day arrival on the Georgia map. Atlanta owes its birth to the coming of the railroad and to the trade and prosperity that followed in its wake.

In 1836 the state of Georgia chartered a rail line that would cross the northern part of the state, connecting the market towns of Augusta and Savannah with the transportation hub of Chattanooga, Tennessee. In September of 1837 civil engineer Stephen Long drove a surveyor's stake into the ground at a location just east of what is now known as Underground Atlanta, marking the spot as the terminus for the railroad. Around this stake grew a town known first simply as Terminus, then as Marthasville, and finally, in 1845, as Atlanta.

Atlanta grew quickly. By the time Georgia seceded from the Union in 1861, Atlanta was the primary transportation hub for the Deep South. The city's strategic importance attracted the eye and ire of Union commanding general Ulysses S. Grant, who in 1864 dispatched Gen. William Sherman and nearly 100,000 men on a mission to sever all Confederate rail and supply lines. From early May until the city's surrender on September 2, Sherman fought Confederate forces in and around Atlanta. Sherman wreaked havoc, pummeling the Confederates at every turn. Fighting raged across what is now the neighborhood of Buckhead, through modern-day Inman Park, and south to Jonesboro.

At the Battle of Atlanta, the culmination of the campaign, over 7,000 boys in gray were killed along with nearly 2,000 in blue. The streets were lined with maimed and mortally wounded soldiers. Gutters ran red with blood. Churches

This painting from the Atlanta Cyclorama depicts the fierce fighting around the Troup Hurd House during the Battle of Atlanta.

Union troops move into Atlanta's Public Square on September 2, 1864. (Library of Congress)

were pressed into service as temporary triage stations. The city was decimated. In the weeks that followed, Sherman pounded the city with artillery, leveling most of the business and residential districts.

Confederate troops fled the city on September 1. On September 7, the remaining 1,500 or so civilians were removed. And in a final blow, upon departing for Savannah on November 16, Sherman ordered the destruction of all but 400 of the remaining 3,600 homes and buildings that had survived the initial onslaught.

Despite the carnage, Atlanta recovered quickly in the years following the Civil War. Fueled by Northern investment and buoyed by journalist Henry Grady's civic salesmanship, Atlanta emerged as an economic force to be reckoned with. Again, transportation proved to be the primary impetus for Atlanta's prosperity. But the real story is that of Grady and his selling of the New South.

In the 1880s, Grady preached a gospel of economic deliverance exhorting Southerners to raise their region up by the bootstraps. Rather than advocating isolationism, Grady sought Northern investment. "Every dollar of Northern money reinvested in the South gives us a new friend in that section," he intoned.

Today, Henry Grady is remembered as the primary proponent of the New South and of a new Atlanta. It was a role in which the Georgia native took great pride. "From the ashes left us in 1864, we have built a brave and beautiful city," he told a gathering of Northern civic leaders in 1886.

By 1890 Atlanta was rebuilt and had begun to prosper, as this photograph of Union Station in that year shows. (Georgia Department of Archives & History)

◆ CAPITAL OF THE MODERN NEW SOUTH

Although the South prospered to some degree in the late 19th and early 20th centuries, much of the region remained rural, agricultural, and poor. At the onset of the Second World War in the early 1940s, the construction of new military bases and an influx of American men from all over the country infused new life into the region. In the 1960s, the Civil Rights Movement shook Georgia's culture to the core, challenging the long-held values and ushering forth a New South of which Henry Grady could not have even conceived. With the emergence of this modern New South, Atlanta came to the fore as the region's most visible, prosperous, and vital city.

◆ RACE RELATIONS

Atlanta has not been without its problems. Race riots swept Atlanta for four days in 1906; anti-Semitism reared its ugly head in 1915 and in 1958; and many blacks were unable to vote well into the 1960s. Yet for the most part, Atlanta's white citizens declined to become involved in the sort of ugly events that stigmatized cities like Birmingham, and much of the credit for Atlanta's ascension is attributable to its relatively stable race relations. This was due in part to the stabilizing influence of Atlanta's well-educated and comparatively wealthy black middle class. Since 1867, Atlanta has been home to a number of the nation's finest black colleges and universities, including such renowned institutions as Spelman College and Morehouse College. African-American businesses have long thrived along Auburn Avenue, once dubbed "the wealthiest Negro street in America."

During the Civil Rights era, the greatest positive influence was that exerted by the local religious community. The Reverend Martin Luther King Jr. (a co-pastor in Atlanta from 1960 to 1968) may have been the most famous advocate of African-American equality, but he was by no means the sole architect. As the Civil Rights Movement gained momentum in the 1960s, preachers and rabbis took to pulpits like politicians to stumps, rallying support among parishioners for what was expected to be a protracted struggle. The right to vote was but one of the issues; there were also neighborhoods, schools, and workplaces to integrate. While Watts and Chicago erupted in riots, Atlanta leaders, black and white, negotiated closed-door settlements, paving the way for an integrated city.

In 1973, Atlanta elected the first African-American mayor of a major Southern city, Maynard Jackson. Jackson served two terms before giving way to Andrew Young, who had made his mark as one of Dr. King's assistants before serving as head of the U.S. delegation to the United Nations during the Carter Administration.

Martin Luther King Jr. preaching at Ebenezer Baptist Church, where his father also served as pastor. (Library of Congress)

♦ PREMIER SOUTHERN CITY

By the 1970s Atlanta was known for its progressive social policies—which resulted from the synergistic efforts of the black and white business and political communities. Success followed success. Corporation after corporation moved to Atlanta, believing that this Southern city had reason to remain above the fray of racial strife and to focus instead on closing deals and making money. Homegrown businesses like Coca-Cola, Delta Airlines, and Turner Broadcasting grew by leaps and bounds. Soon Atlanta was touting itself as "the hometown of the American dream." Anything, it seemed, was possible.

Perhaps the crowning glory in the Atlanta story came in 1996 when the city hosted the centennial Olympic Games. In preparation, Atlanta embarked on a massive public works campaign, building new stadiums, refurbishing old ones, converting urban wasteland into parkland, and installing a good measure of public art. By the time of the opening ceremonies—a spectacle capped by the lighting of the Olympic cauldron by boxing champion Muhammad Ali—Atlanta stood in the klieg lights of the international press and declared its transformation from citadel of the Old South to capital of the New South, a fait accompli.

Over the years Atlanta has reinvented itself a good half-dozen times, never shy about broadcasting its merits (and sometimes selling its soul) in pursuit of the almighty dollar. Today, that huckster spirit prevails. Atlantans will build a strip mall in the middle of far-flung Alpharetta, name it Peachtree Brook, and tell the world what a fine thing they have wrought. Don't buy the bull. Instead, make your way to the in-town neighborhoods that are at the spiritual heart of the city. There you will meet an interesting and diverse cast of Atlantans, and there, along the sun-dappled sidewalks and tree-shaded avenues, you will discover the city's charm.

If you find yourself confused as you make your way around the city, it might be due to the proliferation of roads, areas, and destinations containing the name "Peachtree." Peachtree Street has long been a center of commerce in Atlanta, and it became such a desirable address that, as the city grew, more and more roads and developments were given the name. Adding to the confusion is the fact that, in recent years, several downtown streets have even been *renamed* to provide influential tenants with a Peachtree address.

The gold-domed Georgia State Capitol was constructed in 1889 at a cost of $1 million. Today it serves as the focus of activity in downtown Atlanta.

MIDTOWN

.25 Miles

The Temple

Rhodes Hall

85
75

Beverly Rd
The Prado
Maddox Dr

Center for
Puppetry Arts

17th St
16th Cir
Westminster

ARTS
CENTER

15th St

High
Museum of Art

Woodruff Arts
Center

Atlanta
Botanical
Garden

Piedmont
Park

13th St

12th St

11th St

Lake
Clara Meer

10th St

Alexander
Memorial
Coliseum

MIDTOWN

Margaret
Mitchell
House

9th St

8th St

Georgia
Institute of
Technology

85
75

7th St

6th St

5th St

4th St

3rd St

2nd St

Bobby
Dodd
Stadium

Fox
Theatre

The
Varsity

NORTH
AVE

North Ave

Ponce de Leon Ave

VIRGINIA-
HIGHLAND

.25 Miles

N

Morningside Dr
Wessyngton Rd

Courtenay Dr

N Highland

Amsterdam Ave

Lanier Blvd

Highland Terr

Glen Arden Way

Los Angeles Ave

20th Century
Antiques

Highland Tap

Virginia Ave

Virginia Cir

Aurora
Coffee

Hudson Dr

Rosedale Dr

Highland View

Dish

Drewry St

Briarcliff Pl

Greenwood Ave

St Charles Pl

Frederica

Ponce de Leon Ave

Briarcliff Rd
42

BUCKHEAD

.25 Miles

Roswell Rd
Buckhead
Loop
400
MARTA

Phipps
Plaza

Knollwood

Habersham Rd

BUCKHEAD

Lenox
Square

10

Atlanta
History
Museum

Piedmont Rd

400
LENOX
Rd

Governors Mansion

West Paces Ferry Rd

Chatham

Matheson Dr

Peachtree Rd

LENOX Rd

Cherry-Simms Garden
Garden for Peace

Swan House
Swan Coach House

Tullie
Smith
House

Slaton Dr

Maple Dr

East
Paces Ferry Rd

Buckhead Ave

Pharr Rd

Fay Gold Gallery

DOWNTOWN

.25 Miles

PEACHTREE
CENTER

MARTA

Peachtree
Center
International

St Blvd

Georgia
Dome

International Blvd

Westin
Peachtree
Plaza

191

CNN
Center

High
Museum

GA
Pacific

Ellis St Blvd

Omni
Center

CNN
Center

Candler
Building

J W Dobbs

Marietta St

AT&T

Auburn

FIVE
POINTS

Peachtree St

Woodruff
Park

Edgewood

Courtland

Piedmont Ave

MARTA

OMNI

MLK

Mitchell St

Markham St

Hurt
Park

Hurt
Building

Spring St

Peachtree St

Decatur St

Courtland St

Glimer

Underground
Atlanta

World of
Coca-Cola

Georgia
State Univ

Butler

State
Capitol

GEORGIA
STATE

City
Hall

Forsyth

MARTA

Pryor

Central

Trinity Ave

85
75

GARNETT

LITTLE
FIVE POINTS

.5 Miles

Seminole

Star
Community
Bar

Pavilion
C

Circle of
Flags

Moreland Ave

Ruby

Gregg Davis
Plaza

Little Five
Points

Pavilion B
Pavilion A

Colquitt

N Highland Ave

Variety
Playhouse

Carter
Presidential
Center

Euclid Ave

Seven Stages

Museum of
Jimmy Carter

Washita

Austin Ave

Horizon Theatre
Company

Alta

Degress Ave

N

INMAN PARK/
REYNOLDSTOWN

Austin St

Hurt St

Waverly Way

Elizabeth Ave

Hale St

Springvale
Park

Virgil St

Euclid Ave

Trolley
Barn

Ashland Ave

Druid

Waverly Way

Edgewood Ave

Dekalb Ave

Dixie

Spruce

Delta
Park

MARTA

■ INMAN PARK AND LITTLE FIVE POINTS

Inman Park was Atlanta's first suburb. Established early in the 20th century by developer Joel Hurt, the planned community was linked to downtown Atlanta (three miles to the west) by means of the country's first electrically powered streetcar line. During those years, Inman Park was the most exclusive community in Atlanta, home to, among others, the Candlers and Woodruffs of Coca-Cola fame *(see page 136)*. And yet, with the advent of the automobile age, Inman Park's gilded Victorian mansions lost favor as the moneyed elite made use of their new conveyances, moving farther east and north to the emerging au courant neighborhoods.

By the middle years of the 20th century, Inman Park was a wreck. The adjacent business district known as Little Five Points fared no better. As the neighborhood folk tell it, that all changed when the "hippies showed up in the late '60s," looking for cheap housing close to the city center. Pouring "sweat equity" into the old Victorians, these urban pioneers made Inman Park fashionable once again. Alas, the neighborhood's greatest threat may come from success. Today, Inman Park is one of the city's hippest addresses. To hear the aging urban pioneers tell it, what was once a bohemian enclave is fast becoming a yuppie haven where you can get a great latte, but buying a lug wrench requires a trip across town.

ATLANTA

Little Five Points is known as a prime shopping area for the hipster set.

A rockabilly couple at Atlanta's Star Community Bar. (photo by Kelly Duane)

Greg Davis Plaza

At the heart of Little Five Points is Atlanta's answer to New York's East Village, Greg Davis Plaza (named for a police officer slain in the line of duty during the early 1990s). It is here that Moreland, Euclid, and Seminole Avenues intersect, and it is here that the nose-ring set and the terminally hip mix and mingle with low-key locals. Avant-garde businesses line Moreland and Euclid Avenues and include **Stefan's**, an upscale vintage clothing store; **Wax 'n' Facts**, the city's premier source for used records and CDs; and **A Capella**, a used bookstore that's well stocked with Beat-era novels as well as classics.

Live Music and Theater
in Little Five Points

Live music is a big draw in Little Five Points, ranging from the country-tinged bands featured at the **Star Community Bar** *(437 Moreland Avenue; 404-681-9018)* to an eclectic schedule of touring acts at the **Variety Playhouse** *(1099 Euclid Avenue; 404-521-1786)*. Two theater groups call Little Five Points home: the **Horizon Theatre Company** *(1083 Austin Avenue; 404-584-7450)*, often a showcase for local productions of seasoned Off-Broadway fare, and **Seven Stages Theatre** *(1105 Euclid Avenue; 404-523-7647)*, Atlanta's most consistently innovative, multicultural theater.

Carter Presidential Center

Three blocks west of Little Five Points is the Carter Presidential Center, home to the Museum of the Jimmy Carter Library and the offices of the former President's numerous philanthropic and ambassadorial operations. Although much of this complex of interconnected concrete pavilions is off-limits, exhibits dealing with the Carter presidency are open to the public. *441 Freedom Parkway (at Highland Avenue); 404-331-3942.*

At the rear of the complex, on a ridge overlooking downtown, is a terraced Japanese-style garden and a grassy slope popular with dog lovers, who convene to let their canine companions romp and play.

Inman Park Residential Streets
A 10-minute walk southwest of Little Five Points down Euclid Avenue—along sidewalks shaded by towering oaks—takes you to Inman Park. A few hours wandering the neighborhood is time well spent. Among the highlights are the homes along Edge-wood Avenue, Elizabeth Street, and Waverly Way, built in a hodgepodge of architectural styles and including a number of brick-turreted Victorian follies.

The green- and red-shingled **Trolley Barn**, a High Victorian wonder located in the 900 block of Edgewood Avenue, is the only vestige of Inman Park's days as a trolley-car suburb. It now serves as a community center and special event facility. A number of bed-and-breakfast inns are located in the neighborhood (*see page 154*).

■ VIRGINIA-HIGHLAND

Just a mile or so north of Little Five Points, across Ponce de Leon Avenue (pronounced by Atlantans without a trace of a Spanish lilt), is a neighborhood of comfortable bungalow homes known as Virginia-Highland, so named for the intersection of Virginia and Highland Avenues at its epicenter.

Once a slightly down-at-the-heels, middle-class enclave, the neighborhood now bustles with young professionals—jogging, biking, or pushing the latest model designer stroller down the narrow sidewalks. Some of Atlanta's most eclectic shops and innovative restaurants are grouped along the one-and-a-half-mile stretch of Highland Avenue from Ponce de Leon north to University Avenue.

Among the dining highlights are **Dish**, a futuristic fusion restaurant housed in a former filling station, and the **Highland Tap**, Atlanta's den of drinking iniquity where the city's best martinis are served alongside well-marbled steaks in a cool subterranean setting. *(See page 159.)*

For shopping, **20th Century Antiques** is a perennial favorite, chockablock with chrome-trimmed and leopard-spotted furnishings from the not too distant past.

Perhaps the best way to experience Virginia-Highland is on foot, with a cup of **Aurora Coffee** in hand, wandering the back streets of what many believe to be Atlanta's most engaging in-town neighborhood.

■ DRUID HILLS

Druid Hills, just east of Virginia-Highland, was a late-1890s project of developer Joel Hurt (who also developed Inman Park) and America's foremost landscape architect, Frederic Law Olmsted. The neighborhood is a tangle of looping lanes wedged between two main thoroughfares, Briarcliff Road and Ponce de Leon Avenue (just Ponce to locals). Lushly landscaped and grand in scale, the homes of Druid Hills are among the most imposing in the Atlanta area.

Though planned as a residential enclave, Druid Hills is also home to some of the city's most vital cultural and educational institutions.

Fernbank Museum of Natural History

Tucked into a bank of hardwoods just off Ponce is the Fernbank Museum of Natural History. Opened in 1992, this is the largest museum of natural history constructed since the Roosevelt era. The building itself is a wonder, featuring limestone floors studded with fossils, but the real treats are the permanent exhibits, including "A Walk Through Time in Georgia," a fascinating account of the natural history of Georgia and the Southeast. Also on the premises is a giant IMAX theater. *767 Clifton Road; 404-378-0127.*

Fernbank Forest

Adjacent to the Fernbank Museum is Fernbank Forest, a 65-acre woodland preserve just a small remove from the traffic snarl of Ponce de Leon Avenue. Now maintained by Dekalb County as a teaching center, the forest is home to the **Fernbank Science Center**, which includes a 500-seat planetarium and an observatory that boasts a 36-inch telescope. *156 Heaton Park Drive; 404-378-4311.*

Emory University

North of Fernbank Forest, just beyond the manicured confines of the Druid Hills Golf Club, is the main campus of Emory University. Founded at Oxford, Georgia, in 1836, Emory moved to Atlanta in 1915, lured by a grant of of 75 acres of land and a one-million dollar endowment from Coca-Cola magnate Asa Candler. Ties to the Coca-Cola Corporation remain important to the school, as evidenced by the new Goizuetta School of Business, named for the company's former chief executive.

Today the campus covers almost 600 acres and attracts a liberal student body, many of whom, in the Georgia vernacular, "ain't from around here." Indeed, the university is home to a large international population and, thanks to its sterling academic reputation, has attracted to a good number of students from Northern states lured by the mild winter weather, as well as excellent academics and generous scholarships.

The Michael C. Carlos Museum, recently renovated and expanded, houses the largest collection of ancient art in the South—from Mesopotamian cuneiform tablets to pre-Columbian pottery. The building itself is a delight, an architectural marvel that somehow manages to mix Italian Renaissance and postmodernist styles. *571 Kilgo Drive; 404-727-4282.*

Emory Village, just across the street from the Emory campus, contains a welcoming collection of shops and restaurants, most of which are geared toward the 10,000-plus students.

■ MIDTOWN

A diverse, dispersed collection of shops, restaurants, and homes spreading north and south along Peachtree Street between Buckhead and Downtown, Midtown is the center of Atlanta's thriving gay and lesbian community as well as home to the city's premier cultural institutions. Once a jumble of lovely bungalow homes and neighborhood businesses, Midtown's main thoroughfares are increasingly shadowed by postmodern skyscrapers, but side streets remain relatively undisturbed.

Piedmont Park

At the center of Midtown, sandwiched between Piedmont Avenue and Monroe Drive, is Piedmont Park, Atlanta's largest public green space. Designed in part by Frederic Law Olmsted, the 185-acre park was once the race ground for the Piedmont Driving Club, Atlanta's most exclusive social club. Today, the lakes and lawns are given over to biking, sunbathing, and Rollerblading. At the park's southeastern corner is a cafe serving cold beers and sandwiches, the perfect respite from a dog day summer afternoon.

On the northwest side of the park is the **Atlanta Botanical Garden**, a 30-acre oasis of meandering paths and vast swaths of grass. The gardens are punctuated by the **Fuqua Conservatory** and a new children's playscape, the most arresting feature of

The Fuqua Conservatory in the Atlanta Botanical Garden.

Midtown's skyline, as seen from Piedmont Park.

which is a wrought steel Butterfly Pavilion, designed and constructed by up-and-coming Atlanta sculptor David Landis. Thanks to a variety of plants that grow within the structure and attract the butterflies, the pavilion is less a cage to contain the kaleidoscope of winged creatures than it is a focal point around which they gather, flitting in and out among the foliage. *1345 Piedmont Avenue; 404-876-5859.*

Gone With the Wind Sites

A few blocks west of Piedmont Park is the **Margaret Mitchell House,** a rather ordinary building where the author of *Gone With the Wind* and her husband, John Marsh, lived from 1925 to 1932. Mitchell, disdainful of her onetime digs, often referred to the apartment house as "the

Dump." Nevertheless, preservationists have recently restored the house, now home to an exhibit that details the life of Atlanta's most famous author. Unfortunately, the house seems out of place amid the unappealing new highrise developments all around it. *Intersection of 10th and Peachtree Streets; 404-249-7012.*

Nine blocks south of the Margaret Mitchell House, at the corner of Peachtree and Ponce, is the **Georgian Terrace Hotel,** host hostelry for the stars of the movie version of *Gone With the Wind,* which premiered in Atlanta in 1939.

Five years before, in the marble-lined lobby, Mitchell had handed over the as-yet-uncompleted manuscript for the novel to literary scout Harold Latham of the Macmillan publishing house.

GONE WITH THE WIND PHENOMENA

One of the most popular books in American publishing history, Gone With the Wind *remains a terrific read and a national embarrassment. If Margaret Mitchell's Scarlett O'Hara and Rhett Butler move through the Civil War era with an unforgettable panache, both the author and her characters treat slavery with nonchalance. And yet few who begin to read this story can put it down. Tom Wolfe (whose 1998 novel,* A Man in Full, *centers on Atlanta) recently observed: "I love being in the same paragraph as Margaret Mitchell. In literary circles, you're not supposed to say that. But you could argue, and I would if anyone would listen, that* Gone With the Wind *is the greatest American novel ever written." Whatever its merits,* Gone With the Wind *is irrevocably linked with the state of Georgia.*

❧ ❧

The year is 1861 and 16-year-old Scarlett O'Hara appears in all her vivid glory:

Scarlett intended to marry…and she was willing to appear demure, pliable and scatterbrained, if those were the qualities that attracted men. Just why men should be this way, she did not know. She only knew that such methods worked. It never interested her enough to try to think out the reason for it, for she knew nothing of the inner workings of any human being's mind, not even her own. She knew only that if she did or said thus-and-so, men would unerringly respond with the complementary thus-and-so. It was like a mathematical formula….

If she knew little about men's minds, she knew even less about the minds of women, for they interested her less. She had never had a girl friend, and she never felt any lack on that account. To her, all women, including her two sisters, were natural enemies in pursuit of the same prey—man.

Scarlett meets her match in blockade runner Rhett Butler:

He was dressed in black broadcloth, a tall man, towering over the officers who stood near him, bulky in the shoulders but tapering to a small waist and absurdly small feet in varnished boots. His severe black suit, with fine ruffled shirt and trousers smartly strapped beneath high insteps, was oddly at variance with his physique and face, for he was foppishly groomed, the clothes of a dandy on a body that was powerful and latently dangerous in its lazy grace. His hair was jet black, and his black mustache was small and closely clipped, almost foreign looking compared with the dashing, swooping mustaches of the cavalrymen near by. He looked, and was, a man of lusty and unashamed appetites. He had an air of utter assurance, of displeasing insolence about him, and there was a twinkle of malice in his bold eyes as he stared at Scarlett, until finally, feeling his gaze, she looked toward him.

Later, the upstanding Dr. Meade confronts Rhett on his lack of patriotic sentiment.

𝒟r. Meade's brows were thunderous.

"Nothing may be sacred to you, young man," he said, in the voice he always used when making speeches. "But there are many things sacred to the patriotic men and ladies of the South. And the freedom of our land from the usurper is one and States' Rights in another and—"

Rhett looked lazy and his voice had a silky, almost bored, note.

"All wars are sacred," he said. "To those who have to fight them. If the people who started wars didn't make them sacred, who would be foolish enough to fight?"

⸙ ⸙

The movie premiere of Gone With the Wind *was a national event, and for years people remembered the night of the film's premiere as if it was a high holy day in Atlanta history. In Rebecca Well's 1996 novel,* The Divine Secrets of the YaYa Sisterhood, *a young girl from Louisiana who has made a trip to Atlanta to see the opening writes to a friend:*

𝒲e have just come from the premiere of the greatest movie ever made. …Vivien Leigh *is* Scarlett….The minute I saw Miss Leigh there on the steps of the porch at Tara with the Tarleton twins at her side… well, I was a goner….

I want to live in this movie, Necie! This is the kind of drama I was born for.

The Loew's Grand Theatre hosted the world premiere of Gone With the Wind *on December 15, 1939.*

(Atlanta Historical Society)

Fox Theatre

Almost directly across the street from the Georgia Terrace Hotel is the Fox Theatre, Atlanta's singular architectural jewel. A gaudy mix of faux Moorish and Egyptian architecture, this 1929 theater was initially intended to be the Yaarab Temple of the Ancient Order of the Nobles of the Mystic Shrine. But a financial shortfall forced the Nobles to turn the temple over to movie impresario William Fox, who retrofitted the building to serve as a movie palace.

Threatened with condemnation in the 1970s, today the Fox has been completely restored. As the curtain rises, the ceiling above comes alive with a galaxy of stars, and the trompe l'oeil Moorish-style courtyard that surrounds the seating area echoes with the sounds of Mighty Mo, the Fox's 3,600-pound Moller organ.

Tours are offered most mornings, and performances are scheduled throughout the year. *660 Peachtree Street NE; 404-881-2100.*

Georgia Tech

East of the Fox, across the interstate highway chasm that locals call "the Downtown Connector," is the campus of the Georgia Institute of Technology, known to most everyone as Georgia Tech. One of the premier scientific institutions in the nation, Georgia Tech, like its sister state campuses, has benefited immensely from the influx of dollars courtesy of the Georgia Lottery. During the 1996 Olympic Games, Georgia Tech was the site of Olympic Village, housing more than 15,000 athletes and person-

nel. The dorms they inhabited are visible from the interstate, directly across the way from **The Varsity**—"the world's largest drive-in" and Atlanta's shrine to grease and weenies, founded by Tech dropout Frank Gordy *(see page 156).*

Woodruff Arts Center

A couple of miles north of Georgia Tech is the Woodruff Arts Center complex, Atlanta's version of New York's Lincoln Center. The Arts Center building serves as home base for the **Atlanta Symphony Orchestra,** the **Alliance Theatre Company,** and the **Atlanta College of Art.** *1280 Peachtree Street; 404-733-4200.*

High Museum of Art

Adjacent to the Arts Center building is the High Museum, which opened in 1983. Designed by Richard Meier, the High Museum has won rave reviews from architecture critics across the country. Blockbuster exhibits that once bypassed Atlanta now make a stop at the High, and retrospectives on Picasso, Monet, and Pop art have all attracted large audiences.

Out front on the lawn, an Alexander Calder stabile whirls, a kinetic study in primary colors; *404-733-4400.*

Center for Puppetry Arts

Headquartered in an old schoolhouse, this is one of the few museum and performance spaces devoted solely to puppetry. Though the museum displays vintage puppets from around the globe, the biggest draws are its shows for adults. These range from renditions of theater classics to avant-garde performance pieces that stretch the bounds of puppetry propriety and have been known to raise the ire of self-appointed art critic Jesse Helms. *1410 Spring Street; 404-873-3089.*

Rhodes Hall

There was a time in the not too distant past when Peachtree was a residential street rather than a busy thoroughfare. Rhodes Hall is a vestige of that time. This graceful, turreted granite home, completed in 1904, now houses the Georgia Trust for Historic Preservation and is open for weekday tours. *1516 Peachtree Street NW; 404-881-9980.*

The Temple

Also on Peachtree, just a few blocks north, is the Temple, home of Atlanta's oldest Jewish congregation. The exterior may be neo-classical, but the interior is a rendering of King Solomon's temple in Jerusalem as envisioned by the late Phillip Trammel Shutze, favorite architect of the Atlanta elite. In 1958 the Temple was blown apart by a 50-stick dynamite charge. Intended to intimidate Jews, the blast was set by that era's well-known cast of malcontents—the guys in the long white robes and pointy hoods. Bombing suspects were quickly apprehended and sent to trial, where they were represented by (among others) defense attorney Jimmy Venable, Imperial Wizard of the National Knights of the Ku Klux Klan. The defendants were not convictd and the trial was a circus, but today the rebuilt Temple remains the focal point of Jewish religious life in Atlanta. *1589 Peachtree Street; 404-873-1731*

The High Museum of Art, designed by Richard Meier, hosts large touring exhibits as well as its own substantial collection.

■ BUCKHEAD

Situated five or so miles north of Downtown, spreading outward from the nexus of Peachtree Street, Roswell Road, and West Paces Ferry Road, Buckhead is Atlanta's wealthiest neighborhood. Home to the city's toniest nightclubs, swankest shops, and most refined restaurants, Buckhead serves as the de facto capital of Southern glitz and glamour. And yet its origins are altogether humble. The community earned its moniker in the late 1830s when a deer hunter mounted the head of a buck on a post somewhere near the site of a tavern built by the area's first inhabitant, Henry Irby. Visitors today will be hard pressed to detect a trace of such frontier style in this mannered, moneyed neighborhood, home to the Georgia governor and a passel of the city's power brokers. Author Tom Wolfe wrote of Buckhead in his 1998 novel, *A Man in Full:*

> *H*ere in the gloaming, the white blossoms, arranged in their distinctive planes, swept from green breast, from mansion to mansion, estate to estate, as if some divine artist had adorned the heavenly air itself with them to show that the residents of Buckhead, off West Paces Ferry Road, were the elect, the anointed, the rightful hand-grabbers of whatever Atlanta, Georgia had to offer.

The Swan House, a historic mansion in the Buckhead area.

Detractors are quick to point out that Buckhead seems to reinvent itself every couple of years in a feverish pursuit of the almighty dollar. And they do have a point. Rest assured, if it's in vogue you will be sure to find it in Buckhead. Atlanta's largest collection of upscale retailers and restaurants is grouped along Peachtree Street between Roswell Road and two of the South's most prestigious and luxurious malls, **Lenox Square** and **Phipps Plaza.**

Most of Atlanta's premier **art galleries** are located in Buckhead. These include Timothy Tew Gallery, Jane Jackson Fine Art, and Fay Gold Gallery, all of which are tucked away in a warren of side streets between Peachtree Street and East Paces Ferry Road. At night, particularly on weekends, a young and rowdy crowd descends upon Buckhead, enticed by its lively bar scene. But there is also a more sedate side to Buckhead nightlife, evidenced by the presence of such understated temples of haute cuisine as **Bacchanalia** and **La Grotta** *(see pages 148–149).*

Governor's Mansion

To see where the beautiful people live, turn off West Paces Ferry Road onto a side street such as Blackland or Cherokee, roll your windows down, and drink in the wealth. Among the bigwigs who call Buckhead home is the governor of Georgia. The **Governor's Mansion**, built in 1968 in the Greek revival style, is an imposing edifice surrounded by 18 acres of landscaped grounds. It is open for tours weekdays. *391 West Paces Ferry Road; 404-261-1776.*

Atlanta History Center

Also on West Paces Ferry Road, close to the intersection with Peachtree, is what may be Atlanta's prime attraction, the Atlanta History Center. On the grounds you will find the **Atlanta History Museum**, a decidedly multicultural introduction to Atlanta that opened in 1993, as well as the **Tullie Smith House**, a working farm (complete with outbuildings) where during late summer and fall you will find a cotton crop growing. Another home on the grounds, the 1928 **Swan House**, occupies the opposite end of the economic spectrum from the unassuming clapboard Smith House. Designed by noted Atlanta architect Phillip Trammel Schutze, this storybook mansion casts an imposing, almost baronial shadow over the landscaped grounds. Classical in design but whimsically appointed (a swan motif is evident throughout), the home is now open for tours. *130 West Paces Ferry Road; 404-814-4000.*

Adjacent is the **Swan Coach House,** the favored choice of Atlanta ladies who lunch.

ATLANTA

■ WEST END

A couple miles southwest of Downtown, West End—like Buckhead—grew up around a crossroads tavern. Once home to a wealthy white population, the beautiful Victorian houses at the center of this neighborhood are now home to a thriving black middle class, many of whom teach at the nearby Atlanta University Complex.

Herndon Home

Born a slave in 1858 near Social Circle, Georgia, Alonzo Herndon was an early black Atlanta entrepreneur who founded the Atlanta Life Insurance Company, the largest black-owned business of the early 20th century. Even before founding Atlanta Life, Herndon had been a successful businessman; his Peachtree Street barber shop, which employed only black barbers and catered to an affluent white clientele, was the largest and fanciest in Atlanta, featuring leather benches, marble floors, and crystal chandeliers. Today Herndon Home, the house he built in 1910, is open for tours. Of Beaux-Arts design, this imposing brick home features many of the original furnishings as well as exhibits that detail the life of this influential member of Atlanta's black leadership, the group W. E. B. Du Bois deemed the "talented tenth." *587 University Place; 404-581-9813.*

Among Alonzo Herndon's businesses was this opulent barber shop on Peachtree Street. (courtesy of the Herndon Foundation)

Wren's Nest

Named for a family of birds that once nested in the mailbox, this Victorian jewel of a house was home to journalist Joel Chandler Harris, best known for his interpretations of African-American folklore collected as the *Uncle Remus Tales.* Soon after Chandler passed away in 1908, the house was opened to the public, making it Atlanta's first house museum. Among the items on display are first editions of many of Chandler's books. Those curious about Chandler's childhood should journey to Eatonton *(see page 186),* where he was born in 1848. *1050 Ralph David Abernathy Boulevard; 404-753-7735.*

Atlanta University Complex

The Atlanta University Complex is the heart and soul of Atlanta's west side. Here, more than 19,000 students matriculate at six separate institutions of higher learning, among which are Spelman College, the country's oldest college for black women, and Morehouse College, alma mater of the late Dr. Martin Luther King Jr.

Atlanta University, founded in 1865 and once under the direction of W. E. B. Du Bois, was an early citadel of African-American education. Morris Brown College was built in 1867 and Spelman in 1881. Morehouse Medical School and the Interdenominational Theological Seminary followed, after the turn of the century.

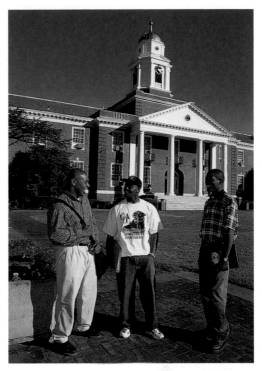

Atlanta University students William Anders, Rashad Boatwright, and Andre Tucker pause for a break between classes.

Long the bastion of the South's middle-class and upper-class blacks, these colleges have fueled Atlanta's growth as a mecca for black entrepreneurs, religious leaders, and educators. Among the redbrick Italianate buildings that comprise the campuses, there stands, on the Morehouse lawn, a modern chapel dedicated to King and fronted by a two-story statue of the slain leader. *James P. Brawley Drive at Martin Luther King Jr. Drive.*

■ GRANT PARK

Named not for the Union general but for one of Atlanta's founding fathers, Lemuel Pratt Grant (who in 1883 donated 100 acres of parkland to the city), Grant Park is a work in progress, a neighborhood of lovingly restored, grand old Victorians homes and sagging Victorian eyesores awaiting the restorer's kind touch. At its center is the eponymous park, home to the Cyclorama and Zoo Atlanta. On its fringes are Atlanta's fabled burying ground, Oakland Cemetery, and Cabbagetown, a onetime mill village now in the throes of restoration.

Cabbagetown

Fulton Bag and Mill is the concrete-and-brick behemoth that sits at the center of Atlanta's Cabbagetown neighborhood. An outpost of Appalachia in the midst of the city, the mill once employed workers who moved south from the mountains in search of jobs. And in typical mill town fashion, the company built the small frame houses that ring the plant for the workers. When the mill closed in 1977 after almost 100 years of operation, the neighborhood went into a tailspin, though most of the residents stayed put. Today, this enclave of narrow streets lined with shotgun houses is experiencing a renaissance of sorts. The old mill is supposed to reopen as a mixed-use apartment and retail complex, but the property suffered a major fire in 1999. *Memorial Drive at Boulevard Road.*

Oakland Cemetery

Oakland Cemetery is the final resting place of Atlantans both famous—author Margaret Mitchell and golfer Bobby Jones—and unknown. Established in 1850 and covering more than 85 acres, the cemetery is integrated by both race and religion. A favorite of picnicking urban pioneers from nearby Cabbagetown, the cemetery is open to the public daily. *Memorial Drive at Oakland Avenue.*

Zoo Atlanta

Long one of the nation's worst zoos, Zoo Atlanta received a major face lift in the mid-'80s, when natural habitats replaced cages and Willie B, the city's prized silverback gorilla, emerged from what amounted to solitary confinement. Today, the zoo is considered to be one of the best in the nation. *800 Cherokee Avenue, 404-624-5600.*

Atlanta Cyclorama

There was a time in the late 1800s when cycloramas, circular paintings that depicted some momentous event, were transported from city to city and displayed with great aplomb. They were, in essence, the IMAX theaters of an earlier time. One of the few still in existence is the Atlanta Cyclorama, a three-ton-plus painting of the Battle of Atlanta that revolves around the viewer. The realism is heightened by a two-dimensional diorama that fades from the foreground into the painting. Also on display is the locomotive *Texas*, one of the two engines involved in the Great Locomotive Chase of the Civil War. *800 Cherokee Avenue in the park; 404-658-7625.*

THE GREAT LOCOMOTIVE CHASE

Georgia is particularly proud of its role in an episode of Civil War history that seems straight out of a Buster Keaton movie. On April 12, 1862, a group of Union raiders boarded a train in Marietta. The passengers and crew, unaware of the Federals in their midst, got off at Kennesaw for a snack, and the raiders departed in the train, planning to destroy the bridges between Kennesaw and Chattanooga. They were foiled, though, by the train's heroic engineer, who doggedly chased his train—first on foot, then by polecar, and finally by commandeering three other engines. Two of these he ran in reverse, since there weren't roundhouses nearby. At one point, the raiders let go two cars, thinking the cars would slam into the pursuers; but the Confederates were able to couple the loose cars with their engine. After 87 miles and eight hours, the raiders were caught. And thus was born the legend of the Great Locomotive Chase.

■ EAST ATLANTA

Those in pursuit of the "next big thing" should make their way east from Grant Park and across Moreland Avenue to the neighborhood of East Atlanta, where funk and food are now the big draws. Over the past few years, urban speculators have begun opening shops and restaurants along Flat Shoals and Glenwood Avenues, drawing a young crowd presumably turned off by the gentrification of Little Five Points. Though there are no "sights" to see, the six-block commercial center is in an almost constant state of entrepreneurial upheaval. Who knows what the future holds?

■ DOWNTOWN

Despite the best efforts of boosters, Downtown is where Atlanta works rather than lives or plays. Home to the headquarters of CNN, Georgia-Pacific, and Coca-Cola, downtown Atlanta is, unfortunately, an after-dark desert, populated primarily by conventioneers plying the streets on weekday nights in search of diversion.

Three distinct districts stretch from north to south along Peachtree Street: Peachtree Center, architect John Portman's skyscraper complex; Five Points (as distinguished from Little Five Points, described on pages 118–120), the onetime heart of the city, now sliding into decline; and Underground Atlanta, formerly a unique subterranean entertainment district, now an urban shopping mall.

Centennial Olympic Park

At the heart of Olympic Park is a fountain fashioned in the shape of the Olympic rings, a gathering spot that is especially popular in the summer months, when children play in the intermittent sprays of water that shoot upward. Walkways leading from the fountain fan out into the park and are paved with commemorative bricks inscribed with the names of the thousands of people who paid $35 for the privilege. A performance pavilion is also on-site, and an Olympic museum is to be built. *Just west of Peachtree Center, wedged between Marietta Street and Techwood Drive and extending north to Baker Street.*

CNN Center

Just south of Olympic Park by way of Techwood Avenue is CNN Center. Once home to an indoor theme park—the World of Sid and Marty Krofft—this glass-and-steel behemoth with a soaring atrium at its center now serves as the headquarters for one of the world's largest news organizations, beaming breaking stories to more than 200 countries around the globe. Studio tours, despite their promotional bluster, provide an entertaining glimpse into the workings of a news-gathering organization. VIP tours, priced at a premium, put you on the newsroom floor and offer the opportunity to grab a snack at the company commissary, where you may just catch a glimpse of Bernard Kalb or Wolf Blitzer. *Corner of Techwood Drive and Marietta Street; 404-827-2300.*

Peachtree Center

Architect John Portman, arguably the man most responsible for reshaping the Atlanta cityscape, was also one of the first architects in the country to aspire to be a developer. Portman's 1961 Atlanta Merchandise Mart was followed in succeeding years by a raft of building projects that sprawled up and down Peachtree Street from its intersection with International Boulevard in a loose assemblage of seven office towers, three hotels, and an urban shopping mall.

Known today as Peachtree Center, the complex is showing its age, maybe even looking a bit kitschy, as evidenced by early buildings like the Hyatt Regency Hotel *(see page 152)*, with its soaring atrium and blue-domed restaurant spinning away up top. The Westin Peachtree Plaza, however—at 720 feet high the tallest hotel in the country—still looks nearly as futuristic as it did when it opened in the mid-1970s.

The complex is interconnected by a series of aboveground passageways that look like little mole tunnels leading from habitat to habitat. There are some that criticize the scale of Portman's master plan. Others take issue with an aesthetic focused on glass and concrete. But none can deny that his developmental zeal played a large part in fueling the building boom that vaulted Atlanta into the top tier of international business centers.

Woodruff Park

Atlanta's other downtown green space, facing on Peachtree Street between Edgewood and Auburn Avenues, is Woodruff Park, a

At 720 feet and 71 stories, Peachtree Plaza dominates the downtown skyline.

pocket oasis among the skyscrapers. On weekdays, park benches are filled with business people toting brown bags, while on weekends, skateboarders rip down the walkways. At the southwestern corner of the park, facing Peachtree Street, stands Atlanta's preeminent symbol: a bronze statue of a woman bearing a phoenix on high, titled *Up From the Ashes*. The sculpture pays homage to the city of Atlanta, which, after the Civil War, arose like the mythical phoenix from the ashes of destruction.

Underground Atlanta

In the late 19th century a series of bridges were built across the center of Atlanta to ease congestion caused by the expansion of the railyards. Over time, the bridges evolved into streets at the second-floor level of the old redbrick buildings in the area; the ground floor was now essentially underground. Merchants moved their operations to the second floor, leaving the first floor to spiders and mice.

In the early 1970s, hedonistic hotspots and subterranean hideaways began flourishing in these cellars, attracting tourists and Atlantans alike to what became known as Underground Atlanta. Clubs like Dante's Down the Hatch hopped 'til the wee hours of the morning. But by the late '70s, the thrill was gone, the nightlife almost nonexistent. In 1981, Underground Atlanta was shuttered, returning to its former state as a dark and dank city beneath a city

But the concept was too good, the appeal too great to let the entertainment district lie fallow. Entrepreneurs reopened Underground Atlanta in 1989 as a mixed-use, family-friendly complex of shops, restaurants, and a few bars. Though there is still an air of mystery about the place, it now feels less like an urban grotto and more like a mall in a semi-subterranean setting. Though the convention trade throngs the area on a good night, Atlantans, for the most part, aren't buying it.

World of Coca-Cola

Just east of the Kenny's Alley entrance to Underground Atlanta, the World of Coca-Cola is housed in a stucco jukebox of a building erected in tribute to that fizzy liquid sold the world over. Inside you will find a replica of a 1930s soda fountain and learn of the role that Coca-Cola Company print advertising played in fashioning our national conception of what Santa Claus looks like. And of course there's plenty of free Coke all around. *55 Martin Luther King Jr. Drive; 404-676-5151.*

A Coca-Cola advertisement dating from 1898.

Georgia State Capitol

One block east is the gold-domed Georgia capitol, constructed in 1889 at a cost of more than $1 million. Visitors are free to roam the marble halls, perhaps making their way to the odd Georgia Museum of Science and History on the fourth floor, where an unlikely assortment of Georgia ephemera is assembled: mounted fish beside meteorites, big ole cotton bales, and—everyone's favorite—the two-headed calf known among some of the lobbyists as Janus.

But the real sights to see are on the grounds that surround the limestone edifice. Here you will come face to face with statues of old-school politicians the Talmadges, both father and son, as well as a compelling sculpture titled *Expelled Because of Color*. Erected in the 1970s on the northeast lawn of the capitol, the artwork is dedicated to the 33 African-American lawmakers who served in the state legislature during Reconstruction before being ousted with the coming of Redemption. The bronze depicts the ascendance of black Georgians from slaves to equals in a participatory democracy. *206 Washington Street; 404-656-2844.*

The museum inside the State Capitol is open to all visitors free of charge.

Turner Field

After the closing ceremonies of the 1996 Olympic Games, the track and field stadium built for the occasion was remade into Turner Field, home of the Atlanta Braves, the winningest major-league baseball team of the 1990s. The field is now known to most locals as simply the Ted, in deference to team owner and media mogul Ted Turner. As much an arcade as a ball field, the stadium offers batting cages and a Braves museum, not to mention numerous spots to eat and drink. That said, it's also a great spot to see a ball game, an intimate facility with great site lines and televisions mounted on the walls at about every five feet to ensure that you won't miss a thing, even if you're in line for a hot dog when someone crushes a home run over the centerfield fence. *755 Hank Aaron Drive at Ralph David Abernathy Drive. Tour information, 404-614-2311; tickets, 404-249-6400.*

ATLANTA

■ Sweet Auburn

Once the economic, social, and spiritual heart of segregated black Atlanta, Sweet Auburn gave birth to the nation's first black-owned newspaper, the *Atlanta Daily World;* the first black-owned radio station, WERD; and the largest black-owned business to emerge from the South, Alonzo Herndon's Atlanta Life Insurance Company. In 1957, *Fortune* magazine deemed Auburn Avenue "the richest Negro street in the world."

Located just a mile or so east of Five Points (not to be confused with Little Five Points), the 12-block stretch along Auburn Avenue declined in the years following desegregation as African Americans, free to work and live in areas not specifically consigned to them, moved their businesses and residences to other parts of the city.

Today, Sweet Auburn retains its role as the spiritual heart of Atlanta's African-American community. It was here that Martin Luther King Jr., arguably the most influential American religious leader of the 20th century, was born. Here were the headquarters of the Southern Christian Leadership Conference, the civil rights organization King headed during the 1960s. And it is here that King's body rests, in a white marble tomb beside a reflecting pool, on the grounds of the Martin Luther King Center for Nonviolent Social Change.

Wheat Street Baptist, Big Bethel African Methodist Episcopal, and Ebenezer Baptist: these are the churches that form the backbone of Auburn Avenue. **Big Bethel,** established in 1847 by slave owners for their slaves, was once the political hub of black Atlanta. A huge "Jesus Saves" sign, tacked to the steeple in the 1920s, advertises the church's philosophy in no uncertain terms. *220 Auburn Avenue; 404-659-0248.*

Wheat Street Baptist Church owes its name to the former name of Auburn Avenue. From the late 1930s to 1988, the humble but influential Rev. William Holmes was pastor of this congregation. *359 Auburn Avenue; 404-659-4328.*

But the best known of Sweet Auburn's churches is undoubtedly **Ebenezer Baptist,** the somber brick-and-masonry building where Martin Luther King Jr. took to the pulpit, and in so doing raised our nation's awareness about the inherent inequity of a segregated society. It was here that a 17-year-old King preached his first sermon, under the watchful eyes of his father, the pastor known to everyone as Daddy King. Here the younger King convened the Southern Christian Leadership Conference, one of the organizations that led the efforts to end segregation. And here was held the memorial service after his 1968 assassination. A recorded program in the sanctuary tells the story of the church and its favorite son. But the best

ATLANTA'S BLACK ELITE

*M*any members of the city's old guard—people like Ella Yates and the men and women she knows—would probably acknowledge that part of Atlanta has become known for its ability to remake itself: to tear up its historical roots every few years and erect a shiny new facade that reflects little of what preceded it....

Yates is old Atlanta. She's fourth-generation. She's Spelman College. She lives in the right neighborhood. She's earned the right graduate degrees, held the right jobs, and married into the right family. She even belongs to the right literary club—one that includes a small and elite group of black Atlanta's old-guard women who have met once a month, without fail, for eighty-nine consecutive years. Yates is the real thing, and she knows where the bones are buried.

But there are many new wealthy blacks in Atlanta who wouldn't know that. Some of the new black money that has landed in Stone Mountain, in Guilford Forest, in Buckhead, or in Dunwoody wouldn't know about the Yates family, or the bank or the drugstore they founded. The wouldn't know about the book party that was just given for Julian Bond's mother...or about the medical contributions of Asa Yancey or the business accomplishment of the Blayton family.... In fact, many members of the new elite don't live within the city limits. They are not among the 260,000 blacks that make the city only one-third white. The new black elite are on the outskirts of old Atlanta—both geographically and socially.

—Lawrence Otis Graham,
*Our Kind of People: Inside
America's Black Upper Class,* 1999

*Judie Dobbs, photographed here
around 1885, was the matriarch
of what became one of Atlanta's
celebrated black families. Born a
slave in the 1820s, she is said to
have lived to be 101.
(Muriel Gassett James files,
Sacramento, CA)*

way to gain an understanding of the importance of this church—or Big Bethel or Wheat Street—is to come to a Sunday morning service. As the gospel music rises to a crescendo, and the pews themselves seem to shake with the power of the pastor's message, you will come to appreciate how churches served as places of both solace and strength during the Civil Rights Movement. No matter your religious belief, you will be moved. A newer, larger Ebenezer was recently built nearby. *407 Auburn Avenue; 404-688-7263.*

APEX

This museum, formally known as the African-American Panoramic Experience, seeks to trace the lineage of black Atlantans from Africa to the modern day. The most compelling parts of the museum are the exhibits dedicated to the little postage stamp of urban Atlanta known as Sweet Auburn, including a re-creation of Yates & Milton, the drugstore that was once a gathering place for black Atlanta. *135 Auburn Avenue; 404-521-2739.*

Martin Luther King Jr. Center for Nonviolent Social Change

The National Park Service now manages a complex of interrelated buildings with this structure at its core. Founded in 1968 by Coretta Scott King, wife of the assassinated civil rights leader, the center was intended to serve as an organ of change, to further King's agenda of racial and social reform. In years past, the center has sponsored concerts that were cross-booked with rap and rock bands in order to draw a racially mixed crowd. And through the years Mrs. King and her children have remained staunch defenders of Martin Luther King's legacy. But today, the center is not as much an organ of change as a representation of it, a place for reflection rather than activism.

The focal point of the center is King's final resting place, a simple white marble tomb surrounded by a reflecting pool and framed by a stepped waterfall. The inscription repeats King's prescient pronouncement from a civil rights speech:

> FREE AT LAST
> FREE AT LAST
> THANK GOD ALMIGHTY
> I'M FREE AT LAST

Inside the main building is a small exhibition hall displaying mementos from King's short and turbulent public life. There are plans afoot to expand the center's displays. *339 Auburn Avenue; 404-524-1956.*

Martin Luther King Jr. Birthplace

One block west is the clapboard and shingle house where King was born on January 25, 1929. Unadorned, simple even, the nine-room house was home to Daddy King and his wife, Alberta, for the first 12 years of young Martin's life. National Park Service rangers now lead tours through the home as well as up and down this stretch of Auburn Avenue, providing visitors with a lively narrative of King's life. *501 Auburn Avenue; 404-331-5190.*

■ GREATER METROPOLITAN ATLANTA

Spreading outward from Atlanta's core, the interstate highway system hurtles travelers north, south, east, and west. Come quitting time, the roadways are thronged with commuters, cell phones in hand, hopping from lane to lane, their horns blaring out a chorus of frustration.

For the most part, the towns that ring metropolitan Atlanta are bedroom communities, their identities long lost to suburban sprawl that reaches across 18 counties and more than 5,000 square miles. But there are a few exceptions, communities of charm and diversity that boast attractions worthy of a detour, like Stone Mountain, Decatur, Kennesaw Mountain, and Moreland. Also of interest, though not detailed here, are Roswell, an old mill community turned toney suburb; Newnan, a thriving town centered on a courthouse square; and Jonesboro, a south-side community chockablock with antebellum homes. Just don't venture out at rush hour!

◆ **MARIETTA** *map page 141, A-2*
Marietta, on the northwestern fringe of Atlanta, retains an attractive square with a grass-ringed gazebo at center. Gathered around the green space is a collection of lively shops and restaurants. But most visitors never make it this far; they're still stopped out on Cobb Parkway,

"The Big Chicken"—a Cobb County landmark in Marietta.

Two young drummers at a Civil War battle re-enactment.

gawking at the Big Chicken, a hen-shaped edifice erected during the heyday of roadside excess. With its rolling eyes and pecking yellow beak, it's a favorite of children, and thanks to it height of nearly 60 feet, pilots use it as a landmark. (Today, Kentucky Fried Chicken has the Big Chicken franchise.)

♦ **KENNESAW MOUNTAIN NATIONAL BATTLEFIELD**   *map page 141, A-2*

West of Marietta, down Highway 120, is the Kennesaw Mountain National Battlefield. Part of the Atlanta Campaign *(see page 110-111)* was waged here, and more than 11 miles of earthen breastworks remain. Though Union General Sherman would eventually push through Confederate defenses, at Kennesaw Mountain his advance was stalled for more than two weeks. His victory came with a stunning price: the lives of more than 3,000 Union troops.

Today the spot is popular with day hikers and picnickers alike who explore the trails that wend through the park. *770-427-4686; 900 Kennesaw Mountain Drive.*

Closer to downtown Marietta, the National Cemetery on Washington Drive is the final resting place of more than 10,000 boys in blue who lost their lives in the Atlanta Campaign. Nearby, the Confederate Cemetery on Cemetery Street is home to more than 3,000 boys in gray, a full third of whom remain unknown.

UNCONQUERABLE KENNESAW MOUNTAIN

*I*n the warm wet summer nights, Atlanta's homes stood open to the soldiers, the town's defenders. The big houses from Washington Street to Peachtree Street blazed with lights, as the muddy fighters in from the rifle pits were entertained, and the sound of banjo and fiddle and the scrape of dancing feet and light laughter carried far on the night air. Groups hung over pianos and voices sang lustily the sad words of "Your Letter Came but Came Too Late" while ragged gallants looked meaningly at girls who laughed from behind turkey-tail fans, begging them not to wait until it was too late. None of the girls waited, if they could help it. With the tide of hysterical gaiety and excitement flooding the city, they rushed into matrimony. There were so many marriages that month while Johnston was holding the enemy at Kennesaw Mountain, marriages with the bride turned out in blushing happiness and the hastily borrowed finery of a dozen friends and the groom with saber banging at patched knees. So much excitement, so many parties, so many thrills! Hurrah! Johnston is holding the Yanks twenty-two miles away!

Yes, the lines around Kennesaw Mountain were impregnable....

With the loss of the supposedly unconquerable position, a fresh wave of terror swept the town. For twenty-five wild, happy days, everyone had assured everyone else that this could not possibly happen. And now it had happened! But surely the General would hold the Yankees on the opposite bank of the river. Though God knows the river was close enough, only seven miles away!

—Margaret Mitchell, *Gone With the Wind*, 1936

Carving of Confederate generals Robert E. Lee and Stonewall Jackson and of Confederate president Jefferson Davis on the side of Stone Mountain.

◆ STONE MOUNTAIN

Located just 15 miles east of Atlanta, this 825-foot-tall dome of stone rises from the Piedmont like an apparition. Though quarrying operations over the years have removed some of the granite for use in projects as varied as the Panama Canal and the U.S. Capitol, what stuns the first-time viewer is what remains: a massive rock, gray and imposing, with tufts of greenery jutting out improbably from the sides and top.

At the foot of the rock is the town of Stone Mountain, which, despite its obvious tourist bent, exudes a great deal of charm. Old storefronts face on the railroad tracks. White clapboard homes line the narrow streets. The city was late to develop, but by 1839 a settlement had begun to grow at the base of the mountain, soon becoming home to stonecutters and other laborers.

In the early years of the 20th century, when the South was awash in efforts to commemorate the Lost Cause, Helen Plane, a charter member of the United Daughters of the Confederacy, began what would be a nearly 60-year campaign to honor the Confederate heroes with a grand sculpture. The result of her efforts is a

ATLANTA

Sculptor Gutzon Borglum shows a Cherokee princess his work on Stone Mountain in 1924. (Underwood Photo Archives, San Francisco)

90-foot-tall bas-relief on the face of Stone Mountain depicting Confederate president Jefferson Davis and Generals Stonewall Jackson and Robert E. Lee. Among the early sculptors to work on the project was Gutzon Borglum, who designed the carving on Mount Rushmore. When finally completed in the 1970s, this sculpture became the world's largest bas-relief.

Today, the effect of the sculpture is somewhat peculiar—what with Davis, Lee, and Jackson mounted on horseback and presiding over a metropolitan Atlanta area so far removed from its Old South. Beneath them, the park teems with visitors who have come to ride the railway, hike the 1.3-mile trail to the summit, view the antique cars on display, or bask on a white-sand beach and swim and fish in the lakes that ring the mountain. *770-498-5600; Stone Mountain Freeway.*

◆ DECATUR   *map page 141, C-3*

Six miles west of Stone Mountain—six miles closer to Atlanta—is the graceful town of Decatur. At once antiquated and up to date, Decatur is a great mix of yesterday's charm and today's attitudes. Suburban sprawl seems not so much absent as arrested here. At the center of town stands the imposing Old Dekalb County Courthouse, built in 1898, while the surrounding blocks are filled with sidewalk cafes, antique shops, and galleries. Ponce de Leon Avenue, the same thoroughfare that cuts slices through Atlanta's in-town neighborhoods, is the main drag.

Home to a sizeable contingent of post-hippies, longhair intellectuals, and college students—the latter attending Emory University or Agnes Scott, a women's college—the town has a reputation as the most tolerant of Atlanta's suburban communities. For evidence, look no further than the local gardening and social club, The Digging Dykes of Decatur, who have been known to march in local parades, pushing toy lawnmowers and chanting playfully, "We're here. We're queer. We garden!"

◆ MORELAND   *map page 163, A-3*

At the lower end of the socioeconomic scale is the little burg of Moreland, some 25 or so miles southwest of Atlanta. The village center is a forlorn place where simple storefronts look as timeworn as the stray dogs that loll about on the front porches of the town's simple clapboard homes. Hard by the railroad tracks is writer Erskine Caldwell's birthplace, known as the **Little Manse**. Caldwell, author of such works as *Tobacco Road* and *God's Little Acre,* was one of the most popular novelists of the first half of the 20th century; his 55 novels sold more than 80 million copies altogether. *Chamber of Commerce, 770-253-2270.*

Caldwell used his bully pulpit to decry the harshness of rural life. In *You Have Seen Their Faces,* a project he undertook with his wife, photographer Margaret Bourke-White, he wrote: "Tobacco Road is a thoroughfare of indeterminable length through every state in the Union. Sometimes it is an alley, sometimes it is a paved highway; now it is a dirt road through Arkansas, now it is a boulevard through Massachusetts." Erskine Caldwell Birthplace Museum: *One East Camp Street; 770-251-4438.*

Sunset over Atlanta, as seen from the top of Stone Mountain.

Atlanta Food & Lodging

✗ **Restaurant Prices:** $ = under $10; $$ = $10–20; $$$ = over $20
Restaurant price designations indicate the approximate cost of an entrée and an appetizer or desert, exclusive of drinks, tax, and tip.

🛏 **Lodging Rates:** $ = under $75; $$ = $75–150; $$$ = over $150
Lodging rate designations indicate the approximate cost of a double occupancy room for one night, exclusive of surcharges and taxes.

Atlanta Neighborhoods

Please consult the maps on pages 116–117 to locate the neighborhoods listed below.

Buckhead

Atlanta's temples of haute cuisine are found here, in the city's most exclusive suburb. Trends come and go—as do a great number of restaurants—but for the most part, the restaurants profiled below have been around a while, enduring the vicissitudes of the marketplace more because they transcend trendiness than because they reject it.

✗ **Anis Café**
404-233-9889; 2974 Grandview Ave.
An unpretentious little restaurant, serving the foods of Provence to a loyal cadre of French expats and in-the-know Atlantans. The salad niçoise and shrimp a l'anis are favorites. Lunch, dinner. $-$$

✗ **Atlanta Fish Market**
404-262-3165; 265 Pharr Rd.
Set in a building that looks like an old railroad station passenger shed but was

actually built for the restaurant, this is the place to find impeccably fresh seafood, simply prepared. Try the grilled grouper cheeks—they have the texture and sweetness of lobster—served on a bowl of grits. Lunch and dinner. $$-$$$

✕ **Bacchanalia**
404-365-0410; 3125 Piedmont Rd.
Tables at this restaurant, in a renovated Tudor home, are some of the hardest-won in town. A prix fixe menu of such delights as a crab fritter in orange broth and foie gras atop charred scallops is well paired to the inventive—and exclusively American—wine list. For dessert try a cheese plate featuring the best from regional American fromageries. Dinner. $$$

✕ **Bone's Restaurant**
404-237-2663; 3130 Piedmont Rd.
Regulars are treated to a car wash while dining at this clubby steakhouse. Thick cuts of beef are dry-aged, and the service is superb but not fawning. You enter through the bar, where blue-suited swells swill martinis and smoke bootlegged Cuban cigars. Lunch and dinner. $$$

✕ **Brasserie Le Coze**
404-266-1440; 3393 Peachtree Rd., Lenox Square
Though set in the midst of a shopping mall, this stylish restaurant is the most genuinely Gallic in Atlanta, with mirrors lining the wall and an authentic French menu. Cassoulet, rillettes, and fish dishes are best bets. Lunch, dinner. $$-$$$

✕ **Buckhead Diner**
404-262-3336; 3073 Piedmont Rd.
A stunning tribute to the roadside diners of old, albeit with super-luxe food. Favorites include homemade potato chips, with Maytag blue cheese crumbled atop, and a sublime veal meatloaf laced with wild mushrooms. Lunch and dinner. $$$

✕ **Buckhead Bread Company**
404-240-1978; 3070 Piedmont Rd.
Under the same ownership as the diner —part of the omnipresent Buckhead Life restaurant chain. Turns out more than 20 varieties of artisanal breads as well as muffins, cookies, and pastries galore. And there's a cafe on-site, serving sandwiches and the like. Breakfast, lunch, and dinner. $

✕ **Fellini's Pizza**
404-266-0082; 2813 Peachtree Rd.
This local mini-chain started out next door in a narrow storefront. Now they have a corner lot and a huge courtyard out front with a fountain. But the simple formula endures: cheap, tasty, thin-crust pizza with a myriad of toppings available, served by the slice or pie. Monstrous calzones and iffy salads are also offered. Lunch, dinner, and late-night. $

✕ **Imperial Fez**
404-351-0870; 2285 Peachtree Rd.
As much a show as a restaurant. Belly dancers shimmy through the dining room amid patrons feasting on lamb shish kabob and partridge beesteya. Be prepared to shed your shoes, take a seat on the floor, and eat Moroccan-style: with your hands. $$

✕ **La Grotta Ristorante Italiano**
404-231-1368; 2637 Peachtree Rd.
Atlanta's oldest grand Italian restaurant. Located in the basement of a chi-chi apartment building, the dining room exudes a grotto-like charm. And the cuisine, ranging from a simple grilled veal chop to ravioli stuffed with goat cheese, is near perfect. Great wine list, heavy on Italian reds. Dinner. $$$

✕ **Prime**
404-812-0555; 3393 Peachtree Rd.,
Lenox Square
Sushi and prime steaks are proffered at this latter-day version of the surf-and-turf house. The bar makes a fine martini, perfect for taking the edge off a day of shopping. Lunch and dinner. $$-$$$

✕ **Seeger's**
404-846-9779; 111 West Paces Ferry Rd.
When chef Guenter Seeger left his long-time post at the Ritz-Carlton Dining Room, he made headlines in the local paper. Set in a converted home on the edge of the Buckhead business district, his new restaurant is decorated in a style that fuses austerity and opulence, old and new. The prix fixe menu features such seasonal offerings as a beet salad with shrimp and champagne, and sea urchin soup. Since day one, the national food press has fallen at Seeger's knees, heaping accolade upon accolade, award upon award. But all this excellence and opulence comes with a price: the tab for three- and six-course dinners is the highest of any restaurant in Atlanta. Dinner. $$$

✕ **Soto Japanese Restaurant**
404-233-2005; 3330 Piedmont Rd.
The best sushi restaurant in Atlanta—and perhaps one of the top five in America. The interior is drab, but behind the bar, chef Sotohiro Kosugi sparkles. In addition to impeccably prepared—and artfully arranged—maki and sashimi, this quiet perfectionist creates daily specials that look almost jewel-like. The fatty tuna is always exceptional. Dinner. $$$

⌂ **Beverly Hills Inn**
404-233-8520; 65 Sheridan Dr.
Eighteen rooms, each with a balcony, are available at this lovely inn, tucked away on a residential side street just off Peachtree. Well equipped for business travelers— dataport phones and fax services available—this European-style hotel is a wonderful alternative to the nearby high-rise hotels. Continental breakfast is served in the garden room each morning. $$

⌂ **Embassy Suites Hotel**
404-261-7733; 3285 Peachtree Rd.
This 16-story hotel has a towering atrium at its heart. More than 300 suites are available, each with refrigerator, microwave, and coffeemaker. In the morning, there is a complimentary breakfast buffet. And in the evening, cocktails are on the house. $$-$$$

⌂ **Four Points Sheraton**
404-261-5500; 3387 Lenox Rd.
Across the street from sprawling Lenox Square, this low-rise hotel is not as luxu-

rious as its neighbors, but it does offer amenities like free continental breakfast and evening cocktails. There are more than 175 rooms and two outdoor swimming pools. It's the best bargain in Buckhead. $$

GRAND HYATT

⌂ **Grand Hyatt Hotel**
404-365 8100; 3300 Peachtree Rd.
This 25-story postmodern skyscraper was built by a Japanese concern before being taken over by Hyatt. There's still a dash of the Orient about the place, as evidenced by the Japanese rock garden just beyond the lobby. Rooms, however—appointed with such luxuries as marble bathrooms—are pure American indulgence. $$$

⌂ **Ritz-Carlton Buckhead**
404-237-2700; 3434 Peachtree Rd.
This is the flagship of the Ritz-Carlton chain. It may look like yet another high-rise hotel, but the level of service ranks

perennially among the best in the world. Tasteful elegance prevails in the lobby and in the well-appointed rooms. Atlanta's power brokers gather in the lobby bar for early evening cocktails. $$$

⌂ **Swissôtel Atlanta**
404-365-0065; 3391 Peachtree Rd.
Modern art and Swiss efficiency meet in this streamlined beauty of a hotel, located between Lenox Mall and the Atlanta Financial Center. The Biedermeier-style furniture gives the ultramodern facility a human scale and warmth. 365 rooms. $$$

SWISSÔTEL ATLANTA

Downtown/Auburn Ave.

✗ **Barker's Charbroiled Red Hots**
404-584-8518; corner of Peachtree and Ellis, and various locations
Served from little portable carts, these incised, grilled tubes of beef are heaven on a bun. Lunch. $

✗ **City Grill**
404-524-2489; 50 Hurt Plaza
An elegant oasis in the middle of Down-

town, housed in the former lobby of a landmark neoclassical granite building, with an interior graced by pastoral murals. Favorites are crab cakes atop a bed of lemon linguini, and trout stuffed with sage-scented dressing and napped with a brown butter vinaigrette. The wine list is diverse and well priced. Lunch and dinner. $$$

✗ Mumbo Jumbo
404-523-0330; 89 Park Place
Run by one of Guenter Seeger's protégés, this is the hottest lunch spot downtown. Look for lobster bisque or truffle-laced chicken salad. The interior is an urbane mix of gothic and modern, trendy and tasteful. At night, the beautiful-people-in-black make this their haunt. Lunch and dinner. $$-$$$

✗ Thelma's Kitchen
404-688-5855; 768 Marietta St.
Owner Thelma Spurlock is famous for her okra patties—and rightly so. Truth be told, just about everything that emerges from her tidy kitchen is a paragon of soul food excellence. Locals grumble that the price—$6-plus per head—is steeper than it should be. Lunch. $

⛨ Omni Hotel at CNN Center
404-659-0000; 100 CNN Center
Conveniently located, the Omni has 458 rooms and caters to business travelers. Full-service health club. $$$

⛨ Westin Peachtree Plaza
404-659-1400; 210 Peachtree St. NW
One of the tallest hotels in the world, this steel-and-glass tower has more than 1,000 rooms and a five-floor atrium lobby that bustles with activity. $$$

⛨ Hyatt Regency Atlanta
404-577-1234; 265 Peachtree St. NE
Built in 1967, this 1,200-room hotel was the first ever to be designed around a huge interior atrium. Top-of-the-line amenities and services. $$$

⛨ Ritz-Carlton Downtown
404-659-0400; 181 Peachtree St. NE
Downtown's most opulent hotel, with 450 rooms and a lobby that drips with luxurious details including marble floors and Persian rugs. Impeccable service. $$$

⛨ The Suite Hotel at Underground Atlanta
404-223-5555; 54 Peachtree St. NE
All the rooms at this understated, elegant, 16-story hotel are suites. $$$-$$$

Emory/Decatur

✗ Burrito Art
404-377-7786; 1451 Oxford Rd.
An outpost of the original East Atlanta location, serving upscale burritos stuffed with Thai chicken and other unlikely but tasty ingredients. Lunch and dinner. $-$$

✗ Floataway Cafe
404-892-1414; 1123 Zonolite Rd.
From the folks who brought you Bacchanalia *(see page 149)*, this hotspot is casual and chic, rather than formal—you'll have to look for it among the warehouses, and it *is* loud—but the food is absolutely perfect. Try the piccolo fritto, then a hanger steak with frites. $$

ATLANTA

FOOD & LODGING

✗ Our Way Cafe
404-373-6665; 303 East College Ave.,
Decatur
These folks do vegetables proud. Cream
corn is a paragon of flavor: fresh-scraped
kernels simmered in a sauce tasting of
butter and cream and little else. Squash
casserole and butter beans are without
peer in the city. Not to neglect the fried
chicken or meatloaf, both of which are
sure to satisfy. The atmosphere is tidy,
unfussy, like that of a classic small-town
cafe. Lunch. $

✗ The Supper Club
404-370-1207; 308 West Ponce de
Leon Ave, Decatur
This romantic enclave is tucked into a
strip mall just off Ponce. But don't let
that dissuade you; take one step inside
this intimate cafe and you leave reality
behind. The lighting is soft; the decorations are a charming, avant-garde mix of
opulent ornamentation and flea market
bric-a-brac. The wine list is an engaging
showcase for lesser-known varietals like
Syrahs and Malbecs. And the menu features such delights as savory crepes laced
with cheese, and ethereal steamed mus-
sels perfumed with citrus. Dinner. $$-$$$

✗ Violette
404-633-3363; 2948 Clairmont Rd.
This is hearty French food at its best:
meaty house-made patés, garlicky snails,
heady platters of couscous. Try the
quiche Lorraine; it belies the stereotype.
Lunch and dinner. $$-$$$

✗ Watershed
404-378-4900; 406 West Ponce de
Leon Ave., Decatur
As much a gourmet grocery as a restaurant. But with Indigo Girl Emily Saliers
at the helm and consulting chef Scott
Peacock around the stove, this new arrival on the Decatur dining scene shows
great promise. Lunch and dinner. $$

⌂ Emory Inn
404-712-6700; 1641 Clifton Rd.
Situated on more than 10 acres in the
midst of the bustling Emory medical
corridor, this 100-plus room hotel pro-
vides a tranquil and welcome respite
from the harried activity just steps away.
On wintry evenings, the lobby lounge
with its fireplace is a favorite gathering
spot. $$-$$$

⌂ Houston Mill House
404-727-7878; 849 Houston Mill Rd.
Set in a graceful clapboard and field-
stone home near the Emory University
campus, this B&B has two rooms up-
stairs, one with a queen bed and one
with two twins. It's a peaceful retreat,
and quite reasonable to boot. $-$$

Grant Park/ East Atlanta

✗ Burrito Art
404-627-4433; 1259 Glenwood Ave.
Not a survivor of the short-lived "wrap"
craze, but an innovative restaurant
where burritos are stuffed with uncom-
mon combinations like Thai chicken

and jasmine rice. A mixed clientele of local hipsters and adventurous yuppies adds to the scene. Lunch, dinner. $-$$

✕ **Grant Central Pizza**
404-523-8900; 451 Cherokee Ave.
Thin-crust pies are the favorites at this neighborhood dive. The location, just a few blocks from the park, makes it perfect for an afternoon bite and beer. Lunch and dinner. $

✕ **Heaping Bowl and Brew**
404-523-8030; 469 Flat Shoals Rd.
One of the pioneering businesses in the emerging East Atlanta neighborhood. Stews and jumbles of rice and vegetables are the draw at this funky kitchen. Lunch and dinner. $

Inman Park Area

✕ **The Flying Biscuit Cafe**
404-687-8888; 1655 McLendon Ave.
A mile north of Inman Park is the Candler Park area, where you'll find this relaxed neighborhood gathering place. The turkey meatloaf and ethereal biscuits draw crowds, especially at Sunday brunch. Breakfast, lunch, Sunday brunch, and dinner. $-$$

✕ **Son's Place**
404-581-0530; 100 Hurt St.
Run by Lenn Story, heir to the legacy of Atlanta's fabled fry cook, Deacon Burton. Some say Story's fried chicken is almost as good as the late Deacon's. If that's so, it's surely the best in town. For breakfast, try a salmon croquette stuffed inside a biscuit. For lunch, sop up your potlikker with a hoecake. Cafeteria-style service. Breakfast and lunch. $

⌂ **King-Keith House**
404-688-7330; 889 Edgewood Ave.
This Victorian "painted lady" has three guestrooms, each with a private bath. Twelve-foot ceilings and ornate carved fireplaces give this inn a regal, if a bit dowdy, air. A full breakfast is included in the tariff. $$

⌂ **Sugar Magnolia**
404-222-0226; 804 Edgewood Ave.
The most opulent B&B south of Buckhead. Built in 1892, this Victorian has a rooftop deck that offers a panoramic view of downtown Atlanta, and each of the three rooms has a working fireplace. Out back, there's a cottage suite. Business services provided. $$

Little Five Points

L5P is more a place to drink and play than eat. But you will find two drinking establishments with great bar food, as well as a great paella purveyor and a lively Caribbean restaurant.

✕ **Bridgetown Grill**
404-653-0110; 1156 Euclid Ave.
These folks were serving jerk chicken to Atlantans before jerk was cool. Join the hipper-than-thou and slumming suburbanites for a supper of slightly Americanized Jamaican fare. Stick to the basics and you will be well rewarded. The brightly painted courtyard out back booms with the sound of reggae music. Lunch and dinner. $-$$

X **Euclid Avenue Yacht Club**
404-688-2582; 1136 Euclid Ave.
A neighborhood institution, famous for its great beer selection and superior bar food. House-made pimento cheese on marbled rye, near-perfect chilidogs, sloppy cheesesteak sandwiches, and spicy Brunswick stew are perennial favorites. The bar draws an eclectic crowd, from local politicos to bikers; visitors of all hometowns and hues are welcomed. Lunch, dinner, and late-night. $

X **La Fonda Latina**
404-577-8317; 1150-B Euclid Ave.
Serves a great skilletful of cheap paella: yellow rice studded with squid, chorizo sausage, shrimp, and various vegetables. The setting—a courtyard facing on an alley—is either scruffy or charmingly funky, depending on your perspective. Lunch and dinner. $

X **The Vortex**
404-688-1828; 438 Moreland Ave.
A two-story skull, its eyes oscillating wildly, graces the façade of this corner bar. Inside, servers dish attitude and great burgers. And the beer selection is outstanding. Lunch, dinner, and late-night. $

☷ **General lodging information**
There are no hotels in Little Five Points proper, but in Inman Park you will find two lovely B&Bs *(see previous page)*.

Midtown

X **Agnes and Muriel's**
404-885-1000; 1514 Monroe Dr.
This paean to the '50s—located, like many Atlanta restaurants, in a converted bungalow home—serves oversize portions of comfort food for the '90s. Amid a swirl of Jetson-inspired furnishings, servers sling platters heaped high with meatloaf, mashed potatoes, and inventive takes on the traditional—salmon potpie, for instance. Lunch and dinner. $$

X **French Quarter Food Shop**
404-875-2489; 923 Peachtree St.
Muffulettas, po-boys, and etouffée served in a no-nonsense setting that was once home to Atlanta's premier "gentleman's club," this busy New Orleans–style neighborhood eatery packs 'em in at lunch. Lunch and dinner. $$

X **Kool Korner**
404-892-4424; 349 14th St.
The Cuban sandwiches served here are some of the best to be found north of Miami. The setting, a scruffy grocery store, isn't much to look at, and the location isn't very convenient, but the mojo-scented wonders that emanate from this tiny kitchen are worth any inconvenience. Lunch. $

X **Krispy Kreme Donuts**
404-876-7307; 295 Ponce de Leon Ave.
When the "Hot Donuts Now" sign is flashing, and the little yeasty donuts are rolling off the assembly line, dripping

icing and calories, all of Atlanta seems to converge on this one spot. Open 24 hours a day. $

✕ Mary Mac's Tea Room
404-876-1800; 224 Ponce de Leon Ave. A long-lived Atlanta institution, the place to come for a cup of potlikker or a platter of country-fried steak with mashed potatoes and gravy. You fill out your own ticket, hand it to the waitress, and, quick as a wink, she's back with your order. Lunch and dinner.$

✕ Pasta da Pulcinella
404-892-6195; 1027 Peachtree St. Authentic regional Italian pastas for about the price of a trip to the Wendy's salad bar! Place your order at the counter, snag a bottle of good red wine, and wait for the server to bring your entree. Try the tortelli stuffed with Granny Smith apples and sausage, topped with a brown-butter and sage sauce. Lunch and dinner. $$

✕ Silver Grill
404-876-8145; 900 Monroe Dr. An unpretentious place that survived the gentrification of the surrounding neighborhood. Plate lunches and dinners are still served by waitresses who call you honey and darling— without the least hint of affectation. The monstrous fried chicken breasts are the most popular items on the menu. Lunch and dinner. $

✕ South City Kitchen
404-873-7358; 1144 Crescent Ave. Occupies a renovated two-story bungalow just off Peachtree Street. The food is

a twist on Southern traditions: gussied-up standards include fried green tomatoes with a bit of goat cheese. Stone-ground grits are used as a foil for everything from pork to fish. For dessert try the white chocolate banana cream pie. Lunch and dinner. $$-$$$

✕ The Varsity
404-881-1706; 61 North Ave. Opened in 1928 by Georgia Tech dropout Frank Gordy, the Varsity lays claim to the title "world's largest drive-in." Though carhops still work the parking lot, most everyone eats insidenow, feasting on greasy chilidogs smothered in slaw, burgers crowned with pimento cheese, near-perfect onion rings, and fresh, if a bit limp, fries. Wash it all down with an F.O.—a frosted orange drink—and should you have room for dessert, make it the fried peach pie, a crescent of deep-fried dough and sugary peach pulp. Breakfast, lunch, dinner. $

THE VARSITY

✕ Veni Vidi Vici
404-875-8424; 41 14th St. Northern Italian food served in a swank

setting is the draw here. Try the gnocchi in pesto or the grilled suckling pig. Or just order an appetizer and a cocktail to enjoy on the patio while playing a game of bocce ball (yes, they have a court). Lunch and dinner. $$-$$$

✕ Vickery's
404-881-1106; 1106 Crescent Ave.
Recently rehabbed, this Midtown favorite has one of the best outdoor dining areas in town, a brick patio beneath the boughs of a monstrous hardwood. Cuban-influenced menu items excel. And the bar scene rocks late into the night. Lunch, dinner, and late-night. $$

✕ The Vortex
404-875-1667; 878 Peachtree St.
The mother bar to the Little Five Points branch, this Peewee's Playhouse–inspired den of iniquity serves a great pimento cheeseburger (an upscale version of the Varsity's). Great beer selection. Lunch, dinner, and late-night. $

✕ Zócalo
404-249-7576; 187 10th St.
This colorful corner restaurant serves Atlanta's most authentic regional Mexican food. The mole sauce is a paragon of flavor, rich with chocolate and dark as Satan's own heart. And the patio is the perfect place to soak up a little sun and sip a premium tequila. Lunch, dinner. $$

⛫ Ansley Inn
404-872-9000; 253 15th St.
Once the home of retailing magnate George Muse, this 1907 Tudor home is now one of the best B&Bs in town. Tucked away off Peachtree Street in the exclusive Ansley Park neighborhood, the inn has 25 rooms, each with a Jacuzzi bath, while the common areas are rich with Oriental rugs. $$$

ANSLEY INN

⛫ Days Inn
404-874-9200; 683 Peachtree St.
Once known as the York Hotel, this somber, brick-fronted hostelry is directly across the street from the Fox Theatre, making it the perfect choice for concert- and theatergoers. Decorated like a 19th-century men's club, the property displays a charm rarely, if ever, associated with a Days Inn. $$

⛫ Four Seasons Hotel
404-881-9898; 75 14th St.
Recently acquired by the Four Seasons chain, this is the swankest hotel in Midtown and one of the most luxurious in the entire city. Occupying the bottom 20 floors of a 50-plus-story skyscraper of pink granite, the hotel has almost 250 rooms, each dripping with opulence and decorated with original artwork. $$$

⌂ **Georgian Terrace Hotel**
404-897-1991; 659 Peachtree St.
Until recently, this was a super-luxe apartment building. Now a favorite for long-term stays, the hotel boasts such unlikely amenities as a rooftop pool with a commanding view of the city below. Fans of *Gone With the Wind* book rooms here, armed with the knowledge that this was the host hostelry for the movie's premier. $$-$$$

⌂ **Shellmont Bed-and-Breakfast**
404-872-9290; 821 Piedmont Ave.
Just a few blocks from Piedmont Park, this 1891 mansion has five rooms in the main house, as well as a carriage house in the rear. Nicer than its neighbor the Woodruff, the Shellmont is decorated with Victorian-era antiques and serves a gourmet breakfast. $$

⌂ **Sheraton Colony Square**
404-892-6000; 188 14th St.
At the center of the Colony Square retail and office complex, this 450-room hotel is a favorite of conventioneers. The erection of this building in the late 1960s was the catalyst for Midtown's resurgence. With a location across the street from the High Museum, it's a great headquarters from which to begin your explorations of in-town Atlanta. $$

⌂ **Woodruff Bed-and-Breakfast**
404-875-9449; 223 Ponce de Leon Ave.
On the southern fringe of Midtown, this inn was once a house of ill repute.

Today, thanks to a 1989 renovation, the 12 rooms (8 with private bath) are now occupied not by ladies of the evening but by businesspeople seeking an alternative to the chains, along with vacationers who use it as a base for exploring Midtown and nearby Virginia-Highland and Little Five Points. $$

⌂ **Wyndham Hotel**
404-873-4800; 125 10th St.
At the epicenter of Midtown—and just a short stroll from the park, the High Museum, and a number of restaurants and bars—this 11-story property feels small in scale despite its nearly 200 rooms. Rooms are well appointed, equipped with such amenities as coffeemakers and dataport phones. $$-$$$

Virginia-Highland

A stroll along North Highland Avenue from Ponce de Leon to University Avenue offers up a two-mile buffet of culinary options, from simple to fancy, from tuna salad sandwiches to sesame-crusted grilled ahi tuna with a citrus beurre blanc.

✗ **Alon's Bakery**
404-872-6000; 1394 N. Highland Ave.
Home to Atlanta's best cookies—with chunks of pecans and chocolate—as well as superior roster of sandwiches, the best of the bunch being smoked turkey with pesto on house-baked French country bread. Take-out only. Breakfast, lunch, and early dinner. $

X **Aurora Coffee**
404-607-1300; 992 N. Highland Ave.
Run by Seattle expatriates, Aurora proffers the city's best cup of coffee—or espresso or latte for that matter. Three other locations dot the in-town neighborhoods, but this location—at the heart of Virginia-Highland—is the best for people-watching and coffee-sipping. $

X **Camille's**
404-872-7203; 1186 N. Highland Ave.
One of the first restaurants in Atlanta to do calamari right. Fried and dipped in a heady red sauce, the little rings of squid still taste great. as do the pizzas and pastas. An unassuming interior and a welcoming staff make this a wonderful place to kick back for a Sunday evening feast. And there's a good wine list, heavy on Italian and Californian reds. Dinner. $$

X **Dish**
404-897-3463; 870 N. Highland Ave.
They used to pump regular at this Tudor-style former filling station, but now chef Sheri Clarke is turning out accomplished fusion cuisine in a futuristic setting. Fish dishes excel. Great wine selection. Dinner. $$-$$$

X **Highland Bagel**
404-897-5280; 832 N. Highland Ave.
Housed in a former laundromat, and they boil their bagels before they bake 'em. Try an onion bagel smeared with lox spread and a glass of fresh-squeezed orange juice. Or just grab a cup of coffee and a seat on the patio and watch the world whirl by. Breakfast and lunch. $

X **Indigo**
404-876-0676; 1397 N. Highland Ave.
A funky fish camp for urbane in-towners. Popular for fresh daily catches baked en papillotte as well as grilled shellfish and, for dessert, the city's best Key lime pie. Dinner. $$-$$$

X **Majestic Food Shop**
404-875-0276; 1031 Ponce de Leon Ave.
The neon signs reads "Food That Pleases Since 1929," but the entertainment may well be a bigger draw than the straightahead diner fare. There's always a late-night scene at this joint, where clientele and waitstaff provide the show. When it comes to people-watching, the Majestic has it all: snippy waitresses, beat cops, and local freaks galore. Open 24 hours. $

X **Moe's and Joe's**
404-873-6090; 1033 North Highland Ave.
They've been around since 1947, long before Virginia-Highland became in-town Atlanta's most popular neighborhood. The burgers and fries are just okay, but the Pabst is cold, the service is friendly, and a sidewalk table may be the best perch in the city. Lunch, dinner, and late-night. $$

X **Rocky's Brick Oven Pizza**
404-872-9331; 1394 -D North Highland Ave.
Crisp, thin, New York–style pizzas

topped with rosemary potatoes or Gorgonzola cheese emerge from the wood-fired brick ovens. Slide into one of the vinyl booths with a few friends and eat a pie or two. Lunch and dinner. $-$$

✕ Terra Cotta

404-853-7888; 1044 Greenwood Ave.

A casual delight, set in a brick bungalow home where the overhead beams have been replaced by high-tension cables. Try the pork tenderloin with shiitake mushrooms, or any of the vegetarian towers. Dinner. $$-$$$

✕ Virginia's Koffie and Thee Cafe

404-875-4453; 1243 Virginia Ave.

This cozy neighborhood coffeehouse has everything you'd want it to: a funky, comfortable interior, a covered patio, lots of magazines to read, and tasty sandwiches and sweets—plus all the usual coffee drinks, and a huge tea selection. $

⛨ General Lodging Information

There are no traditional hotels in the Virginia-Highland neighborhood. Visitors who prefer such accommodations might stay in Midtown, just a couple of miles to the west.

⛨ Gaslight Inn

404-876-1001; 1001 St. Charles Ave.

A gaslight at the curb lends the name to this two-story bungalow situated near the heart of Virginia-Highland. Six rooms, all with private bath, are available. $$-$$$

GASLIGHT INN

⛨ Virginia-Highland Bed-and-Breakfast

404-892-2735; 630 Orme Circle

This 1920 Craftsman-style bungalow fits in well with its surroundings and is just a short walk from Piedmont Park or the intersection of Virginia and Highland Avenues. Two rooms, each with private bath and separate entrance, are furnished with antiques. $$-$$$

West End

✕ Aleck's Barbecue Heaven

404-525-2062; 783 Martin Luther King Jr. Dr.

Martin Luther King Jr. ate ribs here. So should you. Smoke-imbued and tender as a mother's love, these ribs are among the best to be had in Atlanta. Look for the booth in the back where King and his compatriots once caucused over rib sandwiches and sweet tea. Lunch and early dinner. $

✕ **Harold's Barbecue**
404-627-9268; 171 McDonough Blvd., south and east of West End
A venerable Atlanta 'cue shack, in business since 1947. The smoked pork and Brunswick stew draw fans from across the city. And the cracklin' cornbread is without peer. Lunch and early dinner. $

✕ **Heath's Grocery**
404-755-0543; 787 Cascade Ave. SW
A few miles south of West End, but it's worth the drive. Belly up to the steam table for some of the best collard greens and cornbread on the planet. Decor is nonexistent and the food is available for takeout only, but if you wanted something fancy, you wouldn't be here in the first place. Lunch. $

✕ **Satterwhite's**
404-756-0963; 851 Oak St.
404-758-9825; 590 Cascade Ave.
This simple cafeteria, with two locations in southwest Atlanta, may well serve the city's best macaroni & cheese. Breakfast, lunch, and dinner. $

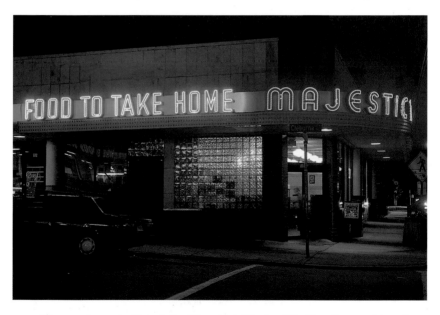

The neon sign at the Majestic Food Store reads "Food to Take Home" on one side and "Food That Pleases" around the corner.

ATLANTA
FOOD & LODGING

MIDDLE GEORGIA

■ TRAVEL BASICS

Running in a line east to west across Middle Georgia are the cities of Augusta, Macon, and Columbus; along with the state's academic citadel of Athens, located to the north, these cities are the heart and soul of the region. Their revitalized downtowns are flanked by lovely tree-shaded boulevards and graceful homes. On the outskirts of each, urban life quickly recedes as you enter pine forests and trace your way down roadways lined with red clay. The region has two significant Native American sites: Rock Eagle Effigy Mound and Ocmulgee National Monument.

Getting Around: Wander the back roads that link the cities. Middle Georgia's towns are all easily explored on foot, so get out of the car and meander the back streets lined with bungalows and Victorian painted ladies.

Climate: Mild winters with occasional cold outbreaks; temperatures in the 50s F; snow rare. Very hot and humid summers with frequent thunderstorms; temperatures in the low to mid-90s. Fall is usually dry and pleasant .

Food & Lodging: With a few notable exceptions, Middle Georgia is not the home of haute cuisine and high-falutin' hotels. That is not to say the region is without charm. You'll find wonderful cafes where country cooking is raised to an art form, and roadside barbecue joints where pork is smoldered for hours before being pulled from the bone and napped with a thin sauce tasting of peppers, vinegar, and just the slightest hint of tomato. You'll also find antebellum inns that have been lovingly restored, and grand old hotels that still sparkle with the charms of yesteryear. For food and lodging listings, see pages 200 to 211.

■ OVERVIEW

The region of Middle Georgia cuts across the center of the state, separating the bustle and boosterism of metropolitan Atlanta from the languor of southern Georgia. At its core are the towns of Augusta, Macon, and Columbus, urban outcroppings in an otherwise rural region.

North and south of the urban corridor that stretches from Augusta on the east, through Macon, and on into Columbus on the state's western border, there are little-populated burgs and vast, open expanses of pine forests. Both can be found just a short detour down narrow two-lane blacktops that snake their way along the state's belly, past roadside produce stands and kudzu-shrouded trees that, in the heat of a sultry summer afternoon, look more like dada topiary than an unfortunate attempt to arrest soil erosion.

It is a region where the past and present seem locked in a slow and fitful dance, where billboards beckoning "Sons of Confederate Veterans Join Now!" share the roadside with the tumbledown houses of the sons of slaves, where ancient wizened women still sweep their dirt yards with handmade brooms and tend day lilies planted in old truck tires.

Along a Georgia two-lane blacktop between Atlanta and Athens. (photo by Kelly Duane)

Georgia Red Clay, *Nell Choate Jones, 1946. (Morris Museum of Art, Augusta)*

In the summer, the sweet perfume of honeysuckle can be almost overwhelming. In the winter, the roadsides bleed red with each heavy rain as the iron-rich soil washes onto the bleached gray pavement.

Though most Native Americans were removed to Oklahoma in the early 19th century, Middle Georgia is awash in physical reminders of a time when they were the sole inhabitants of the area. Near Eatonton stands the Rock Eagle Effigy Mound, a quartz-rock figure believed to date from the Woodland period, which began 3,000 years ago and ended 1,000 years ago. In Macon, the Ocmulgee Indian Mounds stand in mute tribute to the city-building efforts of the Late Mississippian–era people who thrived on the site around 1,000 years ago (the mounds area was settled again by members of the Creek Confederacy by the 1700s).

European settlement of Middle Georgia began in 1736 when settlers made their way up the river from Savannah to establish a trading outpost on the banks of the Savannah River. Like other towns established in the early years of the colony,

Augusta was founded at the fall line, the point at which rapid flowing rivers turn to churning torrents, signaling the end of the Savannah River as a navigable waterway. With the coming of the Industrial Revolution, the choice would prove to be prescient, as the rushing rivers could be harnessed to generate power for mills.

From Augusta, the population moved inland in search of fertile land. And with the people moved the seat of Georgia government, first from Savannah to Augusta in 1784, then west to Louisville, and later to Milledgeville, where it would remain throughout the Civil War.

At the beginning of the Civil War, Augusta, Macon, and Columbus were among the most prosperous towns in the state. Cotton, shipped by rail and river, was traded in local markets or woven by mills into cloth. During the war, munitions plants and other industries thrived. Though much of the region would wither under the onslaught of General Sherman's March to the Sea, the major towns escaped virtually unscathed.

SLEEPLESS NIGHTS—JULY 1864

From the diary of Dolly Burge, who lived on a central Georgia plantation at the time of Sherman's March to the Sea.

29TH

Last night was a sleepless one. At two o'clock I had the carriage at the door. Miss Mary took me out & showed me where she had buried the silver, then she, her brother, & Sally took the carriage for Madison, leaving me all alone again. I feel very much alarmed about them, fearing they will be molested.

All day I have walked about…. The Yankees left Covington for Macon headed by Stoneman to release prisoners held there. They robbed every house on the road of provisions, sometimes taking every piece of meat, blankets, & wearing apparel, silver & arms of every description. They would take silk dresses & put them under their saddles & things for which they had no use. Is this the way to make us love them & their union?

31ST

I slept scarcely none last night. We heard the enemy were below Sandtown destroying everything & that Wheeler was in pursuit. I was looking for them all night. I could hear their cannon. Sadai had the toothache. Mr. Rakestraw come in to dinner & wanted me to send him to Rutledge. I am so very lonely, no one passing.

—Dolly Lunt Burge, 1864, from *Diary of Dolly Lunt Burge*

After the war, rural areas returned to the business of cotton farming while the people of Athens set to work rebuilding a University, scarred by the decimation of its student population and a lack of capital. Through a cycle of boom and bust that lasted until World War II, the landscape and lifestyle remained little changed. But as tenant farmers left the farms for the lure of life in the North, small towns slowly began to sink into oblivion, and the larger cities of Middle Georgia ceased to grow.

The sole economic savior during those bleak years was the U.S. military. Augusta's Fort Gordon, Fort Benning near Columbus, and Warner Robins Air Force Base, just down the road from Macon, boomed during the Cold War years. But their growth, coupled with "white flight" to the suburbs in the 1970s, meant that city centers were virtual ghost towns.

Soon manufacturing concerns were deserting the core as well. Mills closed. Jobs were moved overseas. Until the late 1980s, Middle Georgia was stuck in a rut. At the end of the 20th century, however, the region took on a new vitality, as cities redeveloped their downtown core and manufacturing companies began building plants in the South, lured by the promise of cheap, nonunion labor, inexpensive land, and easy access to the growing distribution network that emanated outward from Atlanta.

Today, the same blacktop road that winds past a row of tumbledown houses—or past a gimme-capped farmer sitting in the shade of an oak tree, selling boiled peanuts—is likely to continue on past a sleek brick-and-steel manufacturing facility perched amid the old cotton fields.

■ AUGUSTA *map page 163, F-2*

Augusta is a city seduced by ghosts, where lineage matters more than acreage and the local genealogical society is housed in finer, more spacious quarters than the main public library. Here, upon encountering a native Augustan of a certain age, you are likely to be greeted with the question, "Who are your people?" rather than, "What do you do for a living?" In Augusta, say some detractors, you had best count three generations of ancestors as natives or be branded an interloper.

That is a far remove from Augusta's birth in 1736 as a frontier trading town and military outpost. At the behest of colonial governor James Oglethorpe, troops were stationed at the post in hopes of better regulating trade with Native American tribes, a venture so successful that by 1740 construction had begun on a road linking Augusta with the colony's other trading center, Savannah.

Sibley Cotton Mill, Augusta, Ga.

Hand-painted photograph postcard of the Sibley Cotton Mill, Augusta, circa 1900. (Augusta-Richmond County Museum, Augusta, collection of Joseph M. Lee, III)

Augusta's role as a center of trade would sustain it through the colonial, antebellum, and Reconstruction eras, as it grew to be the Deep South's largest inland cotton market. By the late 1800s Augusta was also a manufacturing center, boasting a newly built canal that serviced mills and other plants with water-driven power. Concurrently, thanks to the availability of rail travel and Augusta's temperate climate, the city became a vacation destination for frostbitten Northerners and malaria-threatened coastal Southerners.

Today, Augusta is indeed a town that revels in its past and pageantry, eager to showcase the grand mansions of the Summerville neighborhood and inclined to wax poetic about the beauty of the Augusta National Golf Course, home of the yearly Master's Tournament. And yes, there is a drowsy quality to life in this, the second largest city in Georgia.

But that is not the whole story. For an earful of the other Augusta, point your radio dial to native son James Brown's 94.7 FM as you take a turn though the heart of town—down the length of Broad Street, the primary artery of Augusta's urban renaissance. Serenaded by the soulful sounds of Ray Charles or the "hardest working man in show business" himself, you will discover a downtown on the upswing, rich with diversity and cultural adventure, where funky bars and burrito stands coexist with one of the South's great art museums, the Morris Museum of Art.

Riverwalk

The focal point of downtown Augusta's revitalization is the Riverwalk, a five-block promenade stretching along the Savannah River between Fifth and Tenth Streets. Atop the old levee and at water's edge, walkways wend past lush gardens, connecting many of the city's major cultural attractions. *Visitors Bureau: 32 Eighth Street; 706-823-6600.*

The Cotton Exchange.

Cotton Exchange

The graceful, brick-turreted Cotton Exchange was built in 1836 and renovated in 1988. Now serving as both a museum of cotton culture and a visitor's center, this is the place to take a gander at a sample box and learn the difference between fair and middling grades of cotton. Along the back wall, a 45-foot-high chalkboard uncovered during renovations still displays turn-of-the-century market quotes for everything from cotton futures to picnic hams. *Reynolds and Eighth Streets; 706-724-4067.*

Farmers bringing cotton to market, circa 1890. (Georgia Department of Archives & History)

MIDDLE GEORGIA

Augusta-Richmond County Museum

Two blocks east of the Cotton Exchange (at the corner of Sixth and Reynolds), the Augusta-Richmond County Museum— affectionately known as "Augusta's attic"— is bulging at its redbrick seams with an assortment of ephemera that tells the story of the region from prehistoric Indians through the 1970s. Children will delight at seeing the 1914 steam locomotive and tender. *560 Reynolds Street; 706-722-8454.*

National Science Center: Fort Discovery

Facing on the river itself, Fort Discovery is a brand-spanking-new museum that uses virtual reality and other interactive technologies to teach children about natural phenomena such as lightening bolts. *One Seventh Street (at Reynolds); 706-821-0200.*

Morris Museum of Art

Four blocks west along the Riverwalk is the only museum in the world dedicated solely to the art of the American South. Ten intimate galleries are filled with works by, among others, Ida Kohlmeyer, Lamar Dodd, John McCrady, and Benny Andrews. Among the most arresting pieces is a curved mural painted by John Mooney in 1868, titled *Surprise Attack Near Harper's Ferry.* It depicts Union soldiers bathing nude in the river, as seen through the eyes of a Confederate soldier just moments prior to attack. *One 10th Street; 706-724-7501.*

Broad Street

A few blocks south of the river, Broad Street has been undergoing a renaissance of sorts, from Eighth Street west to 13th

The Morris Museum in Augusta is one of the finest art museums in the South.

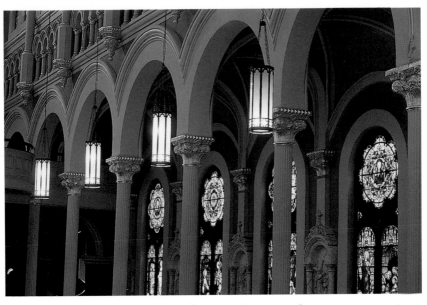

The Sacred Heart Cultural Center now hosts several Augusta performing arts organizations.

MIDDLE GEORGIA

Street. (On the lower end of Broad, signs still beckon servicemen into bars with names like Lucifer's Follies.) Art galleries and restaurants are the primary draw, but the architecturally inclined will want to take note of graceful old theaters like the candy-striped Modjeska and retrofitted skyscrapers like the Lamar Building. The Lamar is a 16-story hodgepodge of Gothic and Italianate styles, built in 1913 and topped in 1973 by a two-story concrete pyramid designed by architect I. M. Pei. Pilgrims hoping for a James Brown sighting may seek out 94.7 FM ("The Boss"), the family radio station at Broad and Ninth, or head down the street for a beer at the Soul Bar, where the walls are lined with posters and ephemera.

Sacred Heart Cultural Center

The most stunning building in this architecturally inviting city may well be the Sacred Heart Cultural Center, a onetime Catholic church that now hosts the Augusta ballet, symphony and other arts organizations. The twin tin-tipped spires of this awe-inspiring, Romanesque revival building, completed in 1900, shine brighter than any other spot on the Augusta skyline. *1301 Greene Street; 706-826-4700.*

Enterprise Mill

At 15th Street, near where a concrete neo-classical bridge spans the Augusta Canal, the old Enterprise Mill stands as a testament to Augusta's past and future. Built in 1848 as a flour mill and later converted to a

The Confederate Memorial in Augusta at sunset.

cotton mill, this 260,000-square-foot brick complex is now a mixed-use residential and retail facility.

Another fixture on the Augusta industrial skyline is the old Confederate Powder Works chimney, a towering brick edifice located along the canal on the site of the present-day Sibley Mill.

Springfield Baptist Church

African Americans, brought to Augusta for cotton cultivation, have been an integral part of Augusta since its founding. Springfield Baptist Church, founded by freedmen in 1787 and perhaps the oldest independent African-American church in America, gave birth to what is now Atlanta's Morehouse University, one of the nation's finest universities. Today, the congregation wor-

ships in a brick building crowned with a copper cupola, and welcomes all comers to Sunday morning services. *Corner of Reynolds and 12th Streets; 706-724-1056.*

Meadow Gardens

Though Augustans are wont to bemoan the loss of some of city's grand old buildings, many fine homes survive, including Meadow Gardens (circa 1791), onetime home of Declaration of Independence signer George Walton. Sandwiched as it is between the Augusta Canal and a hospital parking lot, the white frame home looks threatened, but rest assured: it has been in the safe hands of the Daughters of the American Revolution since 1901. *Open for tours Monday to Friday; 706-724-4174.*

Summerville

During the late 19th century, before Augusta was protected from flood by levees, the community of Summerville began to prosper, since it has a higher elevation than riverside downtown Augusta. Though many of Summerville's frame structures have since burned, two of the crown jewels from the area's heyday as a resort getaway still stand at the crest of the hill on Walton Way: the huge Mediterranean-style Bon Air, and the Partridge Inn, a charming hotel that remains at the center of Augusta social life.

Augusta National Golf Course

Also in the suburbs, along busy Washington Road, is the Augusta National Golf Course. An impenetrable curtain of green foliage separates it from the concrete wasteland of fast-food franchises and gas stations. Conceived as an indigo plantation known as Fruitland, and in later years the site of a nursery, this complex is home each April to the world's most exclusive and prestigious golf event, the Master's Tournament.

Crowds gather around the sixth hole at the Augusta National Golf Course during the Masters Tournament.

MIDDLE GEORGIA

■ WASHINGTON AREA *map page 163, E-2*

Surely there is not another town in all of Georgia with as many historical markers per capita as Washington. Washingtonians are a proud people, proud of their picturesque town and its picaresque history. Chartered in 1780, the town was the first to be named in honor of President George Washington, yet its most significant moment in history did not come until the close of the Civil War.

It was here that in May of 1865 Confederate president Jefferson Davis, while fleeing from Union troops, signed the last official acts of the Confederate government. In effect, it was here that the Confederacy came to an end. And it was near here that the remaining gold from the Confederate coffers was last seen. Treasure hunters still take to the woods each fall in search of the half a million dollars that is believed to have been buried in the red clay of Wilkes County.

Today the town exudes a prosperous air. Spend a few minutes wandering the sun-dappled streets where Victorian painted ladies and Greek revival mansions stand abreast the redbrick façades of stores selling antiques and hardware. There's a brisk efficiency in the air, as though Washington never succumbed to the drowsiness that defines many of Middle Georgia's bucolic little burgs.

MIDDLE GEORGIA

The Campbell Historic Home is one of Washington's many well-maintained Greek revival mansions.

MIDDLE GEORGIA 175

The living room of the Robert Toombs House, where the "respectable" were welcome.

Robert Toombs House

At the time of Georgia's secession from the Union, the primary challenger to Jefferson Davis for the Confederate presidency was Washingtonian Robert Toombs (1810-1895). Though Toombs would serve as the Confederate secretary of state and as commander of a Georgia brigade at Antietam, he is remembered today more for his firebrand oratory than his political acumen. Rather than accept a pardon and regain Union citizenship, Toombs reveled in his status as an "unreconstructed rebel," boasting in 1880, "I am not loyal to the existing government of the United States and do not wish to be suspected of loyalty."

His imposing home, built between 1794 and 1801 and purchased by Toombs in 1837, is supported by two-story Doric columns that line up across the broad front of the house; French windows open into high-ceilinged rooms. Toombs, an avid practitioner of Southern hospitality, always welcomed guests and when, after the Civil War, a hotel was proposed for Washington, Toombs opposed it. "If a respectable man comes to town," Toombs said, "he can stay at my house. If he isn't respectable, we don't want him here."

Today the house is open for tours; the best part is a brief film in which an actor playing Toombs tells his life story to a cub reporter. *216 East Robert Toombs Avenue; 706-678-2226.*

MIDDLE GEORGIA

Washington Historical Museum

Just a block down Robert Toombs Avenue, the Washington Historical Museum offers a fascinating, chauvinistic introduction to local history. The museum is filled with Reconstruction-era carpetbags ("Those Yankees used them to cart away all our silver," says one of the tour guides), a cotton gin from the late 18th century, assorted Civil War ephemera, and a collection of fine furnishings; *308 East Robert Toombs Avenue, 706-678-2105.*

Mary Willis Library

Sitting in the vestibule of the redbrick Mary Willis Library is a battered old chest thought to have once held some of the lost Confederate gold. Though the chest is empty, the graceful, high Victorian building, built in 1888 and home to the first free library in Georgia, is filled with treasures including a floor-to-ceiling stained glass window by Louis Comfort Tiffany. *204 East Liberty Street; 706-678-7736.*

Callaway Plantation

Like much of Georgia, Wilkes County owed its wealth to cotton. Callaway Plantation stands in tribute to the halcyon days. Once at the center of a 3,000-acre plantation, the massive redbrick Georgian home is now open for tours that illustrate well the commerce of cotton in the antebellum era. *Five miles west of Washington on Highway 78; 706-678-7060.*

Azaleas and dogwood in bloom on the Callaway Plantation.

The Louis Comfort Tiffany stained glass window in the Mary Willis Library.

■ THE "BIG LAKE" PARKS *map page 163, F-1*

The damming of the Savannah River north of Augusta created a series of large lakes: Clarks Hill (Strom Thurmond), Russell, and Hartwell. Popular with fishermen and boaters of all types, they can be crammed with jet skis and motorboats on the weekend, but the lakes offer remote and primitive campsites, as well. Five state parks lie along the lakes: **Mistletoe** *(706- 541-0321)*, **Elijah Clark Memorial** *(706-359-3458)*, **Bobby Brown** *(706-213-2046)*, **Richard B. Russell** *(706-213-2045)*, and **Hart** *(706-376-8756)*.

■ ATHENS *map page 163, D-1*

In the late 1970s and early '80s, two Athens bands hit it big. First came the B52s with their campy party-pop send-ups like "Rock Lobster," and later, REM with their moody jangle-rock songs like "Radio Free Europe." By the time the national press corps came calling, the B52s were spending most of their time in New York, and REM was spending all of its time on the road, touring behind albums that had rock critics and pimple-faced high-school kids alike swooning.

Invariably, the articles in *Time, Newsweek,* the *New York Times,* and the *Boston Globe* asked, "Why Athens? Why the South? How is it that the future of postpunk rock 'n' roll finds its taproot in this sleepy little college burg of 50,000 souls?"

While the national press pondered why, bands like Art 'n the Dark, Pylon, Love Tractor, Limbo District, the Method Actors, and the Barbecue Killers slogged it out night after night in cramped, sweaty bars where the rafters were concave from the weight of decades of neglect and the floors shimmied beneath the epileptic writhing of coed dervishes. Though

The rock band REM *named its album* Automatic for the People *after the slogan of Weaver D's in Athens.*

at the time it was little discussed, some observers now argue that, like the Southern literary renaissance of the 1930s, the Athens music scene of the 1980s owed its origins to the self-analysis and self-expression that naturally follows a period of great turmoil. In the case of the literary renaissance, that turmoil was Reconstruction and its aftermath; for rock 'n' rollers in Athens, it was the Civil Rights Movement and the political fallout of Watergate.

And where else but the university-centered town of Athens for such a movement to coalesce?—a place where the staid School of Agriculture and the free-form School of Art held equal sway, a place where those dervishes writhing on the dance floor were but one generation removed from the farm, their parents the protectors of the Jim Crow South.

"Uga V," the bulldog mascot of the University of Georgia, has a camera mounted on his head.

MIDDLE GEORGIA

◆ UNIVERSITY OF GEORGIA

It is to the university that the town of Athens owes its birth. Founded in 1785 as the nation's first chartered state university, the University of Georgia did not open its doors for classes until 1802. North Campus, an oak-shrouded oasis at the heart of the campus, adjacent to Athens' downtown business district, maintains the intimate feel of a small college quad, despite the fact that the university now enrolls more than 30,000 students. And freshmen, bowing to tradition and superstition, still avoid passing through the cast iron arch that frames the passage between town and gown, lest they be rendered sterile. *General information: 706-542-3000.*

Fueled by investment from the Georgia Lottery, the campus is awash in new buildings, among them the **Georgia Museum of Art,** a modern teaching and exhibition center that boasts a sizable collection of modern American painting including works by Jacob Lawrence and Georgia O'Keeffe; *706-542-4662.*

It is now recognized as one of the better public universities in the nation, but for many of the University of Georgia faithful, the university exists for but one reason: football. Each fall 86,000 cheering fans descend upon Athens on home-game Saturdays to watch the Bulldogs do battle "between the hedges" of Sanford Stadium. Those who visit during the off-season make their way to the glass-and-granite Butts–Mehre Sports Museum to relive past triumphs and view the Heisman trophies won by Frank Sinkwich and Herschel Walker.

Tucked into a little-visited corner of North Campus, the boxwood-bordered **Founders Memorial Garden** pays tribute to America's first garden club, established at Athens in 1881. Another tribute to Georgia's wealth of flora is located just a few miles south of town: the **State Botanical Garden of Georgia**, a living laboratory established by the university. *2450 South Milledge Avenue, North Campus; 706-542-1244.*

Perhaps Athens' most unusual—and enduring—tribute to the natural environment is The Tree That Owns Itself, whose property rights were established by Professor William Jackson when he willed to the white oak all land within eight feet of its trunk. Today the tree, ringed by a concrete retaining wall, juts out into Finley Street at the corner of Dearing.

Partygoers await the Magnolia Ball at the University of Georgia. (photo by Kelly Duane)

◆ SEEING ATHENS

Athens' primary attraction might well be its street life. Downtown is a circus of cafes and coffee shops, watering holes and live music venues, record stores, and restaurants, where the modern-day inheritors of the early-1980s renaissance still throng the streets and the 40 Watt Club still hosts live music six days a week.

Any tour of Athens should include a drive down Milledge Avenue, a lush greensward of a street lined with stunning examples of antebellum architecture. Fronted by massive magnolia trees and adorned with wrought iron, many of these former mansions now do service as sorority and fraternity houses.

Athens City Hall

Pointing north from a perch on the grounds of Athens City Hall is an infamous and ineffective Civil War curiosity, a double-barreled cannon. Designed by Athens native John Gilleland and first tested in 1863, the cannon was made to fire two chain-linked balls simultaneously. Rather than whirl out, bola-style, the chain broke, the balls sputtered left and right, and the cannon was quickly retired. *College Avenue at Hancock Street.*

Morton Theatre

Just down the street from city hall is the Morton Theatre, built in 1890 and longtime home to performances by African-American greats like Cab Calloway. Recently restored, the warm wood auditorium now hosts a variety of community events and conferences. *195 West Washington Street; 706-613-3770.*

Taylor-Grady House

Out on Prince Avenue, at a small remove from the downtown core, is the home where the New South booster spent his college years of 1865–1868. Grady referred to the house as "an old Southern home with its lofty pillars, and its white pigeons fluttering down through the golden air." Today it is filled with period antiques and available for tours. *634 Prince Avenue; 706-549-8688.*

(left) Statue and garden on the campus of the University of Georgia.

(opposite) Street scene in Athens.

■ MADISON *map page 163, D-2*

Madison, established in 1807, is not alone in claiming to have been spared by General Sherman because he considered it "too beautiful to burn"—an oft-told story. In the case of Madison, the story goes that Sen. Joshua Hill, a local Union sympathizer of sorts, persuaded one of Sherman's men, General Slocum, to spare the town. Some attribute Hill's success to the men's common bond as members of the Mason order, others to a gentlemen's agreement forged some time previously. Others say it's all a bunch of hooey. No matter, after a tour of the town, you will come to share with the good people of Madison the belief that it was indeed too lovely to torch.

Time was that Madison flourished as the seat of government in a cotton-rich county. During the antebellum boom, planters built opulent homes along the streets of this compact village. Today, more than 30 graceful period homes lie within the confines of the historic district. Most of the homes are within a few blocks of one another, set on the narrow roads just north and south of Main Street. The local welcome center supplies maps and cassette tapes for a narrated tour. *115 East Jefferson Street; 706-342-4454.*

As the seat of government for Morgan County, the city bustles with energy, yet its center is anything but typical of courthouse squares in Georgia. The courthouse itself is a Beaux-Arts beauty, built relatively late—1905—and oddly situated not it the middle of a square of green, but catty-corner from the square itself, as if it were an afterthought rather than the focal point.

The locus of cultural life in this town is the **Morgan County Cultural Center.** Housed in a towering Romanesque revival building constructed in 1895 to house the first school in the state to have separate grades, the center now hosts plays and musical concerts as well as a series of historical exhibits; the latter include the Box-wood Parlor installation, a dramatic re-creation of upper-class home life of the late 19th century. *434 South Main Street; 706-342-4743.*

On the opposite end of the economic spectrum, the **Morgan County African-American Museum** pays homage to the hardscrabble life of black Georgians. This simple frame home, built in 1895, is filled to overflowing with mementos of black American folklife and its African roots. Works by world-renowned artist Benny Andrews and his father, George "Dot Man" Andrews, are of special note. *156 Academy Street; 706-342-9191.*

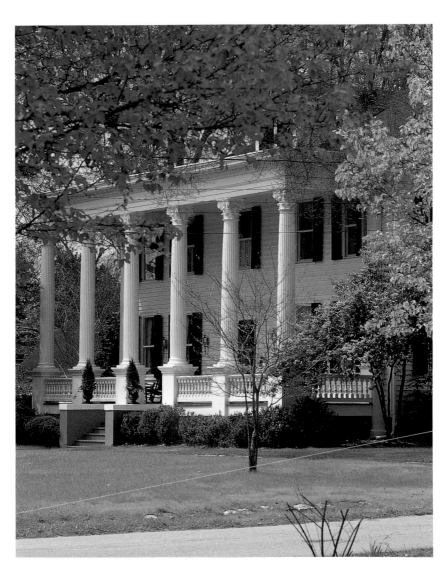

The Kelly House, on Main Street, is one of the fine antebellum mansions built by wealthy cotton planters in Madison.

■ EATONTON   *map page 163, D-2*

Proof of the hold writer Joel Chandler Harris has on this little town is everywhere. On the square across from the beautiful redbrick courthouse sits Briar Patch Office Supply. On the courthouse lawn, a **statue of Brer Rabbit** stands in curious repose, keeping watchful eye over the comings and goings of Eatonton's residents. Harris, compiler of the *Uncle Remus Tales* and often referred to as Georgia's Aesop, was born in Eatonton in 1848.

The first edition of Uncle Remus tales, published in 1881.

Three blocks south of the courthouse is the **Uncle Remus Museum.** Housed in a collection of buildings that one observer claimed are "the world's only air-conditioned slave cabins," the museum brings Harris's African-American folktales to life through dioramas of "The Awful Tale of Mr. Wolf" and "The Wonderful Tar Baby Story," the latter of which was dramatized by the Walt Disney Company as *The Song of the South. 214 South Oak Street, in Turner Park; hours limited, call for information: 706-485-6856.*

Eatonton is the birthplace of another literary lion as well. Born in 1944, Alice Walker, author of *The Color Purple,* grew up on the outskirts of town. Though no monuments pay tribute to her achievements, a driving tour of the Pulitzer Prize–winner's old stomping grounds can be arranged through the local tourist office, and evidence of her Color Purple Foundation's work with underprivileged children can be felt throughout the community.

■ ROCK EAGLE EFFIGY MOUND *map page 163, D-2*

Just north of Eatonton along Highway 441, at the end of an ankle-wrenching flagstone path, is Rock Eagle Effigy Mound, best appreciated from a perch atop the four-story observation platform. More than 100 feet from head to tail, and with a wingspan of 120 feet, this collection of quartz rocks cuts an imposing profile among the pines and oaks of the surrounding forest. Believed to be over 2,000 years old, the mound is one of the most impressive and mysterious Native American sites in the South.

■ MILLEDGEVILLE *map page 163, D-3*

Author Flannery O'Connor, who lived most of her life in Milledgeville, once observed that her native region was "Christ-haunted." Though a half-century of development has certainly changed Milledgeville and Middle Georgia, one can't help but posit that O'Connor would recognize what remains. On Sunday morning and Wednesday evening, churches still bustle with activity, and at almost any time of the day, local radio airwaves crackle with the sounds of a gospel choir or the rants of a country preacher.

Though it was the capital of Georgia from 1803 to 1868, Milledgeville is a sleepy, slow-paced town at heart whose major attractions can be viewed over the course of a leisurely afternoon stroll.

Georgia College is the site of the **Flannery O'Connor Collection.** A small room displays her battered Royal typewriter along with family mementos and early versions of some of O'Connor's greatest works—short stories like "The Misfit" and novels like *Wise Blood.* A 10-minute film puts her life and work in the context of her Middle Georgia surroundings. **Russell Library;** *center of town; corner of Montgomery and Clarke Streets; 912-445-4047.*

The **Old Governor's Mansion,** catty-corner from the Georgia College campus, is undergoing renovations. Built in 1838, this peach-colored citadel of Georgian architecture, ringed by raggedy boxwood gardens, is open for guided tours that give a sense of upper-class life and political machinations in the antebellum era. *120 South Clarke Street; 912-445-4545.*

A few blocks away, at the corner of Green and Jefferson Streets, the Gothic **Old State Capitol** is also undergoing renovations. Built in 1807, this forbidding gray fortress was the seat of Georgia government for more than 60 years.

A VARIED LIFE

*H*e leaned back against the two-by-four that helped support the porch roof. "Lady," he said slowly, "there's some men that some things mean more to them than money." The old woman rocked without comment and the daughter watched the trigger that moved up and down in his neck. He told the old woman then that all most people were interested in was money, but he asked her what a man was made for. He asked her if a man was made for money, or what. He asked what she thought she was made for but she didn't answer, she only sat rocking and wondered if a one-armed man could put a new roof on her garden house. He asked a lot of questions that she didn't answer. He told her that he was twenty-eight years old and had lived a varied life. He had been a gospel singer, a foreman on the railroad, an assistant in an undertaking parlor, and he had come over the radio for three months with Uncle Roy and his Red Creek Wranglers. He said he had fought and bled in the Arm Service of his country and visited every foreign land and that everywhere he had seen people that didn't care if they did things one way or another. He said he hadn't been raised thataway.

A fat yellow moon appeared in the branches of the fig tree as if it were going to roost there with the chickens. He said that a man had to escape to the country to see the world whole and that he wished he lived in a desolate place like this where he could see the sun go down every evening like God made it to do.

"Are you married or are you single?" the old woman asked.

There was a long silence. "Lady," he asked finally, "where would you find you an innocent woman today? I wouldn't have any of this trash I could just pick up."

—Flannery O'Connor, "The Life You Save May Be Your Own,"
from *A Good Man is Hard to Find, and Other Stories*, 1948

■ MACON *map page 163, D-3*

In 1806, the first European settlement in the Macon area was established at Fort Hawkins, on the east bank of the Ocmulgee River. Less than a mile away, the prehistoric Ocmulgee Indian Mounds loomed, a tribute to the architectural acumen of the late Mississippian culture that flourished here more than 3,000 years ago. By 1823 the town of Macon had begun to take shape on the western bank of the Ocmulgee, and as cotton brought prosperity to the Georgia interior, Macon grew steadily.

Early on, Macon served as a riverboat port, shipping cotton to the Georgia coast and on to Europe. After the Ocmulgee River became clogged with silt and detritus, railroads delivered the cotton, and Macon retained its importance in the cotton trade. During the Civil War, Macon suffered relatively little at the hands of Sherman. And yet Macon never became a bustling boomtown like Atlanta. Instead, this prosperous burg, 12 miles north of the state's geographic center, seemed to languish in the summer heat. Boosters spoke of the beauty of the city's columned mansions rather than the size of its labor force.

That all changed in 1942 with the establishment of **Warner Robins Air Force Base,** 12 or so miles down the road. During World War II and throughout the Cold War, the military installation grew. Today more than 15,000 people work at the base, making Warner Robins the state's single largest employer.

◆ MACON AND MUSIC

Of late, Macon has benefited from yet more governmental investment, this time from the state of Georgia. In 1996, the **Georgia Music Hall of Fame** opened, a multimedia tribute to a musical legacy that includes Macon's own Otis Redding, the Allman Brothers, and Little Richard. Arranged by period and genre, and housed in thematic sets (a faux 1960s nightclub for the R&B exhibit), the exhibits are augmented by musical accompaniment delivered via headphones hooked to CD players. In the Gospel Chapel visitors sway to the sounds of "Precious Lord Take My Hand" by gospel pioneer and Villa Ricca native Thomas Dorsey. *200 MLK Jr. Blvd.; 912-750-8555.*

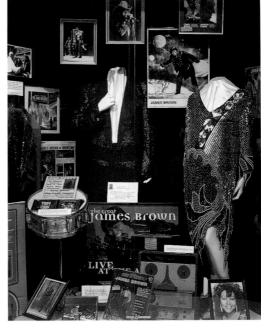

The James Brown exhibit at the Georgia Music Hall of Fame.

Cherry blossoms bloom along a street in downtown Macon.

Dorsey made his name by fusing elements of blues and spiritual music. In the early 1970s, the Macon-based Allman Brothers Band made a name for itself by combining blues with rock 'n' roll to create something called Southern Rock. With songs like "Ramblin' Man" and "Statesboro Blues," they sang of a South in transition, paying tribute to the bluesmen who went before them. Today, fans of the Allman Brothers come to Carnation Ridge at Rose Hill Cemetery on Riverside Drive to visit the graves of band members Barry Oakley and Duane Allman, both of whom died in mid-1970s motorcycle accidents, or to eat at the H&H Cafe, where Mama Louise has fed generations of Macon's musical legends. At the Big House, a Tudor mansion that was once the communal home of the band, Kirk and Kirsten West serve as unofficial keepers of the **Allman Brothers archive and museum***; 2321 Vineville Avenue, 912-742-5005.*

When, in the early 1920s, millionaire entrepreneur Charles Douglas grew tired of being relegated to the balcony bench seats of the local **Grand Opera House,** he built one of the South's "first and finest" African American–owned theaters. After years of neglect, this theater, once host to such luminaries as Duke Ellington and Count Basie, has come to life again, hosting IMAX film screenings and musical performances. *651 Mulberry Street; 912-752-5460.*

◆ MACON SIGHTS

Sidney Lanier Cottage

Sonorous sounds of a different sort are paid homage to at the boyhood home of Sidney Lanier, composer of such poems as "The Marshes of Glynn." This gabled, white frame cottage, built in 1840, is perched high on a brick street packed with beautiful homes. *935 High Street; 912-743-3851.*

Hay House

Near the crest of Coleman Hill stands what may well be Georgia's grandest home, an Italian Renaissance revival mansion known as the Hay House. Completed in 1859, the four-level, 18,000-square-foot home was, at the time of its construction, a marvel of architectural ingenuity boasting an ingenious central heating system and an early tube-based intercom. The 45-minute tour is a spellbinding introduction to the glories of an antebellum home, with enough secret passageways to delight even the most jaded adult or overstimulated child. *934 Georgia Avenue; 912-742-8155.*

Cannonball House

Just down the street, the diminutive Cannonball House looks like a dollhouse reproduction of a Tara stage set. The most interesting things about the house are a cannonball-pierced column and a collection of Civil War memorabilia. *856 Mulberry Street; 912-745-5982.*

A doorway to the picture gallery in the Hay House.

Luther Williams Field

Another downtown fixture is Luther Williams Field, former home of the Macon Peaches, now home to the Macon Braves, the Atlanta Braves' farm team. The 1920s-era steel-and-brick ballpark is the most intimate professional baseball field in the state. *In Central City Park; 912-745-8943.*

Tubman African-American Museum

Macon's African-American heritage is as well documented as that of any city in the state, thanks to the Tubman African-American Museum. Named for a onetime conductor on the Underground Railroad, Harriet Tubman, this is Georgia's largest African-American museum, featuring exhibits on African art as well as a mural of local and national notables that wends its way through the gallery space. *340 Walnut Street; 912-743-8544.*

The Great Temple Mound in Ocmulgee National Monument.

◆ OCMULGEE NATIONAL MONUMENT

What is perhaps the most important site in Macon is also the oldest. Located on the eastern fringe of the city on the site of an old trading outpost, Ocmulgee National Monument is dominated by a series of earthen mounds, including the imposing Great Temple Mound, which rises some 45 feet from a base the size of 14 football fields. People first began living at this site about 10,000 years ago, but it was those who lived here between A.D. 900 and 1100 and belonged to what is known as the Late Mississippian culture, who built the temple mounds and structures such as the clay-floored "Earthlodge."

The Mississippians were a comparatively sedentary people, inclined to farming rather than hunting and gathering. Along the river bluff they built a series of ceremonial mounds, raising them higher and higher over the years as new leaders came to power. At its height the settlement was home to more than a thousand people.

Today, the mounds the Mississippians built—basketful by basketful of dirt—are popular with hikers and amateur anthropologists alike, who travel the trails through the pastoral lands surrounding the temples, formulating their own ideas as to why it all started and how it all ended. *1207 Emery Highway; 912-752-8257.*

■ PASAQUAN *map page 163, B-4*

Just outside Buena Vista at the bend in a curve on a two-lane blacktop looms Pasaquan, a walled compound decorated with a dizzying intensity. Pasaquan was created by Eddie Owens Martin, who was born to sharecroppers here in Marion County on the Fourth of July 1908. Ostracized early on because of his sexual orientation, Martin ran away from home at the age of 14 and traveled to such exotic locales as India and Burma before settling in New York. During an extended illness in 1935, Martin had a vision of a deity whose hair reached from his head to the sky. Compelled by his vision and the voices of this deity, Martin was reborn as St. EOM of Pasaquan.

The core tenet of St. EOM's new religion was a Samsonesque belief that hair was the center of man's being; thus St. EOM bound his hair in a turban and coated it with boiled rice syrup to insure that it would reach astounding heights. In divining this new religion, he borrowed liberally from Sikh, Mayan, and Egyptian religious traditions.

Despite his affinity for the exotic, St. EOM returned home each year at harvest

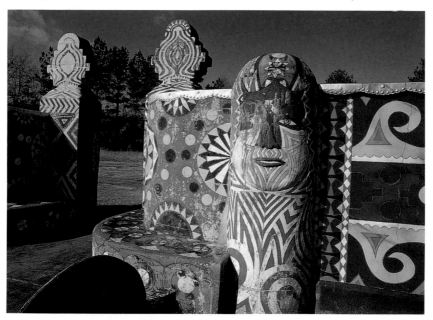

A brilliantly colored exterior wall at Pasaquan.

time to help his family bring in the crop. It was not until 1957, after both his parents passed away, that he took up full-time residence at the family farm just outside Buena Vista.

Fueled by proceeds from a flourishing fortune-telling business, St. EOM began to build the four-acre walled compound that is Pasaquan. He used the simplest of materials: Sherwin Williams house paint was his medium and concrete was his canvas. A tour of the grounds is a humbling experience.

Depictions of prototypical Pasaquayans with upswept hairdos appear throughout the work. In the land of the Pasaquan, all images carry equal weight: religious iconography shares wall space with depictions of oversize genitalia. Christianity and Buddhism coexist. Surprises are everywhere: upon closer inspection, what appeared to be a geometric abstraction is actually a hermaphroditic torso.

St. EOM continued work on his Pasaquayan homeland until his death in 1986, after which the property was given to the Marion County Historical Society. After years of deterioration, the environment has recently been stabilized thanks to the work of caretaker Gwen Martin (no relation to Eddie Owens Martin) and groups of visiting schoolchildren.

■ PINE MOUNTAIN AND ENVIRONS *map page 163, A-3*

At the tail end of the Piedmont Plateau, Pine Mountain rises abruptly from the surrounding plains. At some 1,500 feet in elevation, the area has long provided escape from the heat of summer, and thanks to the heated mineral springs that issue from the mountainside, it has long been a place of healing.

Among those who made their way to Pine Mountain was Franklin Delano Roosevelt, who came to the area in 1924 in search of warm water treatments for his polio-afflicted legs. With Roosevelt's help, the failing resort town of Warm Springs was recast as a polio research center and, in 1927, the Georgia Warm Springs Foundation was born. Roosevelt returned many times in the following years, developing a deep rapport with the local folk. Natives of the area, who were but children when Roosevelt visited, recall him motoring about the countryside, shouting "Hiya neighbor" in his inimitable accent.

◆ ROOSEVELT'S WARM SPRINGS HOME

By 1932 President Roosevelt had built a home at Warm Springs. The six-room dwelling was a simple affair, reflective of his desire for comfort and relaxation on *(above) Kudzu in central Georgia. Native to Asia, the vine was brought to this country to prevent soil erosion. Kudzu can grow up to 60 feet per season, and in much of the Southeast it has become a rampant weed. (below) A Georgia woman weaves a basket of the woody kudzu stem.*

Taken during FDR's 1928 trip to Warm Springs, this photo shows Roosevelt exercising his polio-damaged legs in the enclosed pool. (Underwood Photo Archives, San Francisco)

his Southern sojourns. Today, visitors to the home, now dubbed the **Little White House,** are free to tour the grounds and wander through the home. Among the more touching items on display are the President's wheelchair, various leg braces, and a collection of canes whittled by supporters unaware of just how debilitated he was. In the living room is the portrait for which Roosevelt was posing when he died at Warm Springs on April 12, 1945. *Highway 85 just south of the town of Warm Springs; 706-655-5870.*

◆ CALLAWAY GARDENS RESORT

On the other side of Pine Mountain, at about the same time that Roosevelt was re-making Warm Springs, another vision began to take hold, as textile tycoon Cason Callaway and his wife, Virginia, started buying up depleted cotton fields with the idea of transforming them into a garden of native fauna. In 1952, their private dream turned public with the opening of Callaway Gardens.

Today, Callaway Gardens Resort cuts a lush emerald swath through the red clay of Middle Georgia. Like pearls on a necklace, lakes dot the roadway that encircles the property. Though it may not live up to its billing as the "prettiest garden since Eden," Callaway Gardens delights the senses, with the rust- and orange-hued leaves of oak and elm trees in the fall and the riot of colors that comes when the world's largest collection of azaleas blooms in the spring. Indoor attractions do not disappoint, either. The Day Butterfly Center swarms with more than a thousand tropical butterflies in a crystal palace setting, while the Sibley Horticultural Center is a steamy five-acre oasis that harbors rare and exotic plants. Golf, tennis, and hotel facilities are available. *US 27 south of the town of Warm Springs; 800-282-8181.*

■ COLUMBUS *map page 163, A-4*

Chartered in 1828, Columbus began life as a frontier trading outpost. Like the cities of Macon and Augusta, Columbus owes its location to the fall line that straddles Middle Georgia, marking the dividing line between turbulent waters to the north and navigable streams to the south.

In his 1838 hand-tinted lithograph Pont de Columbus (The Bridge at Columbus), *Francis de la Porte also depicted the city hall of Milledgeville at the top right and the bridge at Augusta in the top left. (courtesy of the Columbus Museum, Columbus)*

While river trade was important when Columbus was founded, it was the textile mills that became central to the city's economic life. The mills were located here because of the power generated by turbulent upstream waters. During the Civil War, Columbus supplied the Confederacy with more manufactured goods than any other city in the Deep South. Today, the city's Swift Textiles is still the world's largest producer of denim, yet the glory days of the textile industry are far behind. Former mills stand vacant, their somber redbrick façades a reminder of days past. Bibb City, a separate municipality once home to a massive mill and row upon row of workers' homes, is in danger of losing its state charter now that the mill has closed, leaving the city without a viable tax base.

And yet Columbus is on the rebound as the city retools, coming to life again as a financial center. Where warehouses once lined the riverfront, a graceful park borders on a revitalized shopping district, and just down the road, Fort Benning, the world's largest infantry base, pumps millions of dollars into the local economy.

Military Museums

Fort Benning is the site of one of the area's most popular attractions, the **National Infantry Museum.** Dedicated to telling the story of American foot soldiers from 1750 to the present, the museum houses an eclectic collection of memorabilia ranging from a stunning display of rifles to an epaulet from Italian dictator Mussolini's uniform. *Fort Benning, off Highway 280 (Victory Drive) southeast of town; 706-545-2958.*

Closer to town, the **Civil War Naval Museum** pays homage to a little-known chapter of Civil War history, the pioneering Confederate deployment of submarines, naval mines, and torpedoes. *Second Avenue at Fourth Street, just southeast of town; 706-327-9798.*

Riverwalk

It was Columbus' location on the Chattahoochee River that made it a manufacturing site for Confederate naval vessels, and the riverbank was also what drew industry to the city. Today, that same riverbank is home to the Riverwalk, a brick promenade at the center of 12 miles of jogging and hiking trails.

Historic District

Just a couple of blocks from the river, the historic district stands in testament to the wealth of the 19th century. At Tenth Street and First Avenue, the **Springer Opera House,** built in 1871 and host to such stage notables as Edwin Booth and Oscar Wilde, is a dignified brick edifice trimmed in cast iron. Also on **First Avenue** is the nation's sole double octagon house, an architectural oddity known as "The Folly."

Notable Homes and Sites

For a glimpse of what the nouveau riche have wrought, locals recommend a trip down to the 1900 block of Wynnton Road, where you can take a gander at another folly, the **home of Ellena Amos,** widow of

AFLAC Insurance Company founder John Amos. Perched atop a six-story parking garage, the red-tile-roofed Mediterranean villa faces down on the loading dock of the adjoining skyscraper.

Set in humble surroundings is the last home of gospel-and-blues singer Gertrude "Ma" Rainey at **805 Fifth Avenue.** Though you would never know it from the present-day appearance of this ramshackle house, Rainey was among the most popular female entertainers of the 1920s.

Atlanta is not the only town that lays claim to being the birthplace of Coca-Cola. Though there is some debate, locals claim it was in Columbus that pharmacist John Pemberton devised the formula for Coke. Today, the simple **Pemberton House** is open for tours. *712 Broadway; 706-322-0756.*

There is no debate as to where RC Cola was created. Long the nation's third most popular cola, RC was first concocted around 1900 in the basement of the **Hatcher Grocery** on 11th Street. Coca-Cola may be king in the rest of the country, but, judging by the billboards that dot this town, RC rules the roost in Columbus.

Columbus Museum

The finest cultural establishment in Columbus is most certainly the Columbus Museum, one of the better art spaces in the Deep South. Folk art and fine art complement one another in this inviting modern facility. Among the highlights of the permanent collection are assemblages by Radcliffe Bailey, and Bo Bartlett's *The Homecoming,* a massive—and ghoulish— oil painting of a football player and homecoming queen posed against the backdrop of a raging bonfire. *1251 Wynnton Road; 706-649-0713.*

A patron views Bo Bartlett's The Homecoming *at the Columbus Museum.*

MIDDLE GEORGIA

Middle Georgia Food & Lodging

X **Restaurant Prices:** $ = under $10; $$ = $10–20; $$$ = over $20
Restaurant price designations indicate the approximate cost of an entrée and an appetizer or desert, exclusive of drinks, tax, and tip.

▥ **Lodging Rates:** $ = under $75; $$ = $75–150; $$$ = over $150
Lodging rate designations indicate the approximate cost of a double occupancy room for one night, exclusive of surcharges and taxes.

A statewide food and lodging **reference map** can be found on page 306, and an **index of towns** with food and lodging listings in this book follows on pages 307–308. Toll-free numbers for **chain hotels and motels** can be found on page 308.

Athens   *map page 163, D-1*

Athens is a college town with many international students, yet most of the best eats in town are traditionally Southern in style or at least inspired by years of eating grits, greens, and every part of the hog but the squeal.

X **Allen's**
706-548-8309; 1294 Prince Ave.
East of downtown Athens, in an area called Normaltown, is the quintessential beer-and-burgers joint. Mind you, the burgers are very good. While you're waiting for your order, you can play a game of pool. Former Georgia governor Zell Miller manned the grill here when he was an undergraduate at the University of Georgia. Lunch and dinner. $

X **Depalma's Italian Cafe**
706-354-6966; 401 East Broad St.
Offers fresh pasta smothered in porcini mushroom cream sauce or pesto; pizzas; and gargantuan calzones. They also serve a different grilled fish nightly. Comfortable and reassuringly dark, this is a favorite haunt of courting college couples. Lunch and dinner. $-$$

X **East West Bistro**
706-546-9378; 351 East Broad St.
Serves fusion cuisine, dishes like salmon in rice paper with a cilantro-ginger pesto, or nori rolls stuffed with goat cheese and then fried. Cool, mustard-colored walls and high-backed booths make for a hip setting. A good selection of wines by the glass is offered. Lunch, dinner. $$

X **The Five Star Day Cafe**
706-543-8552; 229 East Broad St.
This simple storefront cafe features new takes on traditional Southern cooking (the collard greens are cooked with soy and garlic instead of ham hock). The mozzarella-laced meatloaf is a revelation. Counter service. Lunch and dinner. $

X **The Grit**
706-543-6592; 199 Prince Ave.
Serves a melding of international and

Southern-inspired vegetarian fare. Amid a setting of distressed brick walls festooned with funk and folk art, a cadre of tattooed waiters slings some great hash. Try the curries and the daily vegetable plates, and for heaven's sake save room for dessert. Pray for German chocolate cake. Lunch and dinner. $-$$

THE GRIT

✕ The Last Resort Grill
706-549-0810; 174/184 West Clayton Ave.

An informal, brick-walled restaurant that does wonders with grits, cooking the stone-ground variety to a creamy, thick consistency, topping them with a slab of salmon, and gilding the lily with a caper cream sauce. The cooks also do good work with grilled vegetables and other less complicated fare. Good reds are offered by the bottle, including a couple of syrahs. Lunch and dinner. $$

✕ Mayflower Restaurant
706-548-1692; 171 East Broad St.

If the Rotary Club doesn't meet here, it should. With red-and-white checkered tablecloths and black-and-white tiled floor, this downtown favorite looks little changed from the day it opened in 1948. Breakfast biscuits stuffed with hand-patted sausage and BLTs are favorites. Breakfast and lunch. $

✕ Rocky's
706-353-0000; 233 East Clayton St.

A perennial favorite for thin-crust pizzas, including a white pizza with potatoes. Don't let the grubby, college-dive atmosphere dissuade you; this place makes a good pie. Salads and pastas are also available. Lunch and dinner. $

✕ The Varsity
706-548-6325;1000 West Broad St.

A branch of the original Atlanta location. And the chili-slaw dogs, onion rings, fresh-cut fries, and frosted orange drinks taste just as good here. A great place for a quick bite. The line moves fast, even faster if you do as they ask and, "have your order in mind and your money in hand" before you reach the counter. Lunch, dinner. $

✕ Weaver D's
706-353-7797; 1016 East Broad St.

Won national attention when local boys REM named an album *Automatic for the People*—a tribute to the response that Weaver D's owner, Dexter Weaver, gives when somebody asks for a helping of collards, a plateful of pork chops, or just about anything else at this spotlessly clean little cinderblock restaurant. Be sure and try the crusty-top macaroni and cheese. Lunch and early dinner. $

✗ **Wilson's Soul Food**
706-353-7289; 351 North Hull St.
A trencherman's favorite, this old diner has cafeteria-style service, great fried chicken, swine-scented green beans, and moist, coarse cornbread. Try the sweet potato pie or peach cobbler. Lunch. $

⊡ **General lodging information**
A number of motels are clustered on the northern fringe of downtown Athens, including **Courtyard by Marriott** *(706-369-7000; 166 Finley St.)* and **Hampton Inn** *(706-548-9600; 2220 West Broad St.)*. The **Holiday Inn** *(see below)* has the best location in town.

⊡ **The Georgia Center**
706-542-1181; 1197 South Lumpkin St.
Run by the University of Georgia, this on-campus, motel-style facility has more than 200 rooms. What they lack in charm, they more than make up for in convenience (South Campus is at your doorstep). $

⊡ **Holiday Inn**
706-549-4433; 197 East Broad St.
Step out your door and you are on UGA's North Campus or in the midst of Athens' bustling downtown business district. The facilities are a mixture of motel-style lodging and newer rooms in an attached tower, and there's a big pool on-site. $-$$

⊡ **Magnolia Terrace**
706-548-3860; 277 Hill St.
Located in the historic Cobbham neighborhood, this 1912 Colonial-style inn is within walking distance of shops and restaurants along Prince Avenue. Well-appointed rooms and an expansive front porch with comfortable wicker furniture complete the scene. $-$$

Augusta *map page 163, F-2*

✗ **Delta Sandwich Shop**
706-738-5221; 1208 Wilson St.
In this tiny nook of a restaurant tucked behind a now closed drugstore, the Whitaker family has been frying great burgers on a solid-top grill since 1978. Try one slathered with pimento cheese or capped with coleslaw. Lunch. $

✗ **Duke Restaurant**
706-736-6879; 1920 Walton Way
The local greasy spoon—and politico's haunt—where plate lunches of country fried steak, creamed corn, and lima beans draw the faithful. Breakfast is especially tasty, and the grits are good enough, as they say, to make you slap your mama. Breakfast and lunch. $

✗ **La Maison on Telfair**
706-722-4805; 404 Telfair St.
A candlelit Victorian mansion where Austrian native Heinz Sowinski does wonders with wild game and seafood. Among recent specials was a pistachio-crusted pork tenderloin with mango shrimp that was especially toothsome. Dinner. $$$

✗ **Le Café du Teau**
706-733-3505; 1855 Central Ave.
Here things take a decided turn upscale. Jazz echoes through the plush dining room, and escargot, lamb, and venison

are prepared with a flair that borders on pretension. The wine list includes many reasonable California reds. Dinner. $$$

✗ Luigi's
706-722-4056; 590 Broad St.
This vestige of yesteryear is an Italian grotto run by Greeks, where the booths are made of red leatherette and the jukebox cranks out songs by Tony Bennett. Favorites are toasted ravioli, lasagna, moussaka, and spaghetti with fried chicken livers. Chianti, served in those little straw-encased bottles, is a bargain. Dinner. $

✗ Mally's Bagels and Grits
706-736-0770; 2742 Washington St.
They boast that this is the restaurant where "North meets South in perfect hominy." Cheese-topped burgers, lox-smeared bagels, and stone-ground grits are the best bets at this open, airy diner. Breakfast and lunch. $

✗ Nacho Mama's
706-724-0501; 976 Broad St.
A relative newcomer on the Augusta scene. Funky and purposefully hip, this narrow storefront cafe sells Cal-Mex burritos, quesadillas, and tacos. The stereo system lays down a soulful backbeat. Lunch and dinner. $

✗ The Pizza Joint
706-774-0037; 1032 Broad St.
The Italian counterpart to Nacho Mama's, where exposed duct work looms above and hardwood floors run beneath, and the pizzas, calzones, and strombolies

are first rate. The Tree Hugger is a vegetarian pizza topped with, among other ingredients, artichokes, spinach, and mushrooms. Lunch and dinner. $

✗ Sconyers Barbecue
706-790-5411; 2250 Sconyers Way
Opened since 1956, Sconyers is operated by Augusta mayor Larry Sconyers. He cooks his pork over oak and hickory chips and serves up sides of hash and rice as well as coleslaw. For those put off by the "downhome" appearance of many barbecue restaurants, this two-story log cabin will assuage your fears. Lunch and dinner. $

✗ Sunshine Bakery
706-722-9419; 1209 Broad St.
Opened in the summer of 1946 by the Greenberg family, formerly of Minsk, Russia. Today Augustans come to this simple restaurant, with brick walls and gold vinyl booths, for egg salad sandwiches and Reubens on house-baked sourdough rye, as well as breakfast specialties. Breakfast and lunch. $

✗ Treybon
706-724-0632; 520 Reynolds St.
The place to go if you can't decide what sort of barbecue you like best. There's a large selection of sauces, ranging from the ketchupy stuff they serve in western Tennessee to the mustard-laced sauce popular in South Carolina. Chili, Brunswick stew, and a few Cajun specialties round out the eclectic menu at this simple downtown roadhouse. Lunch and dinner. $$

✕ **White Elephant**

706-722-8614; 1135 Broad St.

Features such delights as homemade chicken sausage, grilled fish, and Cuban sandwiches in a charming, plant-filled dining room. An elephant tusk juts out from behind the bar like a prop in a child's dream. And there's a wide-ranging, economical wine list. Lunch; dinner on weekends. $-$$

⌂ **General lodging information**

A phalanx of chain motels, one as nondescript as the next, lines Washington Road near the Augusta National Golf Club. But downtown, and north of town in the Summerville neighborhood, you will find quaint B&Bs, a lovingly restored old resort hotel, and new riverfront towers. Should your travel plans coincide with the annual Master's Golf Tournament, be forewarned: rooms will be as scarce as chicken teeth.

AZALEA INN

⌂ **Azalea Inn**

706-724-9774; 312 Greene St.

Greene Street is lined with restored Victorian homes known as "painted ladies"

for their bright color schemes. At this eggplant-hued bed-and-breakfast—the reception center for a trio of renovated properties —all the guest rooms have private baths (some have Jacuzzi tubs) and the ceilings soar to dramatic heights. Complimentary continental breakfast is included. $$

PARTRIDGE INN

⌂ **Partridge Inn**

706-737-8888; 2110 Walton Way

Built in 1890 at a time when the Summerville neighborhood flourished as a resort community, the Partridge still shines with the opulence of old. Perched high on a hill and fronted by a wide and welcoming veranda, this recently renovated hotel features a wonderful little courtyard pool at its center and a great bar on the second floor. More than 100 rooms are available, many of which are spacious mini-suites. $-$$

☰ **Radisson Hotel Augusta**
706-722-8900; Two 10th St.
Augusta's newest, swankest hotel has more than 200 rooms (many of which have sweeping views of the Savannah River below), a full host of business services at your beck and call, and a heated outdoor pool. For those intent upon exploring downtown, it just doesn't get any more convenient than this— the Morris Museum of Art is literally next door. $$

Columbus   *map page 163, A-4*

✕ **Bludau's Goetchius House**
706-324-4863; 405 Broadway
Housed in a squat, New Orleans–style antebellum home is Columbus's grand old lady of dining. Here the patrons, the menu, and, most of all, the servers, are frozen in time. The setting is charming if just a tad threadbare, and the food is good, if a bit uninspired. Frog legs, duck with cherry sauce, and Veal Oscar are favorites. Dinner. $$-$$$

✕ **Country's Barbecue**
706-596-8910; 1329 Broadway
Sells the best Brunswick stew in these parts, thick with smoky pork, corn, and tomatoes. Housed in a former bus station, the restaurant is a visual treat. Ribs are meaty, fries are fresh-cut, and the sauce comes in three varieties, the best of which is a thin, mustardy, vinegar-based concoction. Lunch and dinner. $

✕ **Dinglewood Pharmacy**
706-322-0616; 1939 Wynnton Rd.
Opened its doors in 1918 as a pharmacy with a small lunch counter. Today, it's the lunch counter that matters. In charge is a man everyone knows as Lieutenant. Grab a seat at the counter and listen to the local banter while savoring one of his famous "scrambled dogs," a culinary train wreck of sliced hotdogs on a bun, topped with homemade chili, oyster crackers, and pickles. Lunch and early dinner. $

✕ **Evelyn's Cafe**
706-322-9436; 2601 Hamilton Rd.
A study in minimalism—and good food. Let the screen door bang behind you and settle into one of the vinyl booths for a breakfast of scrambled eggs and grits, biscuits, and strong, hot coffee. Lunchtime plate offerings are tasty, too. Breakfast and lunch. $

✕ **Garlic Clove Restaurant**
706-321-0882; 6060 Veteran's Parkway
Situated hard by the side of a dusty road in the suburbs, the restaurant has little curb appeal. But the menu is a delight, featuring such dishes as shrimp sautéed with local mushrooms, served over angel hair pasta, and a rib eye steak in an Asian oyster sauce. Dinner. $$-$$$

✕ **Macon Road Barbecue**
706-563-0542; 2703 Avalon Rd.
Housed in a green cinderblock building, this barbecue joint serves chipped or chunked smoked pork along with Brunswick stew and a cheek-puckering

barbecue slaw that is heavy on the vinegar. Piles of white bread are provided for sopping. Lunch and dinner. **$**

✗ **Minnie's Uptown**
706-322-2766; 104 Eighth St.
The country-cooking cousin of the Royal Cafe *(see below)*. Belly up to the steam table for crunchy fried chicken, perfectly lumpy mashed potatoes with gravy, and okra in many guises. The setting is country cute but spic-and-span. Lunch. **$**

✗ **Olive Branch Cafe**
706-322-7410; 1032 Broadway
On a block where the jewelry stores hock cubic zirconium rings, this attractive (if slightly precious) eatery serves an eclectic menu of entrees, ranging from manicotti to pesto-rubbed pork chops with sweet potatoes in a cherry sauce. A good selection of wines (mostly California) are offered. Lunch and dinner. **$**

✗ **Rose Hill Seafood**
706-322-4410; 2621 Hamilton Rd.
Columbus's venerable seafood house. Famous for raw oysters and fried fish, this simple eatery features the freshest seafood in town. There always seems to be a line out front. Lunch and dinner. **$**

✗ **Royal Cafe**
706-322-9149; 600 11th St.
Columbus's plate-lunch palace. Factory workers and stockbrokers alike jostle for a table at this unassuming eatery, set across the street from an old foundry. Fresh rutabagas and collard greens,

toothsome meatloaf, and splendid hoecakes are the best of a stellar bunch. Pay your respects to longtime proprietor Lila Star at the cash register. Breakfast and lunch. **$**

🛏 **Columbus Hilton**
706-324-1800; 800 Front Ave.
Just a step away from the city's historic district and a couple of blocks from the riverfront, this modern hotel claims the best location in town. Set between the walls of an old gristmill, and featuring a nice pool and inviting coffee shop, this property rises above the other chain accommodations in town. **$-$$**

🛏 **Gates House**
706-324-6464; 737 Broadway
This late Victorian cottage is the closest B&B to the Riverwalk. Furnished with Victorian appointments, the rooms all have private baths. Wake up to the smell of fresh-baked banana nut bread and dark roast coffee. **$-$$**

🛏 **Rothschild-Pound House**
706-322-4075; 201 Seventh St.
This is Columbus's premier B&B. Built in 1870, the Victorian beauty was fully renovated in 1994. The eight rooms are decorated with period furniture as well as such modern amenities as coffeemakers. Afternoon cocktails and a sumptuous breakfast featuring a grits soufflé are highlights. **$$**

🛏 **Woodruff House**
706-320-9300; 1414 Second Ave.
Built in 1885, this white frame home was the birthplace of Coca-Cola mag-

nate Robert Woodruff. Thirteen mini-suites are available, all with private bath and fireplace. $$

Macon *map page 163, D-3*

✕ The Bear's Den
912-745-9909; 1191 Oglethorpe St.
May well be the best plate-lunch place in town. Step up to the steam table and select from the daily specials, then carry your tray back to the tidy dining room lined with pictures of Mercer University sports teams. Though the meats are good, your first visit calls for a vegetable plate piled high with cheddar-crowned macaroni, squash casserole, dusky turnip greens, and sage-scented dressing topped with giblet gravy. Lunch. $

✕ Cherry Corner
912-741-9525; 502 Cherry St.
Proof positive that there's good eating to be had outside the plate-lunch and barbecue houses. Salads, fresh-baked European style breads and pastried fortify the downtown workers who flock here. Breakfast and lunch. $

✕ Fincher's Barbecue
912-743-5866; 891 Gray Hwy.
May be a local favorite, but this author just can't taste the appeal. That said, generations of Macon residents swear by the soupy sauce and revel in the knowledge that their favorite was the first barbecue to go into outer space when, in 1989, astronaut Sonny Carter took it aboard a Space Shuttle flight. Lunch and dinner. $

✕ Fresh Air Barbecue
912-477-7229; 3076 Riverside Dr.
A branch of the original in Jackson serving the same tasty, slow-smoked 'cue. Lunch and dinner. $

✕ H & H Restaurant
912-742-9810; 807 Forsyth St.
Proprietor "Mama Louise" used to feed local blues-rockers the Allman Brothers Band, and she'll feed you too. Try the fried chicken, collard greens, and sweet-potato pie at this inestimable, funky landmark. When you see the mushroom painted over the old soft-drink sign, you'll know you've arrived. Breakfast and lunch. $

✕ Jeneane's Cafe
912-743-5267; 524 Mulberry St.
A sparkling clean downtown lunchroom where you can sate your cravings with country fried steak, speckled butter beans, creamed corn, and turkey with dressing. If you show up on Thursday, top off your feast with a bowl of banana pudding. Lunch. $

✕ Len Berg's
912-742-9255; 240 Post Office Alley off Mulberry St.
Berg's has been around since 1908. Try the fresh vegetables and the salmon croquettes, or, during summer, a plate of cold chicken, deviled eggs, and a pimento cheese sandwich. For dessert, sample the oddly satisfying macaroon pie. If you like the food, there's a button you can push that signals a buzzer in the kitchen, telling the cooks that another

happy customer has exited with a full and happy belly. Lunch. $

✕ Midtown Grill
912-745-8595; 3065 Vineville Ave.
Occupies an unimpressive, narrow maroon rectangle in a suburban shopping center, and yet the food is some of the most consistent and tasty to be found in the city. Try the grilled pork chops or the veal-and-spinach meatloaf. A decent selection of wines is offered. Dinner. $

✕ Natalia's
912-741-1380; 2720 Riverside Plaza
The place for Italian-inspired dishes and triple-cut lamb chops charred to a rosy hue. Maconites call this their best restaurant and pack the cheery dining room on weekends. Natalia's is home to Macon's best wine list. Dinner. $$-$$$

✕ Nu Way
912-743-1368; 430 Cotton Ave.
Famous since 1916 for the sweet heat of the chili sauce on the dogs, the parsley-flecked coleslaw, and the flaky ice in the cups of Coke, this "weenie stand" may well have been the model for its more famous rival, the Varsity, 70 miles up the road in Atlanta. Grab a seat at the counter and you're in the middle of the action. Lunch and dinner. $

✕ Old Clinton Barbecue
912-986-3225; Hwy. 129, 10 miles north of Macon
Owned by the Coulter family, who learned their barbecue tricks from the good folks at Fresh Air. Some aficionados (this author included) think they

may even do it a bit better. In good smokeshack fashion, the front porch is covered in sawdust and the amenities are few. Lunch and dinner. $

⊞ General lodging information
For a town of its size, Macon has surprisingly few noteworthy places to lay your head. There are, to be exact, two. For more mundane accommodations, head down Riverside Drive, to where it parallels I-75. There, all the national chains are represented, and rooms seem never to be sold at a premium.

⊞ Crowne Plaza Hotel
912-746-1461; 108 First St.
This businessman's hotel is conveniently located close to downtown attractions and the historic district. And since it's a large hotel (16 stories) that rarely fills up, you can often wrangle a deal. Rooms on the upper floors command a beautiful view of Coleman Hill, to the west. $-$$

THE 1842 INN

⊞ The 1842 Inn
912-741-1842; 353 College St.
This majestic Greek revival home built

in—you guessed it—1842 has 21 rooms, all of which are opulently appointed. Some sport fireplaces and whirlpool tubs. Crystal chandeliers loom above; Persian carpets pad the way below. Breakfast is an opulent affair and there is an afternoon honor bar. $$

Madison Area
map page 163, D-1

✕ **Adrian's Place**
706-342-1600; 325 West Washington St.
Squash casserole, thick with onions, as well as black-eyed peas and okra stewed with tomatoes are vegetable favorites at this unassuming brick storefront cafe close to the railroad underpass. Lunch. $

✕ **Amici Cafe**
706-342-0000; 113 South Main St.
This eatery has a pressed tin ceiling and is decorated with with a mural of Venice on one wall, a scene from the Italian countryside on the other. Calzones and pizzas are the draw, especially the pizza bianca, a white pie with sun-dried tomatoes, onions, mozzarella, and olive oil. Lunch and dinner. $

✕ **Blue Willow Inn**
770-464-2131; 294 North Cherokee Rd., 15 miles west of Madison in Social Circle
Serves a justifiably famous buffet, stocked with perennial Southern favorites like corn pudding, dressing and gravy, fried chicken, stewed tomatoes, good, crunchy fried green tomatoes, and

ersatz oven-cooked barbecue. Popular with tourists and locals alike, this graceful home feels a bit like a small-town country club. Hoop-skirted lasses welcome you on the veranda. Lunch and dinner. $$

✕ **Madison Chophouse**
706-342-9009; 202 South Main St.
This clubby restaurant serves pastas, sandwiches, steaks, and the like to a steady stream of locals and tourists. Lunch and dinner. $-$$

✕ **Ye Olde Colonial Restaurant**
706-342-2211; 108 East Washington St.
Housed in the former Morgan County National Bank. Choose a sausage biscuit for breakfast or a plate lunch and snag a table in the front room where the locals gather, or seek out the old vault in back where a round table in the middle of a room papered with Confederate money. Breakfast, lunch, and dinner. $

⛺ **General lodging information**
A number of motels have opened near the intersection of Highway 441 and Interstate 20, but the better choices are Madison's two historic inns.

⛺ **Brady Inn**
706-342-4400; 250 North Second St.
The heart pine floors are polished to a sheen in this late-1800s Victorian cottage. The seven rooms have private baths, and there are plenty of rocking chairs out on the front porch. A full breakfast is served. $

⌕ **Burnett Place**
706-342-4034; 317 Old Post Rd.
Built around 1830, this Federal-style inn was recently restored by an interior designer who worked with the local historical preservation society to ensure that the home remained faithful to its original design. Rooms are well appointed, with some featuring canopy beds. $$

Milledgeville Area
map page 163, D-3

✗ **The Brick**
912-452-0089; 136 West Hancock St.
A college favorite for pizza, sandwiches, and salads. The music caroming off the brick walls can be deafening, but the food satisfies. $

✗ **Cafe South**
912-452-3164; 132 Hardwick St., Hardwick
Serves cafeteria-style Southern food (look for salmon croquettes on Monday, fried chicken every day but Friday) at weekday lunch, and modified continental fare (roast Cornish hen in a cranberry port sauce with cornbread dressing) on weekend evenings. Housed in a former post office, the restaurant wears its age well. Weekday lunch; dinner on weekends. $$

✗ **Southern Boys Barbecue**
912-453-9444; 2811 North Columbia St.
Just off the main highway, down a dusty road. This tin-roofed smokeshack sells a fine barbecue sandwich and a meaty cup of Brunswick stew. And there are bottles of vinegary sauce on the tables should you need that extra zip. Lunch and dinner, Friday and Saturday only. $

⌕ **Antebellum Inn**
912-454-5400; 200 North Columbia St.
Just a block from the Georgia College campus, this 1890 Greek revival home features five rooms decorated with a feminine flourish. There is a large pool on-site, and a full breakfast is served each morning. $

ANTEBELLUM INN

⌕ **Mara's Tara**
912-453-2732; 330 West Greene St.
Close to campus and downtown sights, this Federal-style 1825 home is a bit less opulent than the Antebellum *(see above)* but no less charming. There are four rooms, but no pool. $

Washington Area
map page 163, E-2

✗ **Another Thyme Cafe**
706-678-1672; 5 East Public Square
The best spot in these parts for pastas and grilled vegetable plates. The

setting—the lobby of an old hotel—is charming. And the pecan pie is flaky, sweet, and chock-full of nuts. Lunch and dinner. $

☶ **General lodging information**
Though most people travel the 40-odd miles north to Athens before bedding down, there is one country inn worthy of a night's stop.

☶ **Holly Ridge Country Inn**
706-285-2594; 2221 Sandtown Rd., Tignall
Five or so miles north of Washington off Highway 44, and set on a 100-acre farm, this country inn offers 10 antique-filled rooms, all with private bath. At night the cicadas serenade you to sleep. In the morning, you wake to a cock's crow. $-$$

Here and There

Three of Middle Georgia's prized barbecue establishments are, in layman's terms, out in the boonies. They may be far afield, but they're worth the drive. All three are between Atlanta and Macon.

✕ **Fresh Air Barbecue**
770-775-3182; Hwy. 42 south of Jackson
The "mother church" of Georgia's barbecue restaurants. Opened in 1929, this Jackson institution—complete with sawdust-covered front porch—is justifiably famous for lean smoked pork spiked with thin, vinegary sauce. Great, finely chopped coleslaw, tooth-achingly sweet iced tea, and okay Brunswick stew round out the menu. Lunch and dinner. $

✕ **Spruce's Barbecue**
770-412-1007; 1201 Meriwether St., Griffin
Housed in a drab, brown cinderblock bunker of a building, Spruce's has been in business since 1938. Cords of wood stacked by the smokehouse attest to the fact that they cook their pork the old-fashioned way. A barbecue sauce piquant with red, black, and white pepper, and a great Brunswick stew, thick with meat, draw the crowds. During the summer, look for the house-made peach cream pie. Lunch and dinner. $

✕ **Tillman's Barbecue.**
706-468-6536; Hwy. 11, Hillsboro
Tillman, a retired welder, cooks hams for 24 hours and simmers his Brunswick stew in big cast-iron wash pots. He's open on Friday and Saturday only, April through December, and he closes up when he runs out of meat—ususally long before the posted hour of 9 P.M. Hailed as one of the best barbecue shacks in Georgia. $

SOUTH GEORGIA

■ HIGHLIGHTS

■ TRAVEL BASICS

In this agricultural heartland, much of the landscape consists of farms and orchards. You'll find fresh peaches, sweet Vidalia onions, peanuts and pecans, and acre upon acre of soybeans and sugar cane. Thomasville has a lovely Victorian historic district. Hunting is still a big draw here, as fishing is at Lake Seminole. Albany is significant for its role in civil rights history; Plains, as the home of former President and peanut farmer Jimmy Carter; and Andersonville as the site of an infamous Civil War prison camp. In the southeast lies the Okefenokee Swamp: a vast, wet world of surreal beauty.

Getting Around: This is no place to be in a hurry. Ease your elbow out the car window and motor down the road, taking time to delight in the graceful turn of a crop row. Though urban sprawl has engulfed Valdosta, towns like Albany and Plains are easily toured on foot. The Okefenokee Swamp is best experienced by canoe.

Climate: Mild winters with occasional cold outbreaks; high temperatures in the 50s and 60s F. Very hot and humid summers with frequent thunderstorms; temperatures usually in the low to mid-90s. Fall is dry and pleasant.

Food & Lodging: Fried mullet, swamp gravy, coleslaw, cornbread: partake of this and you'll eat well here. Somewhere south of Macon, mullet replaces catfish, and grits edge out fries as the favorite accompaniment. Barbecue changes too, with astringent sauces of mostly vinegar giving way to mustard-laced concoctions. Distinctive accommodations are hard to come by, though the turreted Windsor Hotel in Americus is a true delight, and the Melhana Resort near Thomasville will give you a taste of the golden era of plantation life. Lodging is available at many state parks, including Little Ocmulgee. For food and lodging listings, see pages 248 to 253.

■ OVERVIEW

Save actual, physical barriers like rivers and oceans, the boundaries of a region are often difficult to demarcate. And so it is with South Georgia. Middle Georgia is the region that more or less straddles the fall line. Northwest Georgia is the land of the Cohutta Mountains; northeast Georgia, the land of the Blue Ridge. Atlanta is, well, Atlanta. Coastal Georgia hugs the Atlantic seashore. And South Georgia, known to self-satisfied lovers of its rural expanses as "God's Country," is the land beneath the Gnat Line. Above the line, the little beasts rarely venture, but beneath a border that mirrors the fall line, they are a terror.

During the summer months, gnats—two-winged, almost microscopic, fly-like nuisances—swarm the people of the piney woods, buzzing about in ears, crawling across noses, flying unawares and unimpeded into yawning mouths. Fending them off with slaps, flicks, Tourettes-like twitches, and grunts, South Georgians curse them to high heaven. Many a local claims to have taken up cigarette smoking as a means of warding off these offensive and omnipresent airborne pests. And yet, ask a Georgian with a playful sense of her state's geography to define south Georgia, and she's likely to tell you that it's the land beneath the Gnat Line and to the west of what everyone seems to call "the Coast." Should the conversation take place in winter, when all the little creatures have died off, she might even smile when she says it.

This is perhaps the most remote region of the state, with few tourist attractions and more lovely rural vistas than any other. In the east of the region, pine trees rise high and spindly. Bare at the base, branches akimbo near the top, the pines resemble frill-topped toothpicks thrown like javelins into the soil. The farther south you travel, the sandier the soil becomes, and on the region's southeastern fringe lurks the Okefenokee Swamp, a nearly 700-square-mile waterlogged wilderness of black waters, above them towering cypress trees draped with Spanish moss. Dove-white water lilies float on the surface of the dark waters, and a menagerie of animals, among which the alligator is the most menacing and populous, inhabit the swamp. West of Okefenokee lies loamy, almost sandy terrain that in ancient times was covered by an ocean; here palmettos challenge pine trees for dominance. North and west, near Albany, pecan trees growing in red clay soil stretch row after regimented row, mile after empty mile. Two-lane blacktop roads pass trailers parked in wiregrass fields and older, abandoned shotgun or dogtrot homes capped with tin roofs.

Spindly old pines contrast with fuller, young pines in this scene, which is typical of South Georgia.

Agriculture is still big business in these parts, and around harvest time, the roads are clogged with tractors, combines in tow, headed to and from fields white with cotton, green with corn, or blanketed with peanut plants plowed up from their subterranean slumber.

No matter where you go, you can be assured that the stations you pick up on your car radio will play both kinds of music—country *and* western.

◆ SETTLEMENT

Compared to Middle and even northern Georgia, South Georgia was settled late by Europeans, though Spanish explorer Hernando de Soto, in his futile search for gold, marched his troops through Georgia in 1540, possibly along the Flint River.

Long the province of the Creek Indians and their forefathers—who hunted for white tail deer and farmed squash, beans, and corn—the lands of South Georgia were not given over to the slave-fueled cotton monoculture until the mid years of the 19th century, and even then some farmers subsisted by producing cane syrup and turpentine.

Though the region remains rural at heart, the cities of Albany and Valdosta thrive today as much because of industry as agriculture. Valdosta also benefits, economically at least, from its location on I-75, the primary thoroughfare hurtling beach- and Disney-bound travelers south to Florida.

Turpentine is loaded onto a steamboat at Hawkinsville on the Ocmulgee River.
(Georgia Department of Archives & History)

SOUTH
GEORGIA

■ UPPER FALL LINE

On the northern rim of the region, the little burg of Fort Valley is the county seat of the aptly named Peach County, and center of production for the fruit that author Melissa Fay Greene observed "is as thickly furred as a sweater, and so fluent and sweet that once you bite through the flannel, it brings tears to your eyes." During late spring and summer, numerous roadside stands offer fresh-picked peaches by the handful and bucketful. Though Georgia no longer leads the nation in peach harvest poundage, come May, the squat, stunted trees in and around Peach County hang heavy with the blush-colored fruit.

◆ PERRY AND SITES EAST *map page 213, C-1*

Ten or so miles southeast of Fort Valley, across I-75, is the crossroads town of Perry, long a stop for travelers. When the Allman Brothers sang, "I was born in the backseat of a Greyhound bus, rolling down Highway 41," they sang of the old highway just east of the interstate that bisects this town of 12,000. Today the biggest attraction is the columned New Perry Hotel, a dowdy but charming 1925-vintage inn that faces on the courthouse square. At suppertime, the hotel's dining-room tables groan beneath a bounty of Southern vegetables. *800 Main Street; 912-987-1000.*

Driving west from Perry, through Hawkinsville (winter home of horses on the harness racing circuit) you reach **Eastman**, onetime headquarters of the **Stuckey's** chain of stores, famed for pecan logs and other Southern confections. Farther east still is the town of McRae, site of **Little Ocmulgee State Park.** The park boasts an 18-hole golf course that would be the envy of many a country club, plus a tidy lodge and numerous cabins, all at economical rates *(see page 250).*

❖

Spend a few hours traveling these back roads and you will soon find yourself seduced by a languor that borders on laziness. The only thing to do is relax and let your travels be an antidote to the malaise of rush.

◆ VIDALIA   *map page 213, E-1*

North and east of McRae is the agricultural crossroads of Vidalia, capital of the 20-county region where the sweet onions of the same name are raised. Higher in sugar and water content than other onions, Vidalias were once available widely only in the fall; enterprising lovers of the onion were known to extend the shelf life by storing them in nylon pantyhose, hung from the ceiling with a knot separating each bulb. Now, thanks to new storage technologies, the onions some claim to be sweet enough to be eaten raw out of hand are available up to seven months after the harvest. Though Vidalia has no onion museum, intrepid travelers may seek out the historical marker on Highway 280, two miles east of town, that marks the spot where, in 1931, Moses Coleman grew one of the first commercial crops.

Though there are numerous spots in town to purchase onions, those willing to take a detour six miles down Highway 1 toward Baxley will enjoy a visit to **Herndon Farms** roadside produce stand, where, on most mornings, you can purchase vegetables fresh from the farm, with dirt still clinging to the roots and dew still blanketing the leaves—all displayed on gargantuan wooden spools set beneath the eaves of an old country store.

Head east from Vidalia along back roads that parallel I-16 and lead eventually to Savannah, and you'll reach another culinary capitol: Claxton, home of the much maligned Claxton Fruit Cake, a holiday fund-raising favorite made of sodden dough studded with luminescent bits of fruits and nuts.

■ ALTAMAHA RIVER BASIN

South of Claxton stretches the Altamaha River Basin, a land of remote beauty where the people are few and the pine trees many. Here timber is the primary industry, as witnessed by the pulpwood trucks that ply the roads in an eternal loop from forest to town, and the paper plants that belch sulphurous smoke high into the air. Once turpentine mills fueled the economy and Waycross, at the south end of the river basin, was a boomtown. Today the town is worthy of notice only as a spot to eat and perhaps sleep before driving 10 miles south to the wilds of the Okefenokee Swamp.

■ OKEFENOKEE SWAMP   *map page 225*

The largest freshwater swamp in North America, the Okefenokee covers almost 700 square miles of southeast Georgia and is a landscape rich with carnivorous flora such as fly-devouring pitcher plants and equally carnivorous fauna such as the American alligator. (Technically, the Okefenokee is a peat bog, not a swamp, but few save scientists recognize it as such.) Once the home of the Seminole Indians, who knew this as "the land of the trembling earth," this geological oddity is at once forbidding and eerily beautiful, an otherworldly landscape more foreign at times than the lunar images beamed back to us from outer space. Most who visit traverse the swamp by water, for the peat-rich soil does indeed tremble beneath the feet, only fitfully supporting a full-grown man—and occasionally giving way.

The land here was once covered by the Atlantic Ocean, which accounts for the sandy bottom of the swamp. The swamp was, in fact, a large sandbar that trapped the water as the ocean receded. The salt then evaporated, leaving a shallow lake of fresh water hospitable to plant life. As the vegetation decayed, a peat bog was born.

The Okefenokee is known for its abundant flora and fauna—among them
Alligator mississippiensis, *the American alligator.*

(following pages) The cypress-swamp landscapes of South Georgia include Banks Lake National Wildlife Refuge as well as the Okefenokee Swamp.

Though 80 percent of the area is covered by the dense cypress stands that most people associate with the Okefenokee, the geography of the swamp is actually quite diverse. The main physical features, aside from the cypress stands, are hardwood hammocks, larger islands, and watery grass fields called "prairies." The open-water areas that break up the cypress and prairie—rivers, lakes, and ponds or "gator holes"—account for only a tiny portion of the total swamp area. New hammocks and, in turn, islands are continually being formed as methane gas—released from the decaying vegetation at the swamp floor—sends peat beds shooting to the surface; new vegetation grows on these "batteries" or "blowups," finally anchoring them to the sandy bottom. Without the cyclical occurrence of wildfires, the praires and open areas would eventually be entirely filled in.

The Okefenokee is a land of surprises. From a distance, the swamp looks fetid, murky, and immeasurably deep, but a closer look reveals that the water is relatively clean and free of detritus, colored a curious tea-black by the presence of tannins—produced by the decaying vegetation and chemically the same as the tannins in wine—and shallow, with a depth typically between two and five feet. Perched at the bow of a canoe, you'll watch as the swamp glides by quietly, peacefully,

(above) Carnivorous pitcher plants flourish in the Okefenokee Swamp.

(opposite) A white water lily contrasts with the swamp's near-black water.

Needles float around cypress trunks on the still, tannin-dyed waters of the Okefenokee Swamp.

beautifully—an elegant procession of water lilies framed by the black mirror of the water. Reptiles sun themselves on cypress knees beneath the boughs of trees dripping with Spanish moss. Hummingbirds hover beside flowers and whooping cranes gracefully glide by. Innumerable islands dot the swamp's interior, and those exploring the swamp step out of their canoes with tentative steps, hoping the soil they step on will hold.

Within the Okefenokee are the headwaters of two rivers: the St. Mary's, which flows some 200 miles south to the Atlantic Ocean, and the Suwanee, which empties into the Gulf of Mexico. In colonial times the swamp was plumbed by trappers, and later it was invaded by lumber companies who used swamp waters to float out almost 10-million board feet of virgin cypress. Native American tribes inhabited the swamp long before European encroachment. First a mound-building society occupied the area; then came the Creeks and, finally, the Seminoles, who lived and hunted here before being forced to go west on the Trail of Tears. A handful of pioneering settlers practiced subsistence farming in the swamp starting in the 1850s, but by the 1950s, most of these people were gone.

Today, the great majority of the swamp is a federally protected wildlife refuge. But tourism is allowed, even encouraged. For the ecologically and biologically curious, the Okefenokee may well be the state's prime attraction.

◆ Visiting Okefenokee Swamp

Weather: Spring and fall are mild here, with daytime temperatures in the 70s and 80s, and nights in the 40s and 50s. Summers are very hot and humid, with highs consistently in the low to mid-90s; winter temperatures vary between 40 to 80 degrees F in the daytime and occasionally reach freezing at night. If you visit Okefenokee, and especially if you plan to canoe and hike, bring bug repellent, sunscreen, drinking water, and food; wear long pants and long-sleeved shirts.

Most of the swamp belongs to the Okefenokee National Wildlife Refuge and Wilderness Area. *Refuge headquarters and visitors center: 11 miles southwest of Folkston, off Highway 121/23; 912-496-7836.*

There are three entrance points to the swamp:

North entrance. This is the site of the Okefenokee Swamp Park, with its live serpentarium shows and battered powerboats plying the swamp waters. Privately owned, this day-use facility feels a bit like an amusement park, but for those who want a peek at the swamp without taking to a canoe, it will suffice. *Ten miles south of Waycross by way of Highway 1; 912-283-0583.*

East entrance. Motorboats can be rented at this entrance, and guided night tours of the swamp interior are available by reservation (a spooky, surreal experience wherein you glide through the pitch-black night, serenaded by unseen, cacophonous wildlife). *Off Highway 23, 13 miles south of the town of Folkston, at the Suwanee Canal Recreation Area; 912-496-3331.*

West entrance. On the western fringe of Okefenokee is Stephen Foster State Park, the preferred jumping-off point for those inclined to explore the swamp by canoe—the best means of transportation for ecologically conscientious visitors and naturalist voyeurs alike. Here canoes are available for rent, as are campsites and cabins. *Twenty miles from Fargo on Highway 177; 912-637-5274.*

SWAMP HOLLERING

*J*ust as darkness settled in, I returned to camp. Then I heard more of that strange music which always startles me—swamp hollering. I was unversed in the unwritten rules of the matter, and I assumed my friends at the upper end of the island were having fun. Expecting to meet them on the way home, I started out toward them. Soon all of us were together again around our campfire.

Gator Joe asked me somewhat impatiently if I had heard them holler, and if so, why I hadn't answered. "When you hear anybody hollerin', you holler back," he said with undisguised sternness. Clearly he was concerned about my getting lost or being harmed. And so Joe taught me rule one about the art of hollering. Even if I had been aware of what was required, I was then—and am yet—totally incapable of producing a sound at all akin to the marvelous swamp yodeling. Of course I could have made some loud noise, but it would have been a virtual desecration in an atmosphere that had been reverberating with the exquisite music made by two masters, Gator Joe Saunders and Bryant Lee.

—Francis Harper, 1912, from *Okefinokee Album*

A brilliant sunset in the swamp.

MAGICAL OKEFENOKEE

"We tried to destroy it....We didn't know any better." The words of Will Cox, one-time resident of the swamp, allude to the fragile and yet regenerative nature of the Okefenokee. Thanks to the work of biologist Francis Harper and his wife, Jean, who appealed directly to President Franklin D. Roosevelt, the Okefenokee National Wildlife Refuge was established in 1936; in 1974, the most remote region of the swamp was designated a national wilderness area. Visiting the Okefenokee today, one is awed by the unique and magnificent beauty of the environment—and sobered by the thought that, just a generation ago, we came close to losing such a treasure.

The Okefenokee is truly wild and remote. Traversing it is no easy feat; the navigable portion is minuscule compared to the hundreds of thousand of acres of impassable cypress stands, their canopy so dense as to cast dark shadows even by day.

The swamp supports an astonishing variety of plant life: the ubiquitous cypress draped with Spanish moss; slash and longleaf pine; black gum, red maple, bay, wax myrtle, magnolia, bamboo, holly. Meat-eaters such as the pitcher plant go far in advancing the swamp's reputation as a fierce place; but come spring, the swamp is ablaze with the delicate blooms of rare orchids and other wildflowers.

The wildlife selection is equally spectacular. Swamp mammals include the black bear, otter, armadillo, mink, six bat varieties, and the swimming marsh rabbit. The Florida puma is being reintroduced. And Okefenokee is truly a birder's paradise: more than 200 species frequent the swamp, and 75 nest here, including such rare birds as the sandhill or whooping crane, osprey, and redcocked woodpecker. But the real stars are the swamp's reptiles and amphibians, including 15,000 American alligators—which can grow to 18 feet. The swamp is also home to some 150-pound alligator snapping turtles; common snappers (which can also be quite nasty); five poisonous snake species; and a number of less menacing lizards, turtles, and snakes.

Protected from the hand of man, the swamp has healed itself. Though most of the trees are second growth, evidence of former damage is scant. Most prominent is a 12-mile stretch of the Suwanee Canal, centerpiece of an ill-fated attempt, begun in 1889, to drain the swamp for farmland. The lumber industry thought they could log the Okefenokee for hundreds of years; they nearly finished the job in 20, during which time Billys Island was a boomtown. Remnants of structures remain here and on Chesser Island.

The Chesser family belonged to a group of resourceful "swampers" who for several generations, starting in the 1850s, made their home in the Okefenokee. They grew or caught their food, raised pigs and cattle, and traded turpentine (distilled from pine resin) for the few other necessities. Their isolation and their self-sufficient life in this strange environment bred a culture all its own—including a sort of swamp "dialect," traces of which can still be heard in the surrounding area.

Naturalist Francis Harper said that the swampers, being such keen observers of their environment, had more to teach him about biology than he could ever teach them. But over the years he spent here, Harper became more and more interested in the people themselves; he filled his notebooks with their songs and stories and ideas about their world. Ironically, the establishment of the wildlife refuge is what finally drove the swampers out, as they could no longer shoot wild animals to protect their livestock.

But even an old swamper like Will Cox, while saddened by the passing of a culture, recognized the ultimate justice of the situation. After all, the Okefenokee was around long before the swampers. And as Cox put it, the Okefenokee "is God's work. Man couldn't destroy it, and now it's as beautiful as it ever was. It's the most beautiful place on earth."

—Lesley Bonnet

Jean Harper and two of the Chessers navigate a boat on Chessers Prairie, May 1930. (University of Georgia Press)

■ AGRICULTURAL HEARTLAND

◆ AGRIRAMA *map page 213, C-3*

The little burg of Tifton is site of the Agrirama, a state-sponsored living history village, that, despite its location within earshot of the interstate, invokes well the spirit and feel of life in the 1890s. Along well-worn sandy paths are distributed a sawmill, feed and seed store, cotton gin, gristmill, turpentine still, and other businesses of the era, all manned by workers dressed in period costume; *912-386-3344.*

◆ VALDOSTA *map page 213, D-4*

The second largest city in South Georgia, with a population of more than 50,000, Valdosta sits beside I-75 about 20 miles north of the Florida border. Though touted by boosters as the "Azalea City," Valdosta is better known to Georgians as home of the winningest high school football program in the South. With more than 20 state championship titles and six national titles, the Valdosta High Wildcats are a source of pride and entertainment for a rabid cadre of fans who fill the stadium

Peach trees bloom in Peach County.

known as "Death Valley" to capacity on fall Friday nights when the hometown boys take to the gridiron.

Valdosta proper is actually a few miles from the interstate. But along a series of corridors choked with fast-food restaurants, the city sprawls out to meet the thoroughfare, while the downtown area retains the sleepy pace of an earlier era, and a few grand old homes open their doors for tours. The most majestic of these is the **Crescent**. Completed in 1898, this 23-room neoclassical mansion is fronted by a crescent-shaped portico supported by 13 Doric columns, and the interior is furnished with period antiques. Out back an octagonal schoolhouse and other outbuildings are ringed by a boxwood garden. *900 North Patterson Street (at Gordon); 912-244-6747.*

◆ THOMASVILLE   *map page 213, C-4*

An 1887 edition of *Harper's Weekly* magazine proclaimed Thomasville, just 15 miles north of the Florida border, to be the "best winter resort in three continents." During the late Victorian era, this oak-sheltered town was one of the southernmost points accessible by rail, and a favorite retreat for wealthy Northern industrialists who built lavish hotels and converted many of the local cotton

A road through a pecan grove near Fort Valley.

plantations to hunting preserves. Today, though the grand hotels have been replaced by chain motels, there are a number of wonderful bed-and-breakfast inns from which to choose. And the hunting preserves remain, many still owned by descendants of the same carpetbaggers who moved into the town after the Civil War, when grand manor homes and vast tracts of land could be had for a song.

The downtown streets are lined with two-story redbrick buildings, in which antique shops, art galleries, and other businesses geared for the tourist trade coexist with those patronized by locals—such as the **Billiard Academy,** where the chili dogs are just 95 cents apiece and spittoons line the wall for those inclined to dip and chew tobacco *(see page 252).*

Historic District

Thomasville's historic district (centered along Madison, Broad, Crawford, and Dawson Streets) is chockablock with beautiful homes, among them the **Lapham-**

Patterson House, an odd geometric folly featuring fish-scale shingles and Japanese-esque porch decorations. Built in 1884 as a winter retreat by Chicago industrialist C. W. Lapham, today the home is a state historic site open for tours. *626 Dawson Street; 912-225-4004.*

One block north, the **Thomas County Museum** features exhibits on the lavish lifestyles enjoyed by Victorian-era visitors; *912-226-7664.*

The Lapham-Patterson House in Thomasville.

Pebble Hill Plantation.

A few blocks over, on Monroe Street at the corner of Crawford, sprawls **the Big Oak**. With a limb spread of more than 160 feet, the tree covers most of a downtown block, spanning the width of Monroe Street, its ancient boughs held up by a series of trusses and cables.

◆ VACATION PLANTATIONS

Perhaps the grandest examples of Thomasville's golden era are the outlying plantations like Pebble Hill, now a museum, and Melhana, now marketed as "the grand plantation resort."

At **Pebble Hill** you are transported back to a time when ladies rode sidesaddle and dashing, red-frocked huntsmen pursued their prey in the early morning, through the thick pine and magnolia forests, before returning to the grand manor house for an elegant hunt breakfast. Long the winter hunting preserve of the Hanna family of Cleveland, Ohio, the house and grounds are now open for tours. *Five miles south of Thomasville on Highway 319; 912-226-2344.*

Melhana is but one of many resort complexes situated on the grounds of an old plantation and selling the good life to today's well-heeled crowd. *Four miles south of Thomasville; 912-226-4585. (See page 252 for details.)*

SOUTH
GEORGIA

◆ Hunting

Today, hunting—of quail, deer, and other wildlife—remains a big draw in the southwest corner of Georgia. In the 1997 novel *A Man in Full,* Tom Wolfe describes a contemporary hunt scene at Turpmtime, the plantation of his protagonist Charlie Croker:

> No matter how many times you went hunting quail, you never became immune to the feeling that came over you when the dogs set the point and you approached a covey hidden somewhere in the grass. The quail's instinct in the face of danger was to hide in the tall grass and then, all at once, to explode upward in flight with incredible acceleration. Everyone used the same term for it: *explode....*

■ Sugar Cane Country

This far south, the red clay so often associated with Middle and northern Georgia is no more. Instead, the roadways are bordered by sandy, loamy soil, and the tractors that chug slowly along on the blacktop are more likely to be traveling to the next sugar cane patch than a cotton field. Small signs tacked to telephone poles advertise "Cane Juice For Sale," and soon you are in Cairo, (pronounced KAY-ro), epicenter of the sugar-cane processing industry, birthplace of baseball legend Jackie Robinson, and home to the Cairo High Syrupmakers football team (one assumes they are slow). In the blink of an eye the town passes, and eight miles later you come upon the crossroads village of Whigham, home, on the last Saturday in January, to the annual Rattlesnake Roundup. Whigham's roundup is one of at least two such events in the state, and quite possibly the model for Harry Crews's modern-day gothic novel, *A Feast of Snakes,* wherein he recounts the importance of the annual roundup to the mythical town of Mystic, Georgia:

> The rattlesnake roundup had been going on now as long as anybody in town could remember, but until about twelve years ago it had been a local thing, a few townspeople, a few farmers. They'd have a picnic, maybe a sack race or a horse-pulling contest and then everybody would go out into the woods and see how many diamondbacks they could pull out of the ground. They would eat the snakes and drink a little corn whiskey and that would do it for another year.

AN UNLIKELY CAFE

*T*he town itself is dreary; not much is there except the cotton mill, the two-room houses where the workers live, a few peach trees, a church with two colored windows, and a miserable main street only a hundred yards long....

However, here in this very town there once was a café. And this old boarded-up house was unlike any other place for many miles around. There were tables with cloths and paper napkins, colored streamers from the electric fans, great gatherings on Saturday nights. The owner of the place was Miss Amelia Evans. But the person most responsible for the success and gaiety of the place was a hunchback called Cousin Lymon.

~~~

*I*t was a good meal they had together on that night. Miss Amelia was rich and she did not grudge herself food. There was fried chicken (the breast of which the hunchback took on his own plate), mashed rootabeggers, collard greens, and hot, pale golden, sweet potatoes. Miss Amelia ate slowly and with the relish of a farm hand. She sat with both elbows on the table, bent over the plate, her knees spread wide apart and her feet braced on the rungs of the chair. As for the hunchback, he gulped down his supper as though he had not smelled food in months. During the meal one tear crept down his dingy cheek—but it was just a little leftover tear and meant nothing at all....

Having finished, Miss Amelia tilted back her chair, tightened her fist and felt the hard, supple muscles of her right arm beneath the clean, blue cloth of her shirtsleeves—an unconscious habit with her, at the close of a meal.

—Carson McCullers, *The Ballad of the Sad Café*, 1951
The author was born in Columbus, Georgia, in 1917

◆ LAKE SEMINOLE *map page 213, A-4*

Bainbridge, located near the northern tip of Lake Seminole, is as much a gathering point for fishermen as Thomasville is for hunters. Here, at one of the best bass fishing spots in the country, locals and outlanders alike try their hand at wrenching a large-mouth bass or six from the depths of the 12,000-acre lake, while those inclined to let others dip their poles in the water, head to one of the area's famous fish houses *(see page 249)* and feast on such aquatic exotica as sucker fish, shad roe, and swamp gravy.

Seminole State Park, located 20 or so miles west of Bainbridge by way of Highway 253, is a good point of entry for those interested in a foray into the Georgia outback. Along the two-mile **Goper Tortoise Trail,** you will come upon wildlife skittering through the wiregrass and, in the spring and summer, wild azaleas and other bright flowering shrubs in full bloom. *Seminole State Park, Route 2 Donalsonville; 912-861-3137.*

Heading north along Highway 27, you come upon two towns in quick succession, Colquitt and Blakely—both charming, but in their present incarnations mere shadows of their once grand pasts.

◆ COLQUITT   *map page 213, A-3*

Colquitt is not on most gourmets' lists of culinary capitals, yet this pleasant little town lays claim to being the mayhaw capital of the world, a bit of hyperbole celebrated each May at the Mayhaw Festival. Little known today, mayhaws are swamp-bound trees with tart, cranberry-size fruit that locals gather in the spring to use in red-tinged jellies and other preserves.

The cast of the play Swamp Gravy *hams it up outside the theater in Colquitt.*

Colquitt's other claim to fame is *Swamp Gravy,* a folk opera performed by a cast of locals and named for the stew-like concoction of bacon drippings, fish trimmings, and whatever else happens to be in the pantry.

For a taste of swamp gravy at its best, head back down the road to Andrew's Oyster Bar in Bainbridge *(see page 249).* For information about the folk opera—performed in April and October—call *912-758-5450.*

■ BLAKELY

map page 213, A-3

Blakely sits at the epicenter of Georgia's peanut patch, and, fittingly, on the courthouse square there stands a hunk of

A peanut with a presidential smile.

granite with a concrete peanut perched atop, installed in 1954 and inscribed with these words:

> The people of Early County, the largest peanut producing center in the world, have erected this monument in tribute to the peanut which is so largely responsible for our growth and prosperity.

Deep-felt appreciation for the peanut may seem odd to city dwellers, but to people who make their livelihood from one crop, it's not odd at all. During the early years of the 20th century, when the boll weevil wreaked havoc on the cotton crop, peanuts were the savior of local farm fortunes. Today, though the economic impact of the crop has lessened somewhat, come the fall harvest, roadways are still clogged with little tractor-towed peanut wagons, trailing a cloud of dust and peanut shells. And most any social gathering calls for a big black kettle of freshly dug peanuts, boiled in the shell and well salted.

■ KOLOMOKI INDIAN MOUNDS *map page 213, A-3*

Six or seven miles north of Blakely are the Kolomoki Indian Mounds, a 13th-century ceremonial center for the Kolomoki tribe. Seven temple mounds are preserved here, Georgia's oldest among them. Desolate and haunting, this remote site stands in stark contrast to many of the more popular, upstate mound sites. Here all is quiet, serene even; the loudest sound you are likely to hear is the screech and clatter of black crows in the trees overhead. Mound D is the most impressive, rising more than 200 feet in height and now crowned by live oaks. Inside the museum, set incongruously in the side of one of the excavated mounds, a diorama depicts the funeral ceremony of a Kolomoki chief/priest, a bloodthirsty spectacle predicated on the strangling and cremation of his two wives. *Five miles north of Blakely, off US 27; 912-723-5296.*

■ ALBANY *map page 213, B-2*

Albany was founded in 1836 on the banks of the Flint River, and with a population of more than 125,000, it is the largest city in the region. It is also the pecan processing center of the state. During the fall, Rube Goldberg-esque contraptions roll through the rows of the pecan orchards on the outskirts of town, grabbing the trunks of the trees in a bear hug and shaking loose the nuts from the branches. Following on the heels of these behemoths come overgrown riding vacuum cleaners of a sort, which suck up the harvest for transport back to dozens of local processing companies, who in turn transform the nuts into candies and the like. But all this takes place in the rural nether regions of the surrounding counties.

In its early days Albany was the commercial center for sharecroppers who journeyed to town each Saturday to do a little shopping and socializing. Albany still bustles with activity, especially around the Dougherty County Courthouse, where, come summer, seersucker suits are de rigueur for the local cadre of attorneys. In the fall, hunters clad in camouflage coveralls gather in the downtown cafes, hunkered down over steaming cups of coffee. Though many families have moved to the city's suburbs, the old-timers are still called by the square, like bees to a hive.

During the Civil Rights Movement, activists began a grassroots voter registration drive in Albany, hoping to capitalize on the highest concentration of potential African-American voters in the region. Fueled by support from Student Nonviolent Coordinating Committee (SNCC) members and emboldened by the arrival of Martin Luther King Jr. in November of 1961, the black citizens of Albany took to the streets—and allowed themselves to be taken to jail—in an attempt to win the right to equal representation and accommodation under the law. But by the summer of 1963, the Albany Movement was discontinued, the victim of local police chief Laurie Pritchett's use of nonviolent tactics he boasted of having learned by observing King himself.

Pritchett avoided violent confrontation by expanding the capacity of his jail cells (he negotiated space with nearly every county in a 100-mile radius) and by making efforts to see that prisoners were treated in a relatively humane fashion. The chief even gave a course in nonviolence to some of his officers. Pritchett's strategy worked. By the summer of 1963, the Albany Movement was disbanded. "[We thought] we could fill up the jails," SNCC worker Bill Hansen explained. "We ran out of people before he ran out of jails."

Mount Zion Church, at the corner of Whitney and South Jefferson Streets, was the site of many of the mass meetings during the movement. The newly remodeled church is now home to the **Albany Civil Rights Museum.** Glass-cased displays share the space with a stage where local gospel choirs gather on occasion to sing freedom songs made popular in the 1960s by locals like Bernice Johnson Reagon, founder of the modern-day a cappella quartet Sweet Honey in the Rock. *Albany Civil Rights Museum: 326 Whitney Avenue; 912-432-1698.*

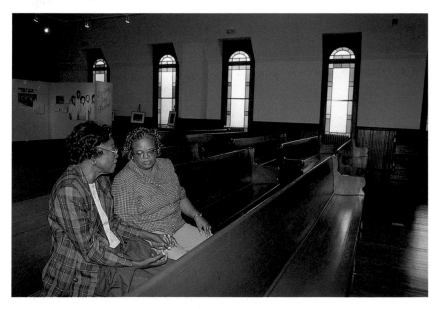

Freedom singers and sisters Rutha and McCree Harris view the exhibits at Mount Zion Church.

A few blocks away, at the corner of Highland and South Jackson Streets, is a fountain built in tribute to the movement. Marble tablets surrounding the fountain are engraved with quotes from people involved in the movement. The most affecting quote is from Martin Luther King Jr.: "When Negroes in Albany decided to straighten their backs up, whenever men and women straighten their backs up, they are going somewhere, because a man can't ride your back unless it is bent."

At the **Albany Museum of Art** the contributions of African peoples are also honored, for here is housed the South's largest collection of sub-Saharan art, a gift of Albany native Stella Davis, a former U.S. Ambassador; *311 Meadowlark Drive; 912-439-8400*. Music fans and chauvinistic Georgians alike might take pleasure in knowing that Albany was once the home of Ray Charles, composer of the state song, "Georgia on My Mind."

■ AMERICUS *map page 213, B-1*
Forty miles north of Albany by way of Highway 19 (and 30 miles west of I-75) is Americus, founded in 1832 on the site of a Creek Indian granary. By the 1890s, Americus, like Thomasville and other towns near the end of the southbound rail

Cotton field and farm near Americus.

The Windsor Hotel in Americus.

lincs, was a booming wintertime resort. Today the only vestige of that era is the turreted, redbrick **Windsor Hotel,** built in 1892 and recently restored to its Victorian grandeur. *125 West Lamar Street; 912-924-1555. (See page 249 for details.)*

Just a couple blocks down Lamar Street is the headquarters of **Habitat for Humanity**, an ecumenical Christian ministry that serves by building low-cost, owner-occupied housing with volunteer labor. Started in 1976 by Linda and Millard Fuller, the organization owes its philosophical origins to another ecumenical experiment started years earlier at **Koinonia Farm,** just south of Americus.

Koinonia means "fellowship" in Greek, and at the time of its founding in 1942 by Clarence Jordan, the farm was an experiment in utopian, agricultural ideals. In the early 1970s, Millard Fuller, after a crisis in his marriage, abandoned a successful law career, sold his house, gave most of his possessions to charity, and moved to Koinonia. He lived and worked there until 1976, when he founded Habitat for Humanity.

Today Habitat occupies a good portion of the office space in downtown Americus and can boast of having partnered with more than 65,000 families to build simple, decent homes in every state in the nation and more than 50 other countries. Visitors may tour the organization's headquarters, where the atrium balconies

SOUTH
GEORGIA

are fashioned from picket fencing and Millard Fuller's Presidential Medal of Honor is on display. There is also a village of the different prototype houses from around the world. *322 West Lamar Street; 912-924-6935.*

Among the advocates of Habitat for Humanity are former President Jimmy Carter and his wife Rosalyn, who were both raised just up the road in Plains and who on occasion pick up hammer and nail to work with other volunteers at a house raising. "I've learned more about the needy than I ever did as governor or President," said the 39th President. "The sacrifice I thought I would be making turned out to be one of the greatest blessings of my life. I don't know of anything I've ever seen that more vividly demonstrates love in action than Habitat for Humanity."

■ PLAINS *map page 213, B-2*

Eight miles west of Americus, Plains is the antithesis of the older county seats of the region. Where those are dominated by a courthouse—grand, looming, and often the largest building in town—Plains resembles a frontier town of the West.

Downtown Plains, home of former President Jimmy Carter.

SOUTH
GEORGIA

In this settlement of less than 750 people, all commerce and life is centered around the rail tracks that bisect the hamlet, and the largest building in sight is a corrugated-metal peanut warehouse. Life here is slow, sublimely so. And a dog sleeping in the middle of the street is a real possibility, not a hackneyed stereotype, so check your rear-view mirror before you back out of that parking space.

But in 1975, this little town came alive when favorite son Jimmy Carter declared his candidacy for President. Carter first entered politics in 1961 and was elected governor of Georgia in 1971, announcing during his inauguration speech, "I say to you quite frankly that the time for racial discrimination is over." When Carter began his presidential campaign after just four years as Georgia's governor, many asked, "Jimmy Who?" Yet thanks to strong grassroots support and tireless campaigning, Carter won the Democratic Party nomination. In the wake of the mendacious mess that was Watergate, Carter promised that he would not lie to the American public, and they believed him. In 1977 he was sworn in as the 39th President.

◆ JIMMY CARTER SIGHTS

Today, the old green-and-white clapboard depot that used to be Carter Campaign Headquarters is open for touring. On display are campaign ephemera like a poster for a July 19, 1976, cattle auction held in Woodbury, Georgia, emblazoned with the slogan, "Got a beef with Bureaucracy? Grind it. Help send Jimmy Carter to Washington."

Also on view are displays that detail Carter Administration accomplishments, from the signing of SALT II treaty with the Soviet Union to limit nuclear proliferation, to the signing of a peace treaty by Egyptian President Anwar Sadat and Israeli Prime Minister Menachem Begin to end hostilities in the Middle East.

Across the tracks are arrayed a series of businesses, some of which sell geegaws. Others, like the Carter Worm Farm Office, are vestiges of past business activity. In the window of cousin Hugh Carter's antique shop, a handwritten sign is posted when the Carters are in town. It reads: "President Jimmy Carter will teach the Sunday school lesson at **Maranatha Baptist Church** this Sunday at 10:00 A.M. You are invited." The church, located just north of town on Highway 45, is a simple brick affair, well suited to this former peanut farmer. On the same road, a bit closer to town, is the graceful redbrick Plains High School, where both President Carter and his wife Rosalynn attended school. Now a part of the 70-acre **Jimmy Carter**

National Historic Site, the school has been converted to a museum dedicated to Carter's education and life. *North of town on Highway 45; 912-824-4104.*

Visitors in search of Carter kitsch will want to stop off at late brother Billy's gas station (now closed) on Church Street, or take a gander at the giant, smiling goober just north of town near Maranatha Baptist Church.

■ ANDERSONVILLE NATIONAL HISTORIC SITE *map page 213, B-1*

North and east of Plains on Highway 49 is the town of Andersonville, site of Camp Sumter, a Confederate prison camp notorious for its inhumane treatment of Union troops. Established in 1864, near the end of the Civil War, the camp housed more than 45,000 troops. Of these, more than 13,000 perished, the victims of dysentery, severe malnutrition, and a range of other maladies. So little food was allowed the prisoners that Confederates were accused of purposely starving the inmates, but officers responded that the Confederate government was virtually broke by 1864, and that they had no funds to buy food.

Over 13,000 Union soldier prisoners died at Camp Sumter in Andersonville.
(Lithograph by John Walker, Library of Congress)

Rows of headstones in Andersonville National Cemetery.

On July 8, 1864, Sgt. David Kennedy, of the 9th Ohio Calvary, recorded these observations in his diary:

Wuld that I was an artist & had the material to paint this camp & all its troops or the tongue of some eloquent Statesman and had the privleage of expressing my mind to our hon. rulers at Washington. I should gloery to describe this hell on Earth where it takes 7 of its occupiants to make a Shadow.

On November 10, 1865, Confederate captain Henry Wirtz, the officer in charge of the stockade, was hanged, the only Confederate to be executed for war crimes after the close of the Civil War. Today many Confederate heritage groups believe—as did many Southerners at the time of his hanging—that Wirtz was a scapegoat. They claim that Wirtz, a Swiss-born physician who had lived in Louisiana prior to the start to the war, was blamed for the atrocities committed under his watch, atrocities that were perhaps abetted by his superiors. Accordingly, in the center of the little village of Andersonville, there stands a marble obelisk, erected not to the Confederate dead of the county or the state, but to Wirtz, in the hope that its presence might help to "rescue his name from the stigma attached to it by embittered prejudice...."

Today, the site of the former prison camp is operated by the National Park Service, and the grounds are open for touring. Also on-site is the **National Prisoner of War Museum,** a bunker-like redbrick fortress housing multimedia displays that poignantly portray the horrors of POW life. As you step into the first exhibition gallery, a spotlight sweeps across the wall, sirens wail, and the staccato crackle of machine gun fire caroms off the ceiling. A tour of the facilities is unsettling, even disturbing. As you hear the voices of soldiers recounting their time in prison, the walls seem to close in around you, and the words give you pause. "War was supposed to be clean...all crisp and decisive," says one Vietnam POW. "Instead I felt like some helpless cornered prey." And though the focus is on POWs from all American wars, there are a significant number of artifacts from Camp Sumter on display, including the original lock, key, and hinge from the south gate of the camp—eerie reminders of what once stood here among the pines. *Highway 49, 10 miles north of Americus; 912-924-0343.*

■ LUMPKIN *map page 213, A-2*

History of a more palatable sort is in the offering west of Andersonville, at the delightful antebellum village of Lumpkin. On the square here you will find the oldest operating hardware store in Georgia—the Singer Company—which first opened its doors in 1838. Just down the street is Hatchett's Drug Store Museum, shrine to the old-fashioned soda fountain, where cherry and vanilla cokes, not to mention banana splits, are served with aplomb.

On the edge of town, a half mile south down Martin Luther King Drive, is **Westville** ("where it's always 1850"), a living history museum where potters, soap makers, and other craftspeople practice their craft. Unlike the Agrirama in Tifton, Westville is far removed from any signs of modern-day life. An afternoon spent wandering the dirt pathways that lead from house to house, from mill to millinery store, is time well spent. And if you're lucky, you will pass by the old Marrett farmhouse just as the cook is pulling a batch of biscuits from the fire. *Off US 27; 912-838-6310.*

■ PROVIDENCE CANYON

On Georgia's western extreme, just a scant few miles from the Alabama border, is a geological curiosity: Providence Canyon, which looks like it belongs in Arizona rather than within a couple of hour's drive of Atlanta. Known to many as Georgia's "little Grand Canyon," it was named for the church that had to be moved when the clay soil continued to erode. But this so-called canyon is, in all actuality, a Brobdingnagian gully. Due to poor farming practices, the gully first began to appear in the 1800s, and it now reaches depths of over 150 feet. At sunset or sunrise, when the sun's rays slant across the walls of the canyon, a kaleidoscope of colors plays across the hoodoo-like rock formations. *Highway 39 C, seven miles west of Lumpkin; 912-838-6202.*

Providence Canyon began as a gully in the 19th century. Today it is a full-fledged canyon, reaching depths of 150 feet in some places.

SOUTH
GEORGIA

South Georgia Food & Lodging

X **Restaurant Prices:** $ = under $10; $$ = $10–20; $$$ = over $20
Restaurant price designations indicate the approximate cost of an entrée and an appetizer or desert, exclusive of drinks, tax, and tip.

▦ **Lodging Rates:** $ = under $75; $$ = $75–150; $$$ = over $150
Lodging rate designations indicate the approximate cost of a double occupancy room for one night, exclusive of surcharges and taxes.

A statewide food and lodging **reference map** can be found on page 306, and an **index of towns** with food and lodging listings in this book follows on pages 307–308. Toll-free numbers for **chain hotels and motels** can be found on page 308.

Albany *map p. 213, B-2*

X **Aunt Fannie's Checkered Apron**
912-888-8416; 826 Byron Rd.
Bright orange slabs of rutabaga, dusky turnip greens swimming in a porcine potlikker, and crusty fried chicken are offered at this cream-colored cinderblock restaurant on a side street in a somewhat derelict neighborhood. At lunch, suits and laborers alike fill the 20-odd tables. Breakfast and lunch. $

X **Carter's Grill**
912-432-2098; 321 West Highland Ave.
Open since 1968, this local institution is famed for its soul food. Served cafeteria-style are butter beans and field peas, pigs' feet and neckbones, all deftly seasoned, all priced at a pittance. At breakfast, salmon croquettes and grits draw a crowd. Breakfast, lunch, and dinner. $

X **Chef Gwen's Bistro**
912-888-0401; 303 West Highland Ave.
The interior, festooned with palm trees, is a riot of color. The Caribbean offerings —oxtails and various jerked meats and curried vegetables—are no less vibrant at this quaint and funky hideaway. Breakfast and dinner. $

X **Fishbone's**
912-439-2261; 1504 Dawson Rd.
Serves just-caught grouper and snapper, baked in parchment or grilled. A good selection of wines and an atmosphere that's two or three cuts above that of the typical fish house make this Albany's favorite for a nice evening out. Dinner. $$

▦ **General lodging information**
Comfort Suites *(912-888-3939)* on Dawson Road has reasonable rates and plenty of amenities. On Highways 82 and 19, you will also find a large number of other hotels including a **Fairfield Inn** *(912-435-6859)* and a **Holiday Inn Express** *(912-883-1650)*. $-$$

▦ **Quality Inn Merry Acres**
912-435-7721; 1500 Dawson Rd.
Though at its heart it's a motor hotel like the rest, this is Albany's nicest place to bed down. There's a pool, too. The inn incorporates an older frame home that was moved to the property. $-$$

Americus *map p. 213, B-1*

✗ Big Jake's Barbecue
No phone; Lee St., across the tracks.
"I got in a little trouble and took a six-year break from cooking," says the proprietor. Be glad he's back. Ribs are the specialty here, served from Big Jake's front yard. Look for the monstrous cookers that sit hard by the road. Late lunch through late-night. $

✗ Monroe's Hot Dogs and Billiards
912-924-4106; 318 West Lamar St.
In a separate, smoke-filled back room, a band of wizened regulars shoots pool from morning to night. In front, Monroe's dishes dogs piled high with chili and capped with coleslaw to office and construction workers alike. The slogan: "Best dogs ever bitten by man." Lunch. $

▦ Windsor Hotel
912-924-1555; 125 West Lamar St.
Built in 1892, this turreted redbrick hotel has been restored to its former glory: an opulent marvel, with fanciful brick and terra cotta work. The three-story lobby, outfitted in gleaming golden oak, is alone worth the visit. Rooms are spacious, while suites (two are set in the tower) are a worthwhile indulgence. $-$$

Bainbridge *map p. 213, B-4*

✗ Andrew's Oyster Bar
912-248-8280; 104 East Calhoun St.
You can get oyster by the bushel or by the dozen, not to mention such local delights as mullet, red roe, and sucker fish, from this tumbledown shack outfit-

ted with four picnic tables. Step up to the window and bark out your order; you won't find better fish in South Georgia. Lunch and dinner. $

✗ Jack Wingate's Lunker Lodge
912-246-0658; 139 Wingate Rd. (off Hwy. 97, 12 miles south of Bainbridge)
This fish camp serves piping hot fried catfish in a rustic setting. Out in the boonies along Lake Seminole, the spot is popular with fishermen, who gather around the tables to swap lies and scarf down hushpuppies. Lunch, dinner. $-$$

▦ Gilded Cage Bed-and-Breakfast
912-243-2040; 722 South West St.
Built in 1855, this Victorian inn is situated in a beautiful little cottage with four rooms for let, two with private bath. Located in the heart of Bainbridge, it holds great appeal for fishermen as well as those who want to just soak up a bit of small-town life. $

Colquitt *map p. 213, A-3*

✗ Tarrer Inn Restaurant
912-758-2888; 155 South Cuthbert St.
At lunch there is a decent buffet, but by dinnertime the chef has pulled out all the stops: pan-seared speckled trout with a brown butter sauce, grilled quail in a mayhaw sauce. The setting is a bit frumpy but pleasant, in a country-club sort of way. Lunch and dinner. $$

▦ Tarter Inn
912-758-2888; 155 South Cuthbert St.
From the veranda of this inn overlooking the courthouse square, all the world

seems at peace. The rooms, which open off a grand central hallway, are high-ceilinged and well appointed. Breakfast biscuits come with a crock of the famous local mayhaw jelly. $

Damascus *map p. 213, A-3*

✗ **The Power Line**
912-725-4138; Hall Place (off Hwy. 45, two miles north of Damascus)
Set off the highway a mile down a dirt road, this tin-roofed, raw-wood building gets its name from the massive power lines that loom above, snapping and humming in the still night air. Crop-duster pilots gather at the bar to talk of recent crashes. Families sit in the dining room eating grilled grouper, sweet and satisfying, or great steaks. Most everyone but the Baptists washes it all down with a bottle or three of beer. Dinner. $$

Homerville *map p. 213, E-4*

✗ **Jimbo's Log Kitchen**
912-487-2142; 600 West Dame Ave. (off Hwy. 84, 25 miles west of Waycross)
Jimbo's has been in business since 1936. At lunch, there's a buffet piled high with vegetables, but most folks still come for the 'cue, which you can see smoldering on the pit just behind the counter. Breakfast, lunch, and dinner. $

McRae Area *map p. 213, E-1*

✗ **Benton Lee's Steakhouse**
912-594-6931; 138 Benton Powell Rd., Uvalda

The owner sits behind the bar in a Lazy Boy, swatting flies and chain smoking. The place is a rambling wreck. And the bench seating is hard and unforgiving. But the monstrous T-bones and sirloins are well marbled and expertly cooked, and the fries are hand cut. Budweiser is the house wine. Not an experience for the effete. Dinner. $$

✗ **Southern Star Grill**
912-868-2507; 752 East Oak St.
Basic American food done right is what you will find at this casual restaurant. Try the catfish, dredged in sesame seeds before frying, or the teriyaki chicken, a surprisingly good take on a much ma-ligned dish. For lunch try a vegetable plate or an overstuffed club sandwich. Decent wine list. Lunch and dinner. $-$$

▥ **Little Ocmulgee State Park Lodge**
912-868-2832 or 800-864-7275; Hwy. 441, two miles north of McRae
A 30-room lodge and a cluster of 10 cabins set around the lake, are available at this underappreciated jewel of a state park. Tennis courts, a swimming pool and an 18-hole golf course give this park the air of a small-town resort.

Perry Area *map p. 213, C-1*

✗ **The Langston House**
912-988-8696; 125 South Langston Cir. (off Hwy. 26, six miles south of Perry)
This newly opened restaurant, set in a beautifully restored 1837 Georgian home, features exquisite local game and fresh seafood as well as many French-inspired dishes, among them an excel-

lent squab with foie gras. The dining room is a study in refined simplicity, with earth-tone walls, hardwood floors, and primitive mantles. Dinner. $$$

✗ New Perry Hotel Dining Room
912-987-1000; 800 Main St.
Open since 1925, on the same spot where the old Perry Hotel once stood—right across the street from the Houston County courthouse. Frumpy furnishings, old-fashioned servers, and reliably good Southern victuals draw diners off the interstate. Stick with standards like stuffed bell peppers and fried chicken. Breakfast, lunch, and dinner. $-$$

✗ White Diamond Grill
912-922-8686; 497 South Hwy. 247, Bonaire
Hand-cut fries, hand-dipped milkshakes and smoke-tinged pork with a mustard sauce are the draws at this country roadhouse open since the '40s. Lunch and early dinner. $

🏨 Henderson Village
912-988-8696; 125 South Langston Cir. (off Hwy. 26, six miles south of Perry)
It's way out in the country, but just a mile from the interstate. Exquisite in every detail, this 24-room country resort is set in 13 different buildings on 22 acres (surrounded by 8,000 acres). Expect to be pampered, and to eat very well, whether it be a dinner in the Langston House *(see above)* or a breakfast of country ham and eggs with Vidalia onion compote. $$-$$$

🏨 New Perry Hotel
912-987-1000; 800 Main St.
The main building is a mint-green concrete take on a Colonial-style mansion, with simple, clean rooms. Out back, there's a motel court. Rooms are basic and affordable, with far more charm than you'd find at a similarly priced chain motel. $

🏨 Swift Street Inn
912-988-9148; 1204 Swift St.
This antebellum cottage has four antique-filled rooms, each with private bath. The nicest is the Magnolia Room, with a four-poster bed and a fireplace. For breakfast, look for stuffed French toast or a cheese-grits casserole. $-$$

Plains Area *map p. 213, B-2*

✗ Mom's Kitchen
912-828-7285; Hwy. 41 & Hwy. 280, Preston
The biscuits here are justifiably famous. Baked by the family matriarch, Evelyn Hollis (Mom's mom), they taste best hot from the oven and burbling with butter. But there are other treats to be had at this simple brick-fronted cafe: crisp fried chicken and sandy-brown fried catfish, baked sweet potatoes and wonderful sweet iced tea. Breakfast and lunch. $

🏨 Plains Bed-and-Breakfast
912-824-7252; 100 West Church St.
This pink-and-cream Victorian lady is well situated in downtown Plains, just across from the old railroad depot. Though a bit worn at the edges, the

four-room inn is quite comfortable—and quite reasonable. A hot breakfast is served daily. $

Thomasville *map p. 213, C-4*

X **Billiard Academy**
912-226-9981; 121 South Broad St.
Ten swivel-back stools face a bar behind which stands the proprietor, dishing out 95¢ hotdogs—and that's all—slathered in a meaty chili topped with mustard and chopped onions. A beer sets you back $1.50. Open since 1949, the four-table poolroom, complete with spittoons, exudes tons of charm. 8 A.M. to 7 P.M.

X **Market Diner**
912-225-1777; 502 Smith Ave.
Appropriately enough, this little restaurant sits next to the local farmer's market, from which the owners purchase their produce. Fried green tomatoes, stewed corn, and mashed potatoes are favorites at lunch. On Friday and Saturday nights, there's an extensive seafood buffet featuring crisp, local mullet, fried to a turn, along with shrimp, oysters, and other treats. Lunch and dinner. $

⊞ **Paxton House Inn**
912-226-5197; 445 Remington Ave.
This bright-blue Victorian home features eight large rooms furnished with all the amenities. Within easy walking distance of the shops of downtown Thomasville, the Paxton House boasts a wide and welcoming front porch as well as a heated indoor pool and hot tub.

⊞ **Melhana Plantation Resort**
912-226-2290; 301 Showboat Lane

For a taste of the opulence that plantation life can offer, try this sprawling resort on the edge of town. You enter along a drive lined with majestic oaks and lustrous magnolias. In front looms the big house, but many of the outbuildings have been retained too. Horseback riding, hunting, polo, and just plain lazing around the beautifully landscaped pool are favorite pastimes. $$$

Valdosta Area *map p. 213, D-4*

X **C. H. Mitchell's Barbecue**
912-244-2684; 515 South Ashley St.
You'll find seeds at the bottom of your tumbler of lemonade, proof of the counterman's boast that it is fresh-squeezed. Though barbecue is the claim to fame here, you're better off sticking to collard greens and the like. On Fridays and Saturdays, chitlins are available. Breakfast, lunch, dinner, and late-night. $

X **The Fish Net**
912-559-5410; 3949 Sportsman's Cove Rd., Lake Park
A bit out in the country, on the edge of a cypress swamp, just where a good fish camp should be. Fried catfish is the star here, and should you wish to experience this Dixie dish at its best, have yours with a side order of grits. (Avoid the phosphorescent cheese grits.) Dinner. $

X **Ray's Mill Pond Cafe**
912-455-4075; off Hwy. 125, near Ray City
Even farther out in the country—20-plus miles to be inexact. And the fish is better to boot. Fishnets line the walls of

this low-slung restaurant perched on the edge of a 3,500-acre lake studded with Cypress knees. Order fresh fried mullet with grits, or stuffed crab in the shell. Out back, live oaks loom over a bleak but beautiful waterfront scene. Dinner. $

🏨 **General lodging information**
From the interstate, Valdosta looks like a neon jungle of chain motels. Exit 5 is the monster, where you will find three of the better ones: **Jameson Inn** *(912-253-0009; 1725 Gornto Rd.)*, **Fairfield Inn** *(912-253-9300; 1309 St. Augustine Rd.)*, and **Holiday Inn** *(912-242-3881; 1311 St. Augustine Rd.)*, the latter distinguished by a country cooking restaurant favored by locals, **The Simmering Pot.**

Vidalia *map p. 213, E-1*

✗ **Hilton's Restaurant/ Sweat's Barbecue**
912-537-3934; 215 Northwest Main St.
For years Sweat's Barbecue in nearby Soperton was counted among the state's best. Alas, the original location has closed. Somehow the 'cue doesn't taste quite as good here, but it's still the best in town. On the weekends they serve a seafood buffet that is not really up to snuff. Lunch and dinner. $

Vienna *map p. 213, C-1*

Site of the Big Pig Jig—Georgia's "official" barbecue championship cook-off, held annually on the second weekend in October —this small Georgia town is better known among true barbecue aficionados as the home of Mamie Bryant's barbecue shack.

✗ **Mamie Bryant's BBQ Pit**
912-268-4179; Eighth Street
Each Thursday, J. B. Bryant puts a mess of hams on the pit to smoke and his wife, Mamie, stirs up a pot of Brunswick stew. Starting at around 10 o'clock Friday morning, a line forms out in the front yard of the small cinderblock building. And by Friday afternoon— maybe Saturday morning—it's all gone. Sweet smoky 'cue and stew is all they sell. It's worth a 50-mile detour.

Waycross *map p. 213, E-3*

✗ **DK's Barbeque**
912-283-9898; 701 Pittman St.
Nearly as good as The Pig (see below). And if you hanker for something a bit sweet with your meal, this may be your best bet: the sweet-potato pie with homemade crust is justly famous. Breakfast, lunch, dinner, and late-night. $

✗ **The Pig**
912-283-4875; 768 State St.
Opened its doors in 1947. Five red vinyl booths hug the wall, and seven stools face the counter. Chopped or sliced pork, ribs, and chicken are all that emerge from the pit. This is barbecue at its best—and simplest. Icy bottles of Coke are the beverage of choice. Lunch, dinner, and late-night. $

🏨 **General lodging information**
Along Memorial Drive are arrayed a number of chain hotels. The **Holiday Inn** *(912-283-4490; 1725 Memorial Dr.)* and **Comfort Inn** *(912-283-3300; 1903 Memorial Dr.)* are good bets.

SOUTH GEORGIA FOOD & LODGING

S A V A N N A H
& T H E   G E O R G I A   C O A S T

■ HIGHLIGHTS

■ TRAVEL BASICS

Savannah is a city splendid enough to seduce even the most jaded traveler. Verdant, almost tropical in its lushness, it is a place of great natural beauty. And for those who come in search of architectural jewels, Savannah does not disappoint, with its regal redbrick townhouses and Gothic-spired cathedrals. South of the city stretches a coastline more remote than might be imagined, what with controlled-access enclaves like Cumberland and Sapelo Islands. Down around Jekyll and St. Simon's Islands, white-sand beaches call. As you make your way closer to the sea, dull gray sand gives way to sparkling white, pine trees to palmettos, and soon the beach beckons, calm and peaceful. Thanks to the miles of coastline, the Georgia beaches are rarely overcrowded. There's always a spot to throw down a blanket, soak up some sun, maybe meander a mile or two down to where the pier juts out into the lolling surf. At night, there's usually a ramshackle fish house just down the road, where the beer is ice cold and the fresh boiled shrimp are delicious.

Between South Carolina and northern Florida, the Atlantic coastline arcs pronouncedly inward. In all of this area, known as the Georgia Bight, the tidal fluctuation is extreme. In Georgia, tides vary up to 10 feet between high and low tide—which accounts for the wide salt marshes found all along the coast. High tide brings seawater as much as 40 miles up the coastal rivers, creating extensive brackish estuaries. These distinctive habitat types make Georgia's coast an amazing place to view wildlife, especially birds.

SAVANNAH &
THE COAST

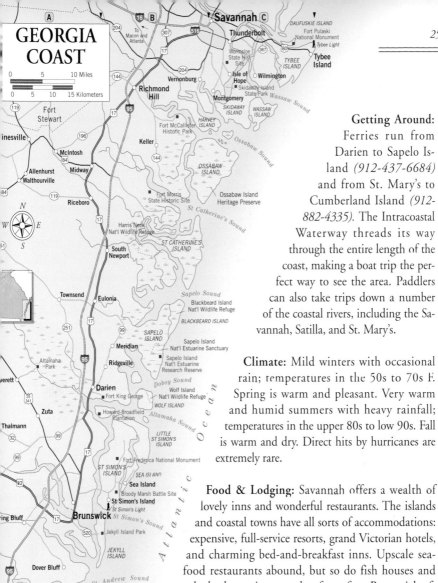

Getting Around: Ferries run from Darien to Sapelo Island *(912-437-6684)* and from St. Mary's to Cumberland Island *(912-882-4335).* The Intracoastal Waterway threads its way through the entire length of the coast, making a boat trip the perfect way to see the area. Paddlers can also take trips down a number of the coastal rivers, including the Savannah, Satilla, and St. Mary's.

Climate: Mild winters with occasional rain; temperatures in the 50s to 70s F. Spring is warm and pleasant. Very warm and humid summers with heavy rainfall; temperatures in the upper 80s to low 90s. Fall is warm and dry. Direct hits by hurricanes are extremely rare.

Food & Lodging: Savannah offers a wealth of lovely inns and wonderful restaurants. The islands and coastal towns have all sorts of accommodations: expensive, full-service resorts, grand Victorian hotels, and charming bed-and-breakfast inns. Upscale seafood restaurants abound, but so do fish houses and crab shacks serving tasty, less fancy fare. Brunswick offers a number of chain motels that lack charm but are inexpensive. And Jekyll Island has 200 spots at an ideally situated, oak-shaded campground. *(Jekyll Island Campground:* 912-635-3021). For food and lodging listings, see pages 296 to 305.

SAVANNAH &
THE COAST

■ OVERVIEW

Savannah is a city of many charms and many contradictions. Azaleas and camellias, dogwoods and crepe myrtle trees flourish in the semitropical swelter of a Savannah spring afternoon. Moss-draped oaks lend a shadowy, almost brooding quality to a bright winter morning. Regal redbrick buildings stand in haughty repose, proud testament to the city's past.

Like New Orleans, Savannah is a house-proud city, a city seemingly drunk on architecture. Unlike New Orleans, this is not a city prone to public displays of hedonism. Here, for the most part, drinking and debauchery are private affairs, taking place far from prying eyes. Walking the streets of Savannah, you get the feeling that something very devilish is going on behind the doors of those lovely townhouses.

And yet, it is the serenity of the city, indeed the gentility, that will seduce you. There is order and beauty to be found here, a sense of man and nature as complementary forces. Nowhere is this gentility more evident than in the vest-pocket parks that dot the city, enclaves of green not so much contained by redbrick borders as protected by them. These squares, part of founder James Oglethorpe's original

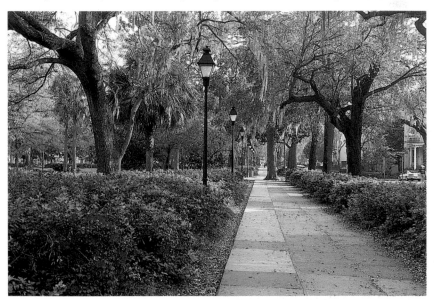

(above) Vest-pocket parks add charm and serenity to Savannah's historic districts.
(opposite) The First Lady *is one of the old-fashioned riverboats that plies the Savannah River.*

plan for the city, are the jewels in Savannah's architectural crown.

South of Savannah lies a marshy coastline where golden-tipped marsh grass waves in the salty breeze and Spanish moss drips from the boughs of live oak trees. Rivers curve through these marshlands, creating a series of low-lying islands, each with its own charm—from Sapelo Island with its dense tropical overgrowth and crumbling ruins, to luxurious resort enclaves like Sea Island.

■ HISTORY

In 1566, a battle-tested Spanish conquistador named Pedro Menendez de Aviles came ashore on St. Catherine's Island, south of Savannah. His intention was to set up missions and presidios off the southeastern coast of North America, to encourage Spanish settlement and protect Spain's most important trade route from the French and British.

At St. Catherine's, Mendendez met with an Indian chief, Guale, whose name the Spaniards thereafter gave to the entire area. Menendez left behind a garrison of 30 men, and soon Spanish Jesuit missionaries were landing on the sea islands.

The native Creeks, farmers who lived in small villages along the coast, initially showed interest in what the missionaries had to teach, but after a few years they grew hostile and drove the Jesuits out. Franciscan missionaries followed the Jesuits, but the Spanish influence remained negligible.

When James Oglethorpe and a group of 114 British settlers arrived off the coast of Georgia on a February morning in 1733, they were welcomed by Tomochichi, chief of the the Yamacraws, a member tribe of the Lower Creek Confederacy. With Tomochichi's guidance Oglethorpe selected a spot on a 40-foot bluff overlooking the Savannah River some 17 miles from the Atlantic coast. "The last and fullest consideration of the Healthfulness of the place was that an Indian nation, who knew the Nature of the Country, chose it for their Habitation," Oglethorpe later reported to the colony's sponsors in England.

Oglethorpe's early description of Savannah's setting still rings true. He wrote in a 1733 letter to the trustees:

> The river has formed a half moon, around the side of which the banks are about forty feet high, and on the top a flat which they call a bluff.... Upon the river-side, in the center of the plain, I have laid out the town,

In this painting by William Verelst, James Oglethorpe presents Yamacraw chief Tomochichi to the trustees of the colony of Georgia in London in 1734. (Henry Francis DuPont Winterthur Museum, Delaware)

opposite to which is an island of very rich pasturage. The river is pretty wide, the water fresh, and from the quay of the town you can see its whole course to the sea.

Oglethorpe had the most profound effect of any one person on the city of Savannah, and his original plan for the city, which artfully fits its setting, endures to this day. With its fine avenues and public squares, the plan focused the life of the new city on its common green spaces, making for an urban environment of physical beauty and pleasing interaction.

Oglethorpe left Georgia in July of 1743, never to return, but the year before he left he fought a final battle with the Spanish, defeating them at the Battle of Bloody Marsh on St. Simon's Island and driving them from Georgia.

In the ensuing years, the utopian community Oglethorpe had envisioned—free from the ill effects of slavery or land speculation—succumbed to economic and

Rice cultivation on the Ogeechee River near Savannah, after a wood engraving by A. R. Ward for Harper's Weekly. *(Library of Congress)*

political pressures. Early attempts to raise wine grapes and silkworms failed, and Georgian whites looked enviously toward South Carolina, where crops of rice and indigo, tilled by slaves, were bringing large profits.

By the time of the Revolutionary War, slavery was legal in Georgia and the port city of Savannah was thriving. But the town's location at the tail end of the colonial territory left it susceptible to attack, and in December of 1778, the city was captured by the British; it would remain in the hands of the redcoats until after the close of the war in 1782.

The years between the Revolutionary War and the Civil War would prove to be Savannah's heyday as cotton and the slave trade brought untold wealth to the port city. As Savannah prospered, the city's residents began constructing many of the elegant homes that now grace the town squares. By 1820, Savannah was among the 20 largest cities in the United States.

During the Civil War, Union blockades cut off Savannah from trade, but the city did not suffer the physical damage that many Georgia towns did. Gracious Savannah remained above the fray, enduring Yankee occupation as if it were a prolonged visitation from a particularly uncouth uncle, rather than a hostile invasion.

It would be a grand oversight to say that nothing of import has transpired in the near century and a half since the close of the Civil War. During World War II, the city's shipyards built boats by the score. And during the Civil Rights Movement, black citizens of Savannah, through a series of boycotts, won a series of decisive battles in the struggle for equal accommodation under the law. The real story, though, is not what has changed but what has endured.

■ SAVANNAH *map page 264*

The original plan for Savannah called for 24 squares, spaced at regular intervals throughout the business and residential districts of the city. Twenty-one of those squares remain, due to preservation efforts spearheaded by the Historic Savannah Foundation. Faced in the 1950s with the prospect of losing many of the squares and not a few of the grand old buildings at the city center to "urban renewal," a dedicated band of urban guerrillas in petticoats worked to engineer a solution, soliciting federal grants and twisting the arms of local loan officers in an effort to

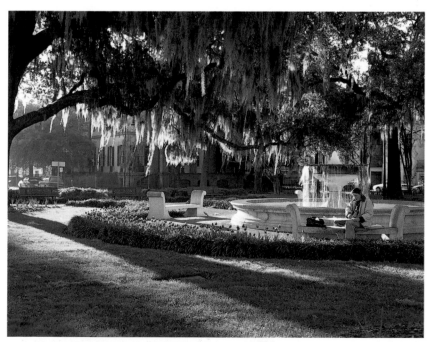

An early morning haze lingers above Orleans Square in the city's historic district.

This engraving by P. Fourdrinier, after a drawing by Peter Gordon, shows Savannah as it stood on March 29, 1734. Bull Street runs north to south through the center of the plan, which shows five of Savannah's original 24 squares. (Library of Congress)

SAVANNAH'S ANCIENT PLAN

*T*he plan of Savannah was based on a sketch in *Villas of the Ancients* by Robert Castell, who died in one of the English debtor prisons that Georgia was founded to relieve. From this sketch Oglethorpe, founder of the city, and Colonel William Bull, an engineer of South Carolina, designed the Colonial city on a plan which has persisted.

For all their contrasting details there is a certain unity in the older Georgian Colonial, Classical Revival, Greek Revival, and Victorian houses, which are built on a level with the sidewalk and often joined in rows. Usually they have three or four stories, including a raised basement, and stairs ascending to a high stoop. Some were constructed of crude brick brought from Europe as ballast in early sailing vessels, others show in their soft colors that they were built of the celebrated Savannah grey brick from the old kiln of the Hermitage, etc.

 exⁿ∞ ∞ⁿ

*A*long Bull Street, which forms the central axis of the city, are five squares that in the original plan were designed as centers of defense against Spanish and Indian invasion. Now two centuries old, these small parks embody Savannah's characteristic, semitropical and hence lush growth, subdued to the precise lines of a formal beauty. Italian cypresses, tall cabbage palmettoes, blossoming bays, and English yews are among the trees that increase the depth of a natural growth of oaks....Flower beds are bright in season with flame and other azaleas, with glossy green-leaved and white wax-blossomed gardenias, and with both single-colored and variegated camellias. Paths through the grassy plots are lined with benches that offer an invitation to rest and contemplation, and in many of the parks monuments to past heroes create a sense of the continuous ebb and flow of life.

—George G. Leckie, *Georgia: A Guide to its Towns and Countryside,* 1940

An 1855 view of Savannah by J. W. Hill, looking north on Bull Street, Savannah's central thoroughfare, from Monterey Square. In the foreground stands the Pulaski Monument, and at the far end of Bull Street is the Cotton Exchange. (Collection of the Mariners Museum)

revitalize row upon row of antebellum homes.

Savannah's architecture spans both distance and time, as early vernacular architecture gives way to Greek revival and then Victorian. At the southern end of the historic district, at DeRenne Avenue, the 20th century arrives with monotonous commercial buildings. An aged local perhaps put it best when she said, "Darling, anything south of DeRenne might as well be Jacksonville, Florida."

Calhoun Square 23
Chatham Square 21
Chippewa Square 15
Columbia Square 11
Crawford Square 16
Elbert Square 13

Ellis Square 2
Franklin Square 1
Green Square 12
Johnson Square 3
Lafayette Square 19
Liberty Square 7

Madison Square 18
Monterey Square 22
Oglethorpe Square 10
Orleans Square 14
Pulaski Square 17
Reynolds Square 4

Telfair Square 8
Troup Square 20
Warren Square 5
Washington Square 6
Whitefield Square 24
Wright Square 9

DOWNTOWN
SAVANNAH

The three-square-mile historic district stretches south from River Street to the southern tip of Forsyth Park. Plan to spend an afternoon ambling from square to square enjoying verdant parks, inhaling the scent of magnolia, and admiring regal redbrick homes and stately public buildings.

The old Cotton Exchange is perched on Yamacraw Bluff.

◆ BAY AND RIVER STREETS

At 100 East Bay Street, near the intersection with Drayton, stands the old **Cotton Exchange**, a Romanesque beauty perched on Yamacraw Bluff. Once the hub of activity for the cotton warehouses that line River Street below, this 1886 building with a fanciful terra cotta front now stands in noble repose beside the Bourbon Street–like circus that unfolds at the riverside. Stretching east and west from the Exchange is a series of brick buildings, once the offices of the cotton factors who made their millions trading long-staple Sea Island cotton, and now home to antique dealers and attorneys.

River Street, a cobblestone lane that runs the width of the historic district, affords an unparalleled view of the Savannah River. The other side of River Street is lined with rough ballast-and-brick buildings, where barkers hawk quart-sized draft beers and any manner of T-shirts. And if your visit happens to coincide with the celebration of St. Patrick's Day (Savannah's celebration is second in size only to New York City's), then you can bet that the beer will be dyed an Irish green.

But River Street is an anomaly, a ticky-tacky blight upon what is truly one of the most serenely beautiful cities in the South, indeed in the whole of the United States. Even in the dead of winter, the city resembles an oasis of green, profuse with giant oaks and the lustrous sheen of azalea and camellia bushes, while during the spring and summer the city flushes with vivid color as crepe myrtles, dogwoods, magnolias, and wisteria vines burst forth in a kaleidoscope of blossoms.

◆ SAVANNAH SQUARE BY SQUARE

Johnson Square

Astride Bull Street between Bryan and Congress is Johnson Square, the first square laid out by Oglethorpe. Named for Robert Johnson, the governor of South Carolina at the time of Georgia's founding, the square is anchored on the east by **Christ Episcopal Church,** the first congregation organized in the colony. The present structure, the fourth at this site, is a study in simplicity, fronted by staid Corinthian columns and noticeably absent of any joyfully bright stained glass windows. It was on this site that John Wesley held the first Sunday school class in North America. Wesley, who came to America as a missionary for the Church of England, proved to be an unpopular and antagonistic sort. He would later leave Georgia after being indicted for interfering in the secular affairs of the colony. Back in England, he rekindled his religious fervor and founded Methodism.

In the center of the square is a monument to Revolutionary War hero Gen. Nathanael Greene, and it is here that you will find his grave.

City Market

West of Johnson Square, past Ellis Square, is the City Market, a pedestrian-only warren of narrow streets lined with some of Savannah's toniest shops and best restaurants. These include the relatively new **Sapphire Grill,** a chic temple of haute cuisine, and **Lady and Sons,** a busy buffet piled high with traditional Southern favorites *(see pages 300–301).*

Reynolds Square

Just a couple of blocks east of City Market, astride Abercorn Street, is Reynolds Square. On the northeast corner you will find the **Old Pink House** restaurant *(see page 301).* The rose-colored stucco building with Palladian windows is one of the few buildings to survive the great fire of 1796, when more than 200 homes were destroyed. Across the square at 27 Abercorn is the **Oliver Sturges House,** an 1818 brick home distinguished by playful dolphin-shaped downspouts that decorate the side of the house.

❖

Farther east are **Warren** and **Washington Squares,** added to Oglethorpe's original 24 in 1790. And just south, astride Habersham Street between State and York, is **Columbia Square,** added in 1799; on the northwest corner you will find the **Isaiah Davenport House Museum,** a Federal-style brick building with wrought iron touches. It was the imminent destruction, in 1955, of the then derelict Davenport home that many credit as the catalyst for Savannah's historic preservation movement. *324 East State Street, 912-236-8097.*

Oglethorpe Square

Just west, on Oglethorpe Square at Abercorn Street, is one of three extant homes designed by noted English architect William Jay: the **Owens-Thomas House,** a Regency-style home of unparalleled opulence, built in 1817 and filled with period furnishings. The National Trust for Historic Preservation calls this "Savannah's

Savannah Market, *by Harry Leslie Hoffman, 1915. (Private collection)*

most sophisticated house, then and now." Today it is operated as a museum by the Telfair Academy of Arts and Sciences. *124 Abercorn Street, 912-233-9743.*

Telfair Square

Also of English Regency style and designed by Jay is the **Telfair Museum of Art,** the oldest art museum in the South, featuring a collection strong in the decorative arts— just what you might expect in house-proud Savannah. *121 Barnard Street; 912-232-1177.*

Wright Square

Wright Square was named for Sir James Wright, the last royal governor of Georgia. But the real reason to visit this green space is to pay homage to Chief Tomochichi. The chief, aided by Mary Musgrove, an inter-preter of mixed European and Native ancestry, signed the formal treaty that allowed Oglethorpe's colonists to peacefully settle among the indigenous tribes. In 1734, Tomochichi traveled with Oglethorpe to England, where he was received by King George II at Kensington and by the Archbishop of Canterbury at Lambeth Palace.

A short stroll south along Bull Street brings you to the **Juliette Gordon Low Birthplace,** an imposing white masonry home completed in 1821, where Girl Scouts founder Low spent her childhood years. In addition to serving as a house museum outfitted in grand Victorian style, the home displays family mementos including a childhood portrait of a precocious-looking Low. *142 Bull Street, 912-233-4501.*

The family parlor in Juliette Gordon Low's birthplace.

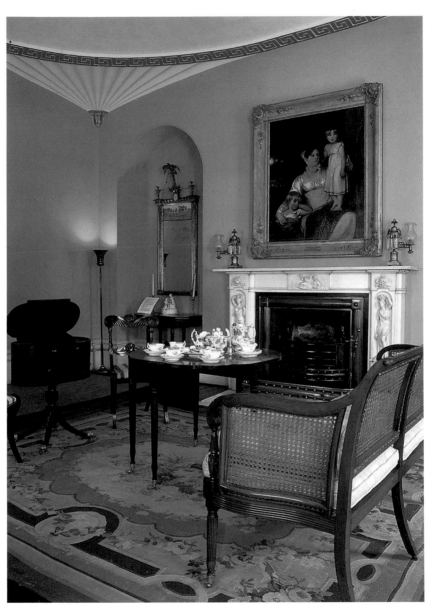

The drawing room of the Owens-Thomas House.

Chippewa Square

Farther south along Bull Street, at Perry, is Chippewa Square, site of a monumental statue of colony founder James Edward Oglethorpe. Attired in the full-dress regalia of a British general, his sword unsheathed, Oglethorpe is shown with his eyes fixed southward toward Florida—long the bastion of the Spanish Empire, England's rival for control of the southeastern seaboard.

And a couple of blocks east, on Abercorn Street is Colonial Park Cemetery, final resting place of many of the town fathers. The cemetery is an outdoor sculpture garden of sorts, thick with beautiful testaments to the dearly departed. Though Bonaventure Cemetery east of town has won praise for its marsh-side beauty and notoriety for its prominence in John Berendt's *Midnight in the Garden of Good and Evil*, Colonial Park casts an equally powerful and timeless spell.

Stretching from west to east between Harris and Charlton Streets are Pulaski, Madison, Lafayette, and Troup Squares; of these, Madison and Lafayette are the most interesting.

Madison Square

The northwest corner of the square is occupied by the **Green-Meldrim House**, a brick Gothic structure that served as Union general Sherman's headquarters during the Civil War. This unusual building is flanked by flagstone piazzas and festooned with ironwork. Here the general and his officers met with local blacks, working to devise the ill-fated "40 acres and a mule" plan intended to guarantee freed slaves a means of support. And it was from here that Sherman sent his now famous telegram to President Lincoln announcing the capture of Savannah and offering the city as a Christmas present to his commander-in-chief.

Today the building serves as the parish house for neighboring St. John's Episcopal Church, and is open for tours. *One Macon Street; 912-233-3845.*

Catty-corner from the parish house is the old **Savannah Volunteer Guards Armory**, a redbrick Romanesque building that now houses the headquarters for the **Savannah College of Art and Design**—known to locals and students alike as SCAD. Founded in 1979, the college is the single largest landholder in the historic district. Its 3,500-plus students pursue bachelor and master of fine arts degrees in topics such as art history, architectural history, graphic design, photography, video, and historic preservation. Students of the latter discipline use Savannah itself as a laboratory. On display at the administration building are student art and design projects ranging from the surreal (computer-generated landscapes) to the absurd (packaging proposals for cartons of flea killer).

Across Bull Street is the **Gryphon Tea Room**, an early-1900s drugstore, refashioned under the aegis of SCAD into a school-operated restaurant. Though there are numerous other buildings that SCAD now operates as commercial endeavors, this is the newest and grandest of the bunch *(see page 300).*

Lafayette Square

Lafayette Square, east of Madison, is the site of the **Andrew Low House**, a burnished pink, stuccoed mansion built in 1848. It was here that Juliette Gordon Low first called to order a meeting of the Girl Scouts, in March of 1912. The building is now open as a house museum. *329 Abercorn Street; 912-233-6854.*

On the opposite corner is the twin-spired **Cathedral of St. John the Baptist**, the oldest Catholic church in Georgia and scene of the mass celebrated each St. Patrick's Day morning before a parade that wends its way through the historic district.

Across the way is the **Flannery O'Connor Childhood Home**. The author lived at the simple four-story townhouse from her birth in 1925 until 1938, and attended the local Catholic grade school. *(See pages 187-188 for more details on her career.)* Today, precious few mementos of her time here remain. *207 East Charlton Street; 912-233-6014.*

Just about any one of Savannah's city squares is a fine place to wile away an hour or so, soaking up the dappled sunlight that plays through the trees on a late fall afternoon, or seeking the cool spots beneath the towering boughs of an ancient oak on a stultifyingly hot summer day. But perhaps the most pleasant of the squares—the two that boast the finest blend of natural beauty and architectural splendor—are Monterey and Calhoun, sandwiched between Taylor and Gordon Streets just a few blocks north of Forsyth Park.

Monterey Square

Monterey Square commemorates the 1846 capture of Monterey, Mexico, by U.S. forces, and is graced by a statue of Polish-born Revolutionary War hero Casimir Pulaski. On the southeastern corner is **Congregation Mickve Israel**, founded in 1733, the oldest congregation now practicing Reform Judaism in the United States. In a 1790 letter to the congregation, President George Washington expressed his wishes that "the same wonder-working Deity, who long since delivering the Hebrews from their Egyptian oppressors...still continues to water them with the dews of Heaven and to make the inhabitants of every denomination participate in the temporal and spiritual blessings of that people whose God is Jehovah."

Opposite, on the southwestern corner, is **Mercer House**, a private residence once home to the ancestors of composer Johnny Mercer, winner of four Oscars for such songs as "Moon River" and "On the Atchinson, Topeka, and Santa Fe." The redbrick Italianate house with wisteria-draped, wrought iron balconies has won more notoriety of late as the former home of antique dealer Jim Williams, protagonist of John Berendt's *Midnight in the Garden of Good and Evil*, known to locals as simply "The Book."

Calhoun Square

Calhoun Square, four blocks east of Monterey, was named for South Carolina statesman John Calhoun and is the site of soaring, Gothic-spired **Wesley Monumental Methodist Church**. The church was

SAVANNAH CHARACTERS

Best-selling novel Midnight in the Garden of Good and Evil *by John Berendt tells the story of Jim Williams, a socialite antique dealer accused of killing local tough Danny Hansford. Though, at its heart, John Berendt's 1994 nonfiction work is a murder mystery, the enduring appeal of the book is in its portrait of Savannah's hedonistic aristocrats and flamboyant ne'er do wells.*

"Savannah's a peculiar place, but if you just listen to your Cousin Joe you'll get along fine. You need to know about a few basic rules though.

"Rule number one: *Always stick around for one more drink.* That's when things happen. That's when you find out everything you want to know."

"I think I can live with that one," I said.

"Rule number two: *Never go south of Gaston Street.* A true Savannahian is a NOG. NOG means 'north of Gaston.' We stay in the old part of town...."

⋯

Savannahians drove fast. They also liked to carry their cocktails with them when they drove. According to the National Institute of Alcoholism and Alcohol Abuse, more than 8 percent of Savannah's adults were "known alcoholics," which may have accounted for the disturbing tendency of motorists to run up over the curb and collide with trees. The trunks of all but one of the twenty-seven oaks that lined the edge of Forsyth Park on Whitaker Street, for instance, had deep scars at fender level. One tree had been hit so many times it had a sizable hollow scooped out of its trunk. The hollow was filled with pea-size crystals of windshield glass that glittered like a bowl of diamonds. The palm trees in the center of Victory Drive had the same sort of scars, and so did the oaks on Abercorn.

The center of the novel is wealthy, ambitious Jim Williams.

Williams was gaining stature in Savannah, to the irritation of certain blue bloods. "How does it feel to be *nouveau riche?*" he was asked on one occasion. "It's the *riche* that counts," Williams answered. Having said that, he bought Mercer House.

Mercer House had been empty for more than ten years. It stood at the west end of Monterey Square, the most elegant of Savannah's many tree-shaded squares. It was an Italianate mansion of red brick with tall, arched windows set off by ornate ironwork balconies. It sat back from the street, aloof behind its apron of lawn and its cast-iron fence, not so much looking out on the square as presiding over it…[I]n 1970, he gave a black-tie Christmas party and invited the cream of Savannah society. On the night of his party, every window of Mercer House was ablaze with candlelight; every room had sparkling chandeliers. Clusters of onlookers stood outside watching the smart arrivals and staring in amazement at the beautiful house that had been dark for so long. A pianist played cocktail music on the grand piano downstairs; an organist played classical pieces in the ball-room above. Butlers in white jackets circulated with silver trays. Ladies in long gowns moved up and down the spiral stairs in rivers of satin and silk chiffon. Old Savannah was dazzled.

—John Berendt, *Midnight in the Garden of Good and Evil,* 1994

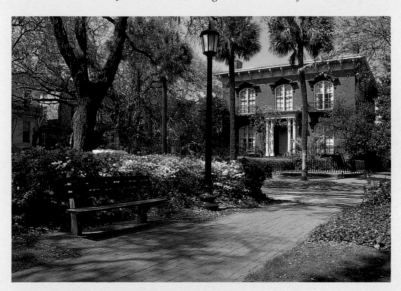

Mercer House, in Savannah's historic district.

The cast-iron Forsyth Park fountain resembles the fountain at the Place de la Concorde.

built in tribute to the brothers John and Charles Wesley, who came to Georgia with Oglethorpe as missionaries for the Church of England and later returned to England to establish the Methodist Church.

Forsyth Park

On the southern fringe of the historical district, where antebellum architecture gives way to Victorian and then early bungalow-style buildings, is Forsyth Park, a 26-acre green space laid out in 1851. The landmark cast-iron fountain near the center of the park is similar to one that graces the Place de la Concorde in Paris. To the south is the towering marble **Monument to the Confederate Dead**, inscribed with the words, "Come from the Four Winds, O Breath, And breathe upon these slain that they may live."

◆ OUTSIDE THE HISTORIC DISTRICT

Savannah History Center

Housed in the old passenger shed of the Central of Georgia Railway, the museum displays a broad collection of artifacts: everything from old fanners used to separate the rice kernels from the chaff during harvest, to a plaster reproduction of the sculpture whose picture graces the original cover of *Midnight in the Garden of Good and Evil*—a diminutive gray figure nicknamed the Bird Girl. (The original Bird Girl sculpture has been moved from its

SAVANNAH & THE COAST

graveplot at Bonaventure Cemetery and is now on display at the Telfair Museum of Art; see page 268. *History Center: 303 MLK Jr. Boulevard near the Liberty Street intersection; 912-238-1779.*

Ralph Mark Gilbert Civil Rights Museum
A few blocks south is the new Ralph Mark Gilbert Civil Rights Museum, named for the long-serving pastor of Savannah's First African Baptist Church who was a leader of the NAACP during the early years of the Civil Rights Movement. The museum features a reconstructed lunch counter from Levy's

department store, scene of boycotts protesting the store's refusal to serve food to blacks. Also on display is a timeline of black achievement in Savannah and the South, punctuated by film footage of civil rights workers and their activities in Savannah. *460 MLK Jr. Boulevard; 912-231-8900.*

Beach Institute
Black achievement of another sort is honored at the Beach Institute. Established by the American Missionary Association in 1865 as a school for freed slaves, the institute now operates a museum. Among the

After losing his job in the Savannah railroad office, self-taught sculptor Ulysses Davis built a barbershop behind his home, cutting hair by day and carving wood by night. His barbershop (shown here) eventually became a dense artistic environment filled with elaborate sculptures and highly detailed wood reliefs. (photo courtesy Richard Sommers)

museum's holdings of African-American art is a remarkable collection of hand-carved wooden busts of former Presidents, fashioned by the late barbershop owner and folk artist Ulysses Davis. As carved by Davis, Abraham Lincoln has Negroid features and Dick Nixon looks trickier than ever. *502 East Harris Street; 912-234-8000.*

King Tisdale Cottage

Around the corner is the King Tisdale house, an 1896 frame cottage decorated with gingerbread woodwork. Here a collection from the Beach Institute documents the vernacular architecture and cultural achievements of Savannah's long-established African-American community. *514 East Huntington Street; 912-234-8000.*

In this photograph from the 1850s, slaves sit in front of houses made of tabby—a combination of oyster shells, sand, lime, and water. (New-York Historical Society)

SAVANNAH & THE COAST

■ SOUTH AND EAST OF SAVANNAH   *map page 255, C-1*

◆ WORMSLOE

An oak-lined avenue leads from Skidaway Road to Wormsloe, the tabby ruins of a plantation constructed by English physician Noble Jones, who came to Georgia in 1733 with Oglethorpe. Wormsloe was named in honor of the silkworm, which the colony's trustees wished their settlers to raise on mulberry trees (eventually leading to the manufacture silk to grace English royalty). Though the ruins conjure up a picture of colonial life, the real attraction is the canopy of more than 400 oaks that span the narrow lane, punctuated by shafts of light that only occasionally pierce the heavy foliage. Also on-site is a museum where you can learn about the early, hopeful days of the colony. *7601 Skidaway Road, 912-353-3023.*

◆ ISLE OF HOPE

Tucked into a bend on the Skidaway River just north of Wormsloe, the Isle of Hope is perhaps the most picturesque community in coastal Georgia. A collection of two- and three-story frame homes—all of them gleaming white—faces the tidal marshlands, bogs of water-saddled grasses that sway in the salty breeze. Take a drive along these narrow serpentine lanes and you will soon be confoundedly, hopelessly, and pleasantly lost.

◆ THUNDERBOLT

A few miles north of the Isle of Hope is Highway 80, also known as Victory Drive, which leads the way east to the sea. Just before you reach the Wilmington River, take the last left turn into the little fishing community of Thunderbolt, and soon you are snaking along a narrow road that leads its way marshward to **Bonaventure Cemetery.** Fans of *Midnight in the Garden of Good and Evil* know this as the place where author John Berendt was first introduced to the peculiarities of Savannah society, by way of a martini-fueled lecture at the gravesite of the poet Conrad Aiken. Site of a colonial plantation that has long since burned, the cemetery is as famed for the natural surroundings as it is for the spectacular statuary. Berendt described it as looking like a "live-oak forest of a primeval dimension."

❖

East of Highway 80, marshlands looking much like placid plains of grass stretch almost to the horizon. Above, seagulls bank and circle, their cries filling air heady with the rich and rank smell of pluff mud. With the crossing of each bridge, you come upon another small spit of land—Isle of Armstrong, Oatland Island, Talahi Island, and, finally, just before land's end at Tybee Island, the turnoff for Fort Pulaski.

◆ FORT PULASKI   *map page 255, C-1*

Completed in 1847 and fortified with more than 25 million bricks, Pulaski was supposedly indestructible. "You might as well bombard the Rocky Mountains," boasted a general with the Corps of Engineers. One of the fort's engineers was young Robert E. Lee, stationed here soon after his graduation from West Point.

The fort, which faces the sea, was captured by Confederate troops early in the Civil War and protected blockade runners from attack by the Union navy. Thus it became one of the priorities of the Federals. In 1861, they secretly hauled 36 cannon over mud flats to Tybee Island and concealed them in 11 batteries.

The fort fell to Union bombardment in April 1862, the casualty of new bullet-shaped artillery shells fired from more than a mile away. This success ushered in a new era in fort construction strategy. Today, the formidable pentagonal redbrick fort, surrounded by a seven-foot-deep moat, is maintained by the National Park Service and is open for tours. *Off Highway 80, 16 miles east of Savannah on US 80. 912-786-5787.*

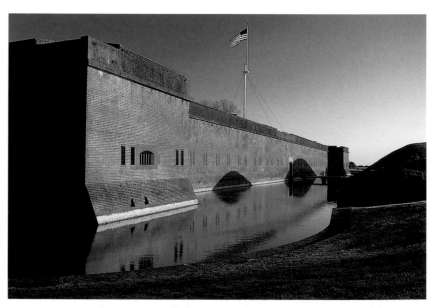

(above) The northwest wall of Fort Pulaski National Monument at sunset.
(opposite) Spanish moss serves as a moody background for this statue in Bonaventure Cemetery.

◆ TYBEE ISLAND   *map page 255, C-1*

Long known as "Savannah's Beach," Tybee Island is a shabbily genteel seaside community, blessed with two long, wide beaches, a low people-to-pelican ratio, and a central business district that exudes a tawdry Coney Island-esque charm. Though the landmark DeSoto Hotel was recently torn down in favor of a condominium development, residents have rallied to enact a moratorium on new multiple-unit construction, thus ensuring that the community does not go the way of South Carolina's Hilton Head Island.

Most of the activity centers on Butler Avenue, on the island's eastern edge, where a pier juts out into the surf. On the pier is a pavilion, originally built in 1891 and reconstructed in 1996. During the 1940s the pavilion was the scene of big-band dances; today it's home to purveyors of cotton candy and corndogs. Here you will find ample parking for beach excursions, and, during the summer high season, a carnival-like atmosphere.

North of "the strip" along Pulaski and Taylor Streets is a second beach scene more popular with locals than with tourists. This comparatively remote enclave is dominated by the looming Tybee Lighthouse and crumbling Fort Screven, the latter a Spanish American War-era fort, now deserted by the military but maintained in part as a museum. When the lighthouse was originally constructed in 1736, it was the highest in America. A portion of the present structure dates from 1773. A long, 178-step climb ascends from deck to beacon.

Just beyond the fort, the surf beckons, a lazy, rolling blanket of foam that laps the shore. In the fall and winter, this section of the island borders on desolate, and Tybee Islanders revel in their isolation, before preparing once again for the summer tourists, relatively few though they may be.

■ SOUTH BY WAY OF THE COASTAL HIGHWAY

Cars and trucks barrel south along I-95, a ribbon of hot white concrete that can take them from Savannah to Jacksonville, Florida, in less than two hours. Highway 17, the old Coastal Highway, is less hectic, wending its way south past chancy flea markets, ramshackle barbecue joints, and abandoned roadhouses.

About ten miles south of Savannah on Highway 17, just north of Richmond Hill, is the **Bamboo Farm and Coastal Gardens,** operated by the University of Georgia College of Agriculture. Once the site of plant introduction experiments, the farm is now home to the largest grove of bamboo in the States, with some stalks towering more than 75 feet. It's a surreal site, worthy of a detour. *2 Cane-break Road; 912-921-5460.*

Just down the road is the town of **Richmond Hill**, conceived in the 1920s as a winter home by industrialist Henry Ford. Built on the site of the former Richmond Plantation, Richmond Hill was once a "company town" where locals lived off the Ford family largess, inhabiting Ford-built homes and, of course, driving Ford-built Model Ts. Today, Savannah is sprawling southward and Richmond Hill is slowly being transformed into a bedroom community for its neighbor to the north, but the small **Richmond Hill Historical Museum** pays tribute to the bygone days. *11460 East Ford Avenue; 912-756-3697.*

◆ FORT McALLISTER   *map page 255, B-1*

Just south of Richmond Hill on Highway 144 is Fort McAllister, site of the last line of resistance the Confederate forces were able to muster in the face of General Sherman's march on Savannah in 1864. In 1863 alone, the fort withstood seven attacks by Union gunboats hurling hundreds of rounds of ammunition shoreward. No matter the intensity of the bombardment, the fort held. Finally, Sherman's ground troops stormed the garrison and in so doing definitively closed down trade through the port of Savannah, cutting off the Confederacy from a major supply route and ensuring waterborne support for Union troops stationed there.

Today there is a museum on-site, replete with artifacts from the Confederate blockade-runner boat, *Nashville,* which sank in the Ogeechee River during a battle with the Union ironclad *Montauk.*

Many visitors who come here picnic on the bluff high above the river—bringing along a few dozen boiled river shrimp for an afternoon snack.

◆ MIDWAY   *map page 255, A-2*

Settled by Calvinists of English and Scottish extraction in 1754, Midway—on Highway 17 just above Riceboro—was once home to two of Georgia's three signers of the Declaration of Independence, Lyman Hall and Button Gwinett. Today, little remains of this once-thriving community, save the white-framed, three-story Midway Congregational Church (built in 1792 to replace an earlier structure burned by the British in 1778) and a colonial-era cemetery with moss-covered tombstones pitching this way and that. The **Midway Museum**, built in a style reminiscent of nearby plantations, is outfitted with properly austere period furnishings. *912-884-5837.*

♦ Ossabaw Island   *map page 255, B & C-2*

Parallel to the coastline, a string of virtually inaccessible islands stretches south from Savannah. **Ossabaw Island,** rife with feral hogs and donkeys, is a heritage preserve utilized by a variety of nonprofit nature concerns.

♦ St. Catherine's Island   *map page 255, B-2*

Just south of Ossabow is **St. Catherine's Island,** once the center of the Spanish missions built in 16th-century Georgia and later one of several Sea Islands where freed slaves attempted to establish a republic of their own. Following General Sherman's vision that every man was entitled to 40 acres and a mule, the freed slaves attempted to distribute land and to set up an independent kingdom.

The Noble Foundation and the New York Zoological Society, act as stewards of St. Catherine's; the island is closed to visitors.

Thanks to recent digs on St. Catherine's and adjacent islands, archaeologists are

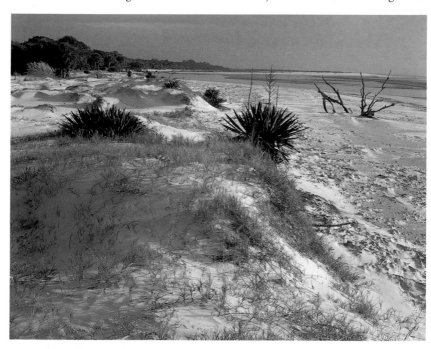

(above) Sand dunes and beach grasses characterize the pristine beaches of Ossabaw Island.
(opposite) A feral hog crosses a road lined with live oak on Ossabaw Island.

SAVANNAH &
THE COAST

learning more about the native people who once thrived on these barrier islands. One of the first travelers to notice evidence of these people was botanist William Bartram, who wrote in 1773:

> *I* observed among the shells of the conical mounds, fragments of earthen vessels, and of other utensils, the manufacture of the ancients; about the center of one of them, the rim of an earthen pot appeared among the shells and earth, which I carefully removed, and drew it out, almost whole; this pot was curiously wrought all over the outside, representing basket work, and was undoubtedly esteemed a very ingenious performance, by the people, at the age of its construction.

◆ BLACKBEARD ISLAND   *map page 255, B-3*

Farther south still are Blackbeard and Sapelo Islands, the former a national wildlife refuge that was once the stomping grounds of pirate Edward Teach, better known as Blackbeard. As the story goes, Teach occasionally used the island as both a hideout and a base of operations from which he carried on a campaign of thievery against English and colonial American merchant ships in the early 1700s. Blackbeard's more permanent lair was at Ocracoke Island, off the North Carolina coast, but while in Georgia waters he settled into an abandoned Spanish mission. Legend has it that Teach beheaded his 16th wife and six members of his crew at this spot, burying them in a shroud of gold doubloons.

◆ SAPELO ISLAND   *map page 255, B-3*

Sapelo, perhaps the most easily accessible and well known of the islands, is home to a sizeable community of Geechees, people descended from the slaves who first worked the island plantations. The Geechee have, thanks to their comparative isolation, maintained a lifestyle that is remarkably African. Their religion, similar to that of South Carolina's Gullah people, is a melding of West African animism and Christianity, while their dialect preserves many African words.

Ferries to the island and bus tours of the interior are available through the **McIntosh County Welcome Center in Darien;** *912-437-6684.*

An excellent introduction to the island's funky, laid-back lifestyle can be arranged by calling Nancy Banks, an island resident who leads tours and runs a lodge for overnight guests *(see page 299)*. In her capable hands, you will tour the sugar mill ruins at Long Tabby and pass by the old R. J. Reynolds mansion near

AFRICAN TRADITIONS

*I*solated on the vast rice plantations of the coast, with their white masters in residence only a short part of the year, the coastal Negroes evolved a unique language—haunting, poetic, and to most whites, almost totally incomprehensible....

The majestic blue heron who sweeps and dives across the emerald marshes at Sapelo is called "poor Joe—Padzo is the name of a similar heron in Africa. The tortoise is called a cooter; near Timbuktu, it is called a kuta. And the small wild horses that roam the coastal islands are known as takis, the West African name for horse. You'll hear them speak of "toting" cotton, a word that derives from tota, in Congo "to pick up." and the Foulah numbers to ten are still in use.

The old plantation books from Kelvin Grove on St. Simon's abound with names still common on the coast—Bina (Tuesday), Cuffy (Friday), Quanimina (Wednesday). The custom of naming children for the day of their birth derives from the Eve tribes of Dahomey and Tago, who borrowed the custom from the Twai people.

*Ghosts abound, as in West Africa, where every man can expect to meet his "duppy" at least once in his lifetime. And in the little settlements like Sandfly, some still talk of being ridden by witches at night, an ancient belief of the Vais.

According to the Vais legend, when a witch comes in the door he takes off his skin and lays it aside in the house, rides the victim through the night and returns him to his bed in the morning.

In Savannah, the Geechee Negroes, who take their name from their birthplace near the Ogeechee River, follow the old Vais custom of sprinkling salt and pepper in the corners of the room, a practice which is supposed to prevent the witch from putting on her skin.

—Betsy Fancher, *The Lost Legacy of Georgia's Golden Isles*, 1970

This walking stick by William Rogers (circa 1938) shows that African-influenced carving traditions lasted in the South long after Emancipation. Considered by many to be coastal Georgia's master carver, Rogers also worked as a farmer, carpenter, state legislator, and preacher. (collection of Mr. and Mrs. Harvey Granger, Jr.)

A swamp estuary near Darien.

Nannygoat Beach before stopping off at B.J.'s Confectionery, the de facto community center for the village of Hog Hammock. *Nancy Banks: 912-485-2277.*

Little evidence remains of the Creek people who once lived here, save a couple of Indian mounds and a ring of oyster shells that may have been used for ceremonial purposes. The Spanish mission built here 400 years ago (by Jesuits hoping to save Creek souls) long ago succumbed to the elements. One of those early missionaries was Pedro Menendez, the scholarly Jesuit of San Jose Mission who authored the first book ever written in America—a little grammar in the Yammassee tongue for the Indian children on the island.

Tangled vine tendrils envelope the ruins of **Le Chatelet** plantation, now referred to by the locals, in a beautiful bit of elision, as Chocolate. Le Chatelet was built by a Marquis de Montalet (by one account an exiled French royalist, by another a Santo Domingo planter kicked out in the 1806 slave rebellion). Montalet carefully trained his black chef in the ways of French cooking and awarded him the cordon bleu when he succeeded in mastering puree of artichoke and poulard in olive oil with sweet cream. The marquis hoped to find truffles growing in the New World, believing they could make men merry and women tender, and civilize barbaric America. To this end he often led a truffle-sniffing pig beneath the moss-draped oaks of Sapelo Island.

Travelers exploring these islands should keep their eyes peeled for notices of performances by the Sea Island Singers, a troupe of Geechee songsters whose polyphonic chanting and clapping has been enjoyed by audiences as far away as Carnegie Hall and as close by as the **Sea Island Festival**, held in August of each year on nearby St. Simon's Island.

■ DARIEN AND ENVIRONS *map page 255, A-3*

On the mainland, Highway 17 snakes ever southward past boggy fields where blond reeds of rice wave in the morning breeze. Soon you are entering Darien, a coastal settlement established in 1736 by Scots Highlanders under the aegis of Oglethorpe himself. During the antebellum years, Darien rose to prominence as a port from which rice and cotton were shipped. Later, lumber replaced rice as the primary export, as huge mills sprang up on the riverbanks to saw trees into board lumber that was then floated downstream. During the late 20th century it has been the shrimping industry that has supported the citizens of Darien and surrounding communities. Today the banks of the Altamaha River are lined with

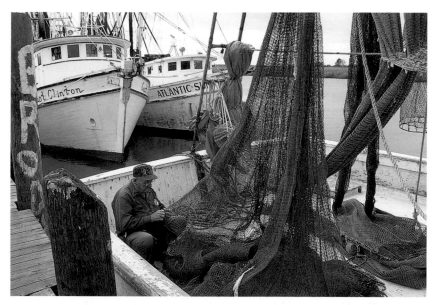

A shrimp-boat operator tends to his nets along the Darien waterfront.

FANNY KEMBLE'S INCENDIARY JOURNAL

It was on Butler Island, just across the bridge from Darien, that Frances Anne (Fanny) Kemble, wife of rice planter Pierce Butler, wrote her *Journal of a Residence on a Georgian Plantation in 1838-1839.* English by birth and a talented Shakespearean actress, she became famous for her portrayal of Juliet at Coventry Garden in 1829, and in 1832 she began touring the United States. One critic wrote of her performance at Park Theater in New York: "Fanny Kemble was to New York something of a divine manifestation…"

In June of 1834 Fanny married Philadelphian Pierce Butler, a member of an eminent American family and owner of two Sea Island plantations tilled by 700 slaves. When the couple and their two small daughters visited in the winter of 1838, little escaped Fanny's interest, even the particulars of rice cultivation at Hopeton Plantation.

Fanny recorded in her journal the sorrowful lives of her husband's slaves. Upon her return to Pennsylvania, she made a copy of it and expressed her desire to have it published. Her husband forbade it, and infuriated by his wife's abolitionist sentiments, he divorced her in the Pennsylvania courts and was granted custody of their children. Fanny returned to Europe, where she continued to act but lived in an emotional limbo, waiting for the day her daughters would gain their majority and she could see them again.

In 1859, 400 of the slaves on Butler's Georgia estate were sold to pay debts. A *New York Tribune* article on the sale included this description of a scene involving two slaves, Dorcas and Jeffrey:

> *I* see Dorcas in the long room, sitting motionless as a statue…and I see Jeffrey, who goes to his new master, pulls off his hat and says, 'I'se very much obliged, mas'r, to you for trying to help me [by buying my wife]…thank you—but—it's—berry—hard'—and here the poor fellow breaks down entirely and walks away covering his face with his battered hat, and sobbing like a child. He is soon surrounded by a group of his colored friends, who with an instinctive delicacy…stand quiet…about him.

Fanny went on to publish her journal in 1863, and it became an abolitionist rallying cry in England and the United States in years leading up to the Civil War.

scruffy shrimp boats, their nets cast high while in port. Fittingly, in the nearby fishing villages of Crescent and Shellman Bluff are three of the state's best fish houses, vestiges of a time when the shrimp you ate that evening had spent the previous night not in an importer's deep freezer but in a nearby river *(see pages 296-297)*.

Five miles south on Highway 17 is **Hofwyl-Broadfield Plantation,** a remarkably intact antebellum rice plantation, where you can wander the levees that controlled the water flow and watch a film on the task system of labor that defined life on a rice plantation prior to the Civil War. *Information: 912-264-7333.*

It's interesting to note that many African farmers from the rice-growing regions of Angola and Gambia were sold as slaves into the Sea Islands and were actively sought out by planters for their skills; in July of 1785 a *Charleston Gazette* advertisement announced the arrival of a "choice cargo of windward and gold coast negroes, who have been accustomed to the planting of rice."

■ GOLDEN ISLES·

Unlike Sapelo and St. Catherine's—islands which can only be reached by ferry— the Golden Isles of St. Simon's, Sea Island, and Jekyll Island can be reached by highway and bridge. Filled with resorts and restaurants, these islands are destinations in themselves.

◆ BRUNSWICK *map page 255, A-4*

Jumping-off point for any island adventure is the seaport of Brunswick, a sad little town where the ships in dock tower over the city, their stacks looming higher than any building in the business district. Yet the natural beauty of the area is stunning. Even on the main thoroughfares, the sea and marsh are ever present. Just north of town, in the median that bisects Highway 17, is the oak under which Sidney Lanier, composer of the poem "The Marshes of Glynn," sat and "looked out over a world of marsh that borders a world of sea."

Cross the causeway that leads east from Brunswick, and within moments you are on St. Simon's Island, a lush, almost edenic oasis of green ringed by white beaches.

◆ ST. SIMON'S ISLAND *map page 255, B-4*

St. Simon's was settled early by the British; the site was staked out in 1734 by Oglethorpe himself. By 1740 Fort Frederica was a thriving military town, and when Oglethorpe repelled the Spanish advance on Georgia at the Battle of Bloody

Marsh in 1742, it was from Frederica that he commanded his troops. But by 1755, with the Spanish no longer a threat, the fort was in shambles. Today, all that remains are a few tabby ruins, now maintained by the National Park Service. *Fort Frederica: 912-638-3639.*

Nearby is **Christ Episcopal Church,** to which Charles Wesley came as a missionary for the Church of England in 1736. The church on the site today dates from 1884. In the neighboring cemetery, seemingly ancient gravestones lean to and fro beneath live oaks dripping tendrils of Spanish moss.

Farther south, on the site of the former Hamilton Plantation, is **Epworth by the Sea,** a retreat operated by the Methodist Church and constructed in part as a tribute to the denomination's founders, brothers John Wesley and the aforementioned Charles. Charles was recruited by Oglethorpe to work with the island's Native American tribes—a task that he quickly abandoned in favor of working with the settlers. His older brother John was assigned duty in Savannah. "I went to America to convert the Indians," he later wrote, "but, Oh! Who shall convert me?" Today, the church operates a conference center, motel, and museum on premises, the latter of which documents the Wesley brothers' disillusionment, return to England, and spiritual rebirth, which resulted in the founding of Methodism. *Epworth by the Sea: 912-638-8688.*

On the eastern edge of the island are the best beaches—flat expanses of hard-packed gray sand touched by a soft, almost placid surf. Here you will find the **King and Prince Hotel** *(see page 299),* as well as public beach access.

At the southern tip of the island is the commercial district, home to the 1872 lighthouse and a collection of low-key restaurants, bars, and shops. Those curious about the island's history should seek out the **Museum of Coastal History** *(912-638-4666),* housed in a bleached-brick Victorian home in the shadow of the lighthouse. Or, better yet, traipse out Demere Road to the **Bloody Marsh Battle Site,** a now quiet patch of wetlands where in 1742 the British repelled a Spanish advance in a battle so vicious that onlookers said the marsh ran red with blood. Little remains to remind us of the fray, save a marker inscribed with the words of Oglethorpe: "We are resolved not to suffer defeat. We will rather die like Leonidas and his Spartans, if we can but protect Georgia and Carolina and the rest of the Americas from desolation."

◆ SMALLER ISLANDS

Two islands nuzzle the St. Simon's coastline: Little St. Simon's and Sea Island.

Little St. Simon's is a private island, maintained as a rustic resort where the emphasis is on isolation and enjoyment of natural beauty. Old rice levees and shell middens can be found here and there, and there are seven miles of beach to enjoy. Access is by ferry; *912-638-1811.*

A narrow bridge crosses from St. Simon's to **Sea Island**, site of the super-deluxe resort known as the **Cloister**. A seaside enclave of manicured lawns, well-trimmed palms, and Mediterranean-style villas, this resort is without peer on the Georgia coast. It has long been the haunt of the rich, bluebloods, and poseurs. *Cloister Resort: 912-638-3611. (See page 304 for details.)*

◆ JEKYLL ISLAND   *map page 255, B-5*

For a look at how these bluebloods once lived, travel south via a seven-mile causeway to Jekyll Island. During the early years of the 20th century, Jekyll was the private playground of families with names like Rockefeller, Pulitzer, Astor, and

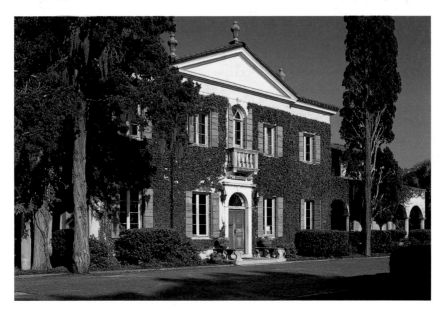

The Crane "Cottage" on Jekyll Island.

Vanderbilt. Similar in style to the northeastern resort town of Newport, Rhode Island, Jekyll was home to a collection of what were termed, quaintly, "cottages." These shingled mansions, most of which were built between 1890 and 1925, now form the basis for an open-air museum of sorts, with their former clubhouse—an asymmetrical, turreted Queen Anne mansion—restored to its former elegance and serving as a resort called the **Jekyll Island Club Hotel** *(see page 297)*. Housed in the former stable is a museum whose exhibits tell the story of the island's heady past. Today, though croquet courts and indoor tennis courts still abound, Jekyll is among the most democratic of resorts on the coast, for the island is now under state control, with businesses operated under a private-public partnership.

The earliest people known to live here were the Muskogean people of the Creek nation. Writes Betsy Fancher in *The Lost Legacy of Georgia's Golden Isles:*

> *A*grarians, their year revolved around the the feast of the First Fire. It opened with the Green Corn Festival in the square of the village Ospo, where trials were held for the year's offenses and culminated with the ritual of the black drink, in a huge bonfire in which the residue of the old year, from old clothes to garbage was burned in a great conflagration with ceremonial dances. But the Muskogeans could be cruel—prisoners were tortured until dead in the town square and scalps were taken and used in orgiastic victory dances....

At a bend in the road along Riverview Drive, the ruins of the island's early plantations stand in eerie repose. Stop here for a peek at the construction methods once used on the barrier islands, techniques that employed a material known as "tabby," a cement-like mixture composed of sand, lime, oyster shells, and water. Linguists believe that the word tabby is of African origin and was originally defined as a wall made of earth and masonry.

At the northern end of the island, along a small creek at a place called Ebo Landing, the slave ship *Wanderer* brought a group of Africans in 1858, half a century after the international slave trade had been banned in the United States. The owners of the ship, the notorious Captain W. C. Corrie of New York, and his partner, Charles A. L. Samar of Savannah, planned to hide slaves on Jekyll until they could be sold. Before federal authorities got wind of the ship's mission, all but 100 of the 300 *Wanderer* slaves who landed on Jekyll had been sold in South Carolina.

At the southern tip of the island is South End Beach, a premier spot for viewing wildlife including brown pelicans, which nest here, and bottle-nosed dolphins.

Between Jekyll Island and Cumberland Island is the wide, marshy mouth of the Satilla River, which canoeists can paddle down for 149 scenic miles starting at Waycross, north of Okefenokee *(for information call the Southeast Georgia Regional Development Center at 912-285-6097).*

■ ST. MARY'S AND CUMBERLAND ISLAND *map page 255, A-6*

Back on the mainland is the little village of St. Mary's, point of departure for the ferry and a charming and storied settlement in its own right. Settled by the British in 1787 on a site long favored by Native American tribes, St. Mary's survives today as a fishing village and as a bedroom community for the nearby King's Bay Naval Submarine Base. Thanks to a number of quaint bed-and-breakfast accommodations, St. Mary's makes a good place to stay for those planning daytrips to Cumberland Island.

South of Jekyll is Cumberland Island, Georgia's largest barrier island. Over the years, numerous attempts have been made to wrest Cumberland Island from the wild. Behind palmetto thickets lurk mansion ruins and rusted car chassis, testaments to a time when the island was little different from St. Simon's or Jekyll.

Starfish on Cumberland Island.

From 1881 until the mid-20th century, Cumberland was a millionaire's retreat, the property of the Carnegie family. One their former mansions, Plum Orchard, now stands vacant, while another, **Greyfield**, serves as an elegant and exclusive inn where one dresses for dinner in the evening yet never feels the arctic chill of an air-conditioner, for the steady breeze of ceiling fans stirs the air *(see page 296)*.

The real attractions are to be found on the island's remote fringes, where feral horses roam and bobcats stalk their prey. Thanks to the National Park Service *(912-882-4335)*, which now oversees a good portion of the island, only 300 visitors are allowed to make the 45-minute ferry ride from St. Mary's each day, ensuring that the miles of beach remain, for the most part, unpopulated. You can literally spend a day wandering the woods or combing the shoreline without seeing another soul. And should you wish to spend the night, campsites are plentiful.

The road to Sea Camp Beach on Cumberland Island.

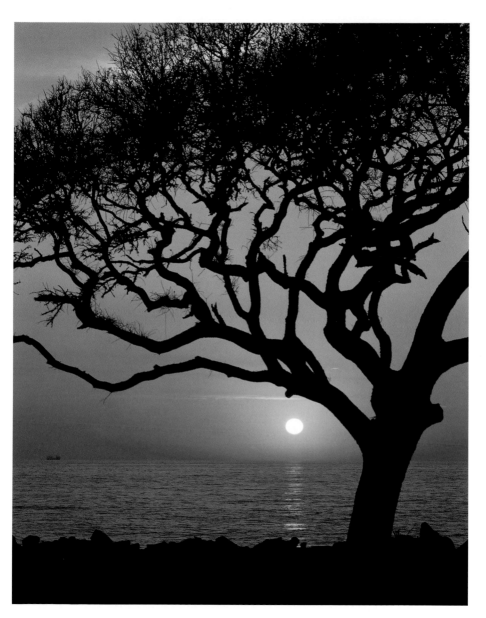

The sun rises behind the twisted form of a live oak on Jekyll Island.

Savannah & Coast Food & Lodging

✕ **Restaurant Prices:** $ = under $10; $$ = $10–20; $$$ = over $20
Restaurant price designations indicate the approximate cost of an entrée and an appetizer or desert, exclusive of drinks, tax, and tip.

🛏 **Lodging Rates:** $ = under $75; $$ = $75–150; $$$ = over $150
Lodging rate designations indicate the approximate cost of a double occupancy room for one night, exclusive of surcharges and taxes.

A statewide food and lodging **reference map** can be found on page 306, and an **index of towns** with food and lodging listings in this book follows on pages 307–308. Toll-free numbers for **chain hotels and motels** can be found on page 308.

Brunswick *map page 255, A-4*

✕ **Georgia Pig**
912-264-6664; Hwy. 17 at I-95
This little barbecue shack is not as good as advertised—their ads quote *New York Times* cake maven Maida Heatter, who wrote lovingly of the place, but what does she know about barbecue? She's a Yankee! But it does serve decent if expensive 'cue, and it's just a few hundred feet off the interstate. Lunch and dinner. $-$$

Cumberland Island
map page 255, A-6

🛏 **Greyfield Inn**
904-261-6408; Cumberland Island
Built in 1901 for the daughter of industrialist Thomas Carnegie, this white clapboard and stone mansion has been an inn since the 1960s. Simple elegance abounds at what many consider to be the nicest, most unique property on the Georgia coast. Accessible by boat only. Rates include all meals. $$$

Darien Area *map page 255, A-3*

✕ **Archie's Restaurant**
912-437-4363; Hwy. 17, Darien
Open more than 60 years, this concrete bunker eatery turns out locally prized fried shrimp. The catfish they fry is river-caught, not pond-raised and anemic. Their motto: "Seafood served in this restaurant slept in the river last night." Breakfast, lunch, and dinner. $$

✕ **Buccaneer Club**
912-832-5171; off Shellman Bluff Rd., Crescent (call for directions)
Once a private club (you still have to ring a buzzer to gain entry), this funky outpost has a pleasing patina of age. The fried shrimp, served in heaping mounds, is the best on the coast. Good cocktails to boot: stop here for a drink and peruse the menu, a delightful doggerel-filled tome. Of the Crabs Galore, the menu says, "If you think we ain't got crabs (HA HA), just listen at this combination!" Dinner and Sunday brunch. $$-$$$

✗ Hunter's Cafe and the Mud Bar
912-832-5771; off Shellman Bluff Rd.,
Shellman Bluff (call for directions)
This fish camp looks the part: screened
door, hardwood floors, ramshackle but
well maintained, reached by a narrow
sandy lane. The menu is simple as can
be: raw oysters; rich, milky crab stew;
and fried seafood (oysters, shrimp, scallops, flounder). This is the real deal, un-
pretentious and good. Dinner. $$

✗ Speed's Kitchen
912-832-4763; off Shellman Bluff Rd,
Shellman Bluff (call for directions)
That this place is a jumble of three bare-
ly disguised trailers shouldn't dissuade
you from visiting this fish camp. Great
crabmeat au gratin and buttery oyster
stew. The food may be a bit better than
Hunter's *(see above)*, but there's no beer
to be had—if that matters. Dinner. $$

▣ Open Gates Bed-and-Breakfast
912-437-6985; Vernon Square
The owner's boat is at your disposal for
dy trips into the marsh or down the Altamaha River. This 1876 home, which
belonged to a timber baron, is one of the
best bargains on the coast. Five rooms
are available. There's a large pool out
back and the house faces on lovely Vernon Square in Darien proper. $

Jekyll Island *map page 255, B-5*

✗ Grand Dining Room
912-635-2600; 371 Riverview Dr., at
the Jekyll Island Club Hotel
Commanding a magnificent view of the
water, this dining room may be valued
more for its ambience than its food.
Graceful columns break up the large
space decorated in pink and white. For
lunch, try the crab cake melt. Dinner
tends toward haute Southern specialties.
Breakfast, lunch, and dinner. $$-$$$

▣ Jekyll Inn
912-635-2531; 975 North Beachview Dr.
Most rooms at this sprawling low-rise
complex—the largest of Jekyll's oceanfront hotels—have their own private
deck. And there's a large pool out back
with a thatched-hut bar serving fruity
drinks. What more could you want in a
beach motel? $$-$$$

JEKYLL ISLAND CLUB HOTEL

▣ Jekyll Island Club Hotel
912-635-2600; 371 Riverview Dr.
The main building, an asymmetrical
Queen Anne–style mansion, was completed in 1887 and refurbished in the
1980s when it reopened as a hotel. A
onetime club for millionaires, this grand
old resort now welcomes one and all.
There's a croquet lawn out front, and
porches envelop the building, giving a
lazy Old World elegance to the place. $$

▦ **General lodging information**

There are also a number of chain motels, most of which are recently refurbished, nondescript relics of the '60s. Among the choices are the **Clarion Buccaneer** *(912-635-2261; 85 South Beachview Dr.)*, the **Comfort Inn** *(912-635-2000; 711 North Beachview Dr.)*, and the **Ramada Inn Oceanfront** *(912-635-2111; 150 South Beachview Dr.)*. $$

Little St. Simon's
map page 255, B-4

▦ **The Lodge on Little St. Simon's**
912-638-7472; Little St. Simon's
Family-owned and eco-sensitive, this naturalist's retreat offers cabins and rooms alike in a setting that will remind you of summer camp. Birding expeditions and nature walks can be arranged. Three home-cooked meals are served each day. And should your group want the ultimate in privacy, the entire island is available to let—at a price. $$$

St. Mary's *map page 255, A-6*

✗ **Greek Mediterrranean Grill**
912-576-2000; 122 Osborne St.
The tabby exterior is painted a vibrant maroon. The interior is splashed with murals of Greek life. Grilled Octopus, spanakopita, and shrimp scampi are favorites. And the owner is a generous and affable host. Lunch and dinner. $$

✗ **Lang's Marina Restaurant**
912-882-4432; 307 West St. Mary's St.
The proprietor operates a fleet of fishing boats, so you can be sure that, in season, the local favorite, rock shrimp, will be fresher than fresh. This little box of a building facing on the river also dishes out various seafood platters and steaks. Lunch and dinner. $-$$

✗ **Seagle's Restaurant**
912-882-3242; 105 Osborne St.
This little restaurant on the ground floor of the Riverview Hotel *(see below)* offers to treat you to your first order of rock shrimp dip. Take them up on the offer, and then move on to sample the boiled shrimp. Keep it simple and you'll eat well. Lunch and dinner. $-$$

▦ **Riverview Hotel**
912-882-3242; 105 Osborne St.
Most days the family pooch lounges on the couch in the black-and-white tiled hallway. The rooms upstairs are calico-cute but nice, befitting what feels like an old railroad hotel. A balcony, also on the second level, is outfitted with rockers and affords a grand view of the river. A cozy bar and restaurant are downstairs. $

▦ **Spencer House Inn**
912-882-1872; 200 Osborne St.
This rambling pink home, built in 1872, is a short walk from the Cumberland Island ferry dock. Each of the 14 rooms has a four-poster bed and a clawfoot tub. A hot Southern-style breakfast is served each morning, and the innkeepers will be happy to pack a picnic lunch if you're headed to the island. $-$$

SAVANNAH & COAST FOOD & LODGING

St. Simon's Island
map page 255, B-4

X **Blanche's Courtyard**
912-638-3030; 440 King's Way
A perennial favorite in these parts, Blanche's, with its flickering gas lamps and shell-packed dirt parking lot, would be a perfect tourist trap if only the food weren't so good. Sweet, meaty scallops, crab soup spiked with sherry, and crisp fried shrimp are favorites. Dinner. $$-$$$

X **Brogen's**
912-638-1660; 200 Pier Alley
Just steps from the waterfront, this is the favorite spot for burgers and beer. Better make that beer and burgers. There's a great porch up top for people watching. Lunch and dinner. $

X **Crab Trap**
912-638-3552; 1209 Ocean Blvd.
Throw your crab shells through the hole in the middle of the table at this purposefully funky seaside dive. Tabby floors and retired outboard motors are the essential design elements. Stick to the simplest seafood and you will eat well. Their motto: "Where the elite eat in their bare feet." Dinner. $$-$$$

X **Dressner's Village Cafe**
912-634-1217; 223 Mallery St.
A good Southern-style breakfast with great grits can be had at this simple little cafe. Thick burgers are grilled to order and served on a toasted bun. Blue-and-white checked tablecloths and a pressed tin ceiling complete the picture. Breakfast and lunch. $

X **Epworth by the Sea**
912-638-8688; 100 Arthur J. Moore Dr.
Owned and operated by the Methodist Church as a retreat for its members, this complex of motel-style buildings rents out rooms to nonbelievers too—at some of the most reasonable rates on the island. $

X **King and Prince Resort**
912-638-3631; 201 Arnold Rd.
Opened as a private club in 1935, the King and Prince is a little less opulent than some other coast resorts, but who's complaining? It's got a lovely indoor pool and a beach with white-gray sand stretching for what seems miles. $$-$$$

X **Yum Yum Shop**
912-634-1108; 600 Sea Island Rd.
A tidy—and tiny—deli set in a strip mall, the Yum Yum Shop is famous for great sandwiches, including the meaty crab cake on croissant and the smoked turkey on rye. For dessert, there's homemade cheesecake. Breakfast and lunch. $

Sapelo Island
map page 255, B-3

▦ **The Weekender**
912-485-2277; Sapelo Island
This no-frills operation, run by island savant Nancy Banks, offers rooms and cabins in a funky, almost forlorn setting. It's a bit expensive for the level of comfort, but, then again, this unvarnished type of hideout is getting harder and harder to find on the coast. And you won't find better hosts. $

SAVANNAH & COAST
FOOD & LODGING

Savannah *map page 255, C-1*

✗ Clary's Cafe
912-233-0402; 404 Abercorn St.
Clary's has been around since 1903. Until recently it was a drugstore with a lunch counter. But this corner cafe now serves everything from burgers to Caesar salads, though many opt for just a malted milkshake. Breakfast is especially good; scrambled eggs are available with either lox and onions, or salami, potatoes, onions, and peppers. Breakfast, lunch, and dinner. $

✗ Crystal Beer Parlor
912-232-1153; 301 West Jones St.
In business since 1933, this dark bar and restaurant with the oversize booths serves great burgers and hand-cut, hand-dipped onion rings. A bit rough around the edges, but for those in search of a place to quaff a beer or grab a snack, it's a jewel in the rough. Lunch, dinner. $-$$

✗ Elizabeth on 37th
912-236-5547; 105 East 37th St.
Savannah's favorite for "new Southern" cuisine. Housed in a bleached-beige, Palladian-style mansion in a sketchy neighborhood, this restaurant turns out amazingly good food, from the simple (pecan-crusted chicken) to the complex (cinnamon-spiced shrimp). Dinner. $$$

✗ Garibaldi's
912-232-7118; 315 West Congress St.
Northern Italian favorites as well as a few unlikely yet tasty dishes–like flounder with an apricot-shallot glaze—are the draws at this rakish restaurant.

There's a good, economical wine list, heavy on California varietals. Dinner. $$$

✗ Geneva's
912-355-5434; 2812 Bee Rd.
The African-American answer to Lady and Sons. Step up to the steam table and order a plate of salmon croquettes or crab cakes. Side dishes include crusty macaroni and cheese, red rice, black-eyed peas, and steamed okra. The surroundings are a bit drab, but the food is as tasty as what the Lady serves—at half the price. Breakfast, lunch, and dinner. $

✗ Gryphon Tea Room
912-238-2481; 337 Bull St.
Once the home of Solomon's drugstore, this ornate building was recently refurbished by the Savannah College of Art and Design, and now functions as a quirkily charming tea room, serving salads, sandwiches, and soups along with an encyclopedic selection of hot teas. Take a gander at the carved mahogany gryphon clock that gives the place its name. Breakfast and lunch. $

✗ Johnny Harris Restaurant
912-354-7810; 1651 East Victory Dr.
Opened in 1924, this is Savannah's oldest restaurant. In the front dining room (a circular, domed affair with booths on the perimeter), big bands once played and Savannah swells danced the night away. These days it's a restaurant that coasts along on a reputation won long ago, serving everything from prime rib to crabmeat au gratin. That said, the smoked pork and lamb aren't bad,

SAVANNAH & COAST
FOOD & LODGING

especially when napped with a bit of the mustardy barbecue sauce. Lunch and dinner. $-$$

✗ Lady and Sons
912-233-2600; 311 West Congress St.
A recent arrival on the Savannah dining scene. There's a menu with such dainty dishes as asparagus sandwiches, but most meals are served buffet style at this favorite of ladies-who-lunch and tourists. Best vegetable bets are the rich, lumpy mashed potatoes, pale creamed corn, and rice flavored with chicken stock. The fried chicken is quite good, though it dies a miserable death after a half-hour or so on the steam table. Fat, crusty hoecakes and thick, cheesy biscuits are remarkably good. Iced tea is spiked with mint leaves. Lunch and dinner. $$

✗ Mrs. Wilkes' Dining Room
912-232-5997; 107 West Jones St.
Locals with jaded palates grumble that the food is slipping, but each weekday at 11 A.M., a line snakes to the street from the basement entrance of this former boarding house. Meals are served family style and you can always count on there being fried chicken—and snap beans, black-eyed peas, and candied yams—on the table. Breakfast and lunch. $-$$

✗ Old Pink House
912-232-4262; 23 Abercorn St.
This landmark restaurant is one of Savannah's best. Fresh seafood and expertly prepared meats are house specialties. The historic building features nine dining rooms, including the cozy and dark tavern downstairs. $$$

✗ Sapphire Grill
912-443-9962; 110 West Julian St.
The place to go for inventive cooking in a setting that feels more SoHo than Savannah. Recent offerings included a "fricassee of local white shrimp, country ham and roasted leek barrels with a lobster scallion fritter, yellow pepper oil, and fried thyme" and "Colorado free range Sapphire Grill lamb lollipops." Fortunately, the chef is as skilled as the menu writer is florid. Dinner. $$

✗ Vinnie Van Go-Go's
912-233-6394; 317 West Bryan St.
Set in a narrow wedge of a building in the City Market area, this low-ceilinged bohemian enclave serves the city's best slice of pizza. Try the pesto sauce. And the spinach salad is squeaky fresh. Lunch weekends and dinner daily. $

✗ Wall's Barbecue
912-232-9754; 5151 East York Lane
Set on a narrow alley in the middle of the historic district, this shack serves good, cheap deviled crabs, red rice, and smoked ribs with mustard sauce. There are only a few tables, so most everyone gets their food to go. Lunch and dinner. $

✗ Yoshi's
912-238-5088; 423 West Congress St.
Minimalist decor, boutique sakes by the score, and super-fresh sushi draw a young, hip crowd. Start your meal with a bowl of edamame—boiled, salted soybeans that taste a lot like that South Georgia favorite, boiled peanuts. Lunch and dinner. $$-$$$

THE BALLASTONE

The Ballastone
912-236-1484; 14 East Oglethorpe Ave.
Snifters of brandy are proffered in the evening, and a continental breakfast with fresh-baked breads in the morning. There are 18 rooms for let at this mansion built in 1838, many of which are furnished with four-poster rice beds. $$$

DeSoto Hilton
912-232-9000; 15 East Liberty St.
Built in 1968 on the site of the venerable DeSoto Hotel, this 15-story hotel is the largest in the historic district proper, and is a short stroll from both Forsyth Park and the Riverfront. Recently renovated, the rooms are luxurious, but lack the charm of those to be found in the historic inns. Rooms on the upper floors command a sweeping view of the city. $$-$$$

East Bay Inn
912-238-1225; 225 East Bay St.
There are 28 guestrooms—the more charming of which have exposed brick walls—at this inn on the northern edge of the historic district. Reproductions rather than antiques fill the high-ceiling

rooms, but then again the prices are reasonable and the location is ideal, just a few steps from River Street. $$

ELIZA THOMPSON INN

Eliza Thompson Inn
912-236-3620; Five West Jones St.
This 1847 Federal-style mansion has more than 20 guest rooms, all with private bath, and was recently renovated. Though the inn offers a complimentary continental breakfast, intrepid travelers hoof it up the street to the venerable Mrs Wilkes' Dining Room for breakfast. $$

THE GASTONIAN

The Gastonian
912-232-0710; 220 E. Gaston St.
Actually two antebellum mansions joined by an aboveground walkway, The

Gastonian is among the most popular of Savannah inns. Each of the 18 rooms has a working fireplace, and Persian rugs cover the hardwood floors. The veranda is wide and welcoming. And there is even a sun deck with a hot tub, one of the few in town. $$$

☷ **Hamilton-Turner Inn**
912-233-1833; 330 Abercorn St.
Until recently a house museum, this striking Victorian Gothic inn faces majestic Lafayette Square. In the parlor, an Empire sofa, acquired from the Mercer estate, faces an ornate white marble fireplace. In the guestrooms, understated opulence prevails, and hardwood floors shine. The carriage house—also available for rent—is a virtual home, complete with 2 bedrooms, living room, dining room, and two and a half baths. $$-$$$

HAMILTON-TURNER INN

☷ **Hyatt Regency**
912-238-1234; Two West Bay St.
This hotel literally straddles River Street, with a tunnel of traffic running between

its foundation supports. Popular with conventioneers, it's a '70s-era, atrium-centered hotel with more than 300 rooms. Unless you can wrangle a deal, the historic inns provide far superior accommodations. $$-$$$

☷ **Jesse Mount Inn**
912-236-1774; 209 West Jones St.
Built in the mid-1800s, this brick rowhouse on a shady side street offers six spacious guestrooms, including a carriage house suite complete with a full kitchen and an inviting view of the courtyard garden. Original oils hang in most rooms. $$-$$$

☷ **Lion's Head Inn**
912-232-4580; 120 East Gaston St.
The innkeepers like to refer to this 1883 Federal-style mansion as a "living history museum." One of the more formal of Savannah inns, it has six guestrooms, two of which are suites. Federal-era antiques are everywhere, and there is a wicker swing out on the veranda, well placed to catch the afternoon breezes. $$

MAGNOLIA PLACE INN

☷ **Magnolia Place Inn**
912-236-7674; 503 Whitaker St.

Overlooking verdant Forsyth Park, this grand Victorian mansion was built in 1878. Twelve guestrooms are available, many featuring a fireplace and Jacuzzi tub. Enjoy afternoon cocktails in the parlor, and pralines and cordials in the privacy of your room before bed. In the morning, breakfast is served on the veranda—or late risers can have it delivered to their room on a silver tray. $$-$$$

The Mulberry Inn
912-238-1200; 601 East Bay St.
Operated by Holiday Inn, this 120-room property was once the site of a livery stable. Though not as quaint as the inns located deep in the historic district, the hotel does boast a wonderful courtyard, and it offers amenities (cofeemakers, VCRs) that will please both businesspeople and tourists. $$

Planter's Inn
912-232-5678; 29 Abercorn St.
Originally opened in 1912 as the Wesley Hotel, this seven-story, 56-room property has all the conveniences of a major hotel, albeit in a setting that is much more intimate. Rooms have four-poster beds and are furnished with antiques and quality reproductions. Complimentary wine is offered in the afternoon. $$

River Street Inn
912-232-4650; 115 East River St.
Ten of the rooms on the backside of this inn have balconies overlooking River Street and are in great demand on St. Patrick's Day. The remainder of the 40-plus rooms rely on graceful appointments and canopied beds as their draw.

Occupying the top floors of an old cotton warehouse, the inn first opened its doors in 1987. $$-$$$

Sea Island *map B-4*

✗ Cloister Dining Room
912-638-3611; 100 Hudson Place
Jackets are required for the evening meal, and big bands often serenade diners at this, the finest dining room south of Savannah. The wine list is superb and service is attentive but never fawning. The menu tends lists towards the more continental side of coastal dining. Dinner. $$$

CLOISTER RESORT

Cloister Resort
912-638-3611; 100 Hudson Place
When you cross the narrow body of water that separates St. Simon's from De Island, you enter a resort enclave like no other in Georgia. Consistently named one of the top properties in the nation, this complex of red-roofed Mediterranean villas exudes an understated elegance. Five miles of beaches, 1,000 acres of woodlands, and world-class golfing. Rates include three meals a day. $$$

Thunderbolt map C-1

✗ **Desposito's Seafood**
912-897-9963; Macceo Dr.
Great steamed oysters at five bucks a dozen can't be beat. This neat-as-a-pin, tin-roofed relic looks like it's been here forever. Yesterday's newspaper serves as today's placemat. Lunch and dinner. $

✗ **Teeple's Restaurant and Market**
912-354-1157; 2917 River Dr.
Steamed oysters by the bucket, in a setting with less charm Desposito's but no less quality. Toss the shells in the hole in the center of the table and cast off your cares. Lunch and dinner. $

Tybee Island map C-1

✗ **Breakfast Club**
912-786-5984; 1500 Butler Ave.
Serving the best meal on Tybee for the money, this warren of interconnected rooms is welcoming—and immensely popular. Breakfast is the best bet, featuring such inventive fare as chorizo and eggs, shrimp and grits, and the Grill Cleaner's Special: a kitchen-sink conglomeration of sausage, cheese, eggs, and whatever else the grill cook rummages up. Breakfast and lunch. $

✗ **George's**
912-786-9730; 1105 East Hwy. 80
Pulled pork over caramelized apples with red cabbage and Vidalia onions in a mustard sauce, or sautéed black grouper over a ragout of lima beans with tasso and cremini mushrooms—such as this is served at this comfortable bungalow,

Tybee's upscale favorite. Dinner and Sunday brunch. $$-$$$

✗ **North Beach Grill**
912-786-9003; 41-A Enddin Dr. (on the beach at Fort Screven)
Set just off the beach, this tropical shack serves jerk chicken, curried lobster, and other Caribbean dishes, and a good measure of Southern specialties to boot. It's funky, fun, and a bit removed from the scene, so tourists are few. Lunch and dinner. $-$$

✗ **Williams Seafood**
912-897-2219; 8010 Tybee Rd.
Set on the bank of the Bull River, this is a Savannah-Tybee institution, serving simple seafood dishes in a utilitarian dining room. Open since 1936, the restaurant may have become just too popular over the years: locals grouse that the prices are too high and the quality has slipped. Lunch and dinner. $$

🏠 **Fort Screven Inn**
912-786-9255; 24 Van Horn St.
On the quieter, north end of the island, this circa-1900 Victorian cottage has been recently refurbished and is just steps from the beach. Above looms the Tybee Lighthouse. $-$$

🏠 **17th Street Inn**
912-786-0607; 12 17th St.
Just a half-block from the ocean, this sturdy little two-story inn, fronted by screened porches, looks like the overgrown beach house that it is. Rooms are furnished simply, with old-fashioned iron beds and antique bureaus. $$

SAVANNAH & COAST
FOOD & LODGING

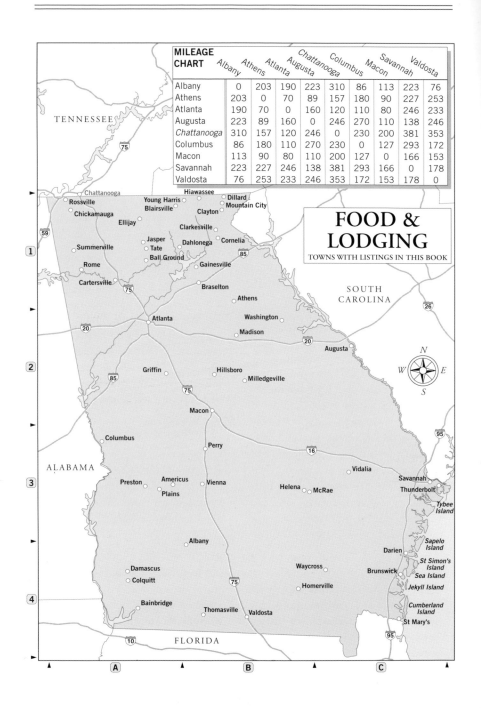

MILEAGE CHART	Albany	Athens	Atlanta	Augusta	Chattanooga	Columbus	Macon	Savannah	Valdosta
Albany	0	203	190	223	310	86	113	223	76
Athens	203	0	70	89	157	180	90	227	253
Atlanta	190	70	0	160	120	110	80	246	233
Augusta	223	89	160	0	246	270	110	138	246
Chattanooga	310	157	120	246	0	230	200	381	353
Columbus	86	180	110	270	230	0	127	293	172
Macon	113	90	80	110	200	127	0	166	153
Savannah	223	227	246	138	381	293	166	0	178
Valdosta	76	253	233	246	353	172	153	178	0

FOOD & LODGING

TOWNS WITH LISTINGS IN THIS BOOK

PRACTICAL INFORMATION

GEORGIA FOOD & LODGING INDEX

CHAIN LODGINGS IN GEORGIA
Toll-Free Numbers

Best Western	800-528-1234	Hyatt	800-233-1234
Comfort Inn	800-228-5150	Marriott	800-228-9290
Day's Inn	800-325-2525	Radisson	800-333-3333
Doubletree	800-528-0444	Residence Inn (Marriott)	800-331-3131
Hampton Inn	800-426-7866	Sheraton	800-325-3535
Hilton	800-445-8667	Suisse Chalet	800-258-1980
Holiday Inn	800-465-4329	Westin	800-228-3000

WEATHER IN GEORGIA TOWNS

WEATHER STATION	AVG. TEMPERATURES (° F)				RECORDS		PRECIPITATION (IN)				ANNUAL	
	JAN	APR	JUL	OCT	H	L	JAN	APR	JUL	OCT	R	S
Albany	62/38	78/53	91/71	78/55	106	-2	4.2	4.0	6.1	2.3	49	0
Athens	50/31	72/50	89/69	72/51	108	-3	4.5	4.2	5.0	3.3	50	2
Atlanta	50/32	73/50	88/70	72/51	105	-9	4.7	4.3	5.1	2.8	50	2
Augusta	58/33	78/50	91/70	78/50	108	-1	3.8	3.3	4.4	2.6	43	1
Clayton	47/28	70/41	85/61	71/42	102	-12	6.1	6.0	6.6	4.6	70	10
Columbus	58/36	78/51	90/70	78/55	104	-2	4.2	4.4	5.7	2.0	50	1
Macon	54/35	75/50	91/71	75/53	105	-4	3.8	3.7	5.0	2.5	44	1
Rome	49/30	72/43	87/66	72/46	107	-7	5.1	4.7	5.0	3.2	54	5
Savannah	60/39	79/55	90/72	79/58	105	3	3.3	3.1	6.8	2.5	49	0
Valdosta	65/43	80/55	91/72	80/56	105	12	3.5	3.6	6.3	2.1	49	0

METRIC CONVERSIONS

To convert feet (ft) to meters (m), multiply feet by .305. To convert meters to feet, multiply meters by 3.28.

1 ft = .30 m	1 m = 3.3 ft
2 ft = .61 m	2 m = 6.6 ft
3 ft = .91 m	3 m = 9.8 ft
4 ft = 1.2 m	4 m = 13.1 ft
5 ft = 1.5 m	5 m = 16.4 ft

To convert miles (mi) to kilometers (km), multiply miles by .62. To convert kilometers to miles, multiply kilometers by 1.61.

1 mi = 1.6 km	1 km = .62 mi
2 mi = 3.2 km	2 km = 1.2 mi
3 mi = 4.8 km	3 km = 1.9 mi
4 mi = 6.4 km	4 km = 2.5 mi
5 mi = 8.1 km	5 km = 3.1 mi

To convert pounds (lb) to kilograms (kg), multiply pounds by .46. To convert kilograms to pounds, multiply pounds by 2.2.

1 lb = .45 kg	1 kg = 2.2 lbs
2 lbs = .91 kg	2 kg = 4.4 lbs
3 lbs = 1.4 kg	3 kg = 6.6 lbs
4 lbs = 1.8 kg	4 kg = 8.8 lbs

To convert degrees Fahrenheit (°F) to Celsius (°C), subtract 32 from degrees F and multiply by .56. To convert degrees C to degrees F, multiply degrees C by 1.8 and add 32.

0°F = -17.8°C	60°F = 15.5°C
10°F = -12.2°C	70°F = 21.1°C
32°F = 0°C	80°F = 26.7°C
40°F = +4.4°C	90°F = 32.2°C
50°F = +10.0°C	98.6°F = 37.0°C

I N D E X

COMPASS AMERICAN GUIDES

Critics, booksellers, and travelers all agree: you're lost without a Compass.

"This splendid series provides exactly the sort of historical and cultural detail about North American destinations that curious-minded travelers need."

—*Washington Post*

"This is a series that constantly stuns us; our whole past book reviewer experience says no guide with photos this good should have writing this good. But it does."

—*New York Daily News*

"Of the many guidebooks on the market, few are as visually stimulating, as thoroughly researched, or as lively written as the Compass American Guides series."

—*Chicago Tribune*

"Good to read ahead of time, then take along so you don't miss anything."

—*San Diego Magazine*

NEW FROM COMPASS:

April 1999	*August 1999*	*December 1999*	*April 2000*
Vermont $19.95 ($27.95 Can) 0-679-00183-2	Southern New England $19.95 ($29.95 Can) 0-679-00184-0	Georgia $19.95 ($29.95 Can) 0-679-00245-6	Pennsylvania $19.95 ($29.95 Can) 0-679-00182-4

Compass American Guides are available in general and travel bookstores, or may be ordered directly by calling (800) 733-3000. Please provide title and ISBN when ordering.

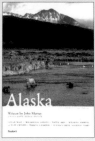

Alaska (2nd edition)
$19.95 ($27.95 Can)
0-679-00230-8

Arizona (5th edition)
$19.95 ($29.95 Can)
0-679-00432-7

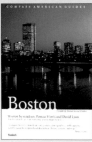

Boston (2nd edition)
$19.95 ($27.95 Can)
0-679-00284-7

Chicago (2nd edition)
$18.95 ($26.50 Can)
1-878-86780-6

Coastal California
$19.95 ($27.95 Can)
0-679-03598-2

Colorado (4th edition)
$18.95 ($26.50 Can)
0-679-00027-5

Florida (1st edition)
$19.95 ($27.95 Can)
0-679-03392-0

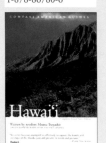

Hawai'i (4th edition)
$19.95 ($27.95 Can)
0-679-00226-X

Idaho (1st edition)
$18.95 ($26.50 Can)
1-878-86778-4

Las Vegas (6th edition)
\$19.95 ($29.95 Can)
0-679-00370-3

Maine (2nd edition)
$18.95 ($26.50 Can)
1-878-86796-2

Manhattan (3rd ed)
$19.95 ($29.95 Can)
0-679-00228-6

Minnesota (1st ed)
$18.95 ($26.50 Can)
1-878-86748-2

Montana (4th edition)
$19.95 ($29.95 Can)
0-679-00281-2

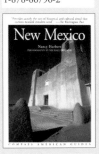

New Mexico (3rd ed)
$18.95 ($26.50 Can)
0-679-00031-3

New Orleans (3rd ed)
$18.95 ($26.50 Can)
0-679-03597-4